TOWARD A THEOLOGY FOR THE FUTURE

TOWARD A THEOLOGY

edited by
DAVID F. WELLS
and *CLARK H. PINNOCK*

for the
FUTURE

Creation House *Carol Stream Illinois*

TOWARD A THEOLOGY FOR THE FUTURE © 1971 by Creation
House. All rights reserved. Printed in the United States of
America. No part of this book may be reproduced in any manner
whatsoever without written permission except in the case of brief
quotations embodied in reviews. For information, address
Creation House, Inc., Publishers, 433 East St. Charles Road, P.O.
Box 316, Carol Stream, Illinois 60187.

FIRST EDITION

Library of Congress Catalogue Card Number: 75-163762

CONTENTS

PREFACE   David F. Wells and Clark H. Pinnock   7

1. PERSPECTIVE ON OLD TESTAMENT STUDY   11
   R. K. Harrison

2. TRADITION OF THE SAYINGS OF JESUS: A CRUX   41
   INTERPRETUM   Everett F. Harrison

3. THE OUTLOOK FOR BIBLICAL THEOLOGY   65
   Palmer Robertson

4. PROSPECTS FOR SYSTEMATIC THEOLOGY   93
   Clark H. Pinnock

5. PROMISE OF PATRISTIC STUDIES   125
   Geoffrey W. Bromiley

6. THE FUTURE OF THE CHURCH   David F. Wells   157

7. ETHICS IN THE THEOLOGY OF HOPE   189
   Bernard R. Ramm

8. PROCLAMATION FOR A NEW AGE   Harold J. Ockenga   217

9. THEOLOGY AND CULTURE: AN EVANGELICAL   239
   CORRELATION   H. D. McDonald

10. RELIGIOUS CERTAINTY AND INFALLIBILITY: A 275
    DISCUSSION WITH HANS KÜNG   Stanley Obitts

11. MISSION AND CULTURAL ENVIRONMENT   293
    Arthur Glasser

    Contributing Authors   320

    Index of Authors   323

ACKNOWLEDGMENTS

The editors make acknowledgment to the following publishers for the use of quoted material: to Thomas Nelson for L. Goppelt: *Jesus, Paul and Judaism;* to Macmillan and Company for W. B. Yeats: *Selected Poetry;* to Faber and Faber for T.S. Eliot: *The Complete Poems and Plays of T. S. Eliot;* To Harcourt Brace Jovanovich, Inc. and T.S. Eliot: *"Little Gidding," Four Quartets.*

PREFACE

Since the Second World War there has arisen a new body of scholarship in the Western world which is committed to the affirmation of historical and biblical faith.[1] Its initial concern has been with the biblical text, but it has now begun to show strength in the philosophical and theological disciplines as well. It would be an exaggeration to call this movement a fully fledged school of thought with a cogent and well-conceived position on every major question. Nevertheless, it is intellectually vigorous and it is moving toward a fully articulated theology.

Characteristic of this movement is a firm hold on the best elements of evangelical Christianity. There is also a matching concern to repudiate the anti-intellectualism, the cultural isolation and the social indifference which, in the public mind at least, have become identified with evangelical Protestantism. This book witnesses again to the determination of Evangelicals to repudiate any trace of a ghetto mentality and to confront the central issues of the day head on. Only as this is accomplished will the gospel of Christ be commended.

The time is propitious for the emergence of this scholarship and for the publication of this book. Theological structures have collapsed three times in this century, leaving behind a debris of shattered convictions. The disintegration of classical liberalism, followed by the fragmentation of neoorthodox theologies and the subsequent polarization between Barthians, Bultmannians and post-Bultmannians, has created a deep and painful ferment. Firm conviction has been replaced by radical doubt, hope by despair, affirmation by repudiation. Contemporary theology has drifted into a dangerous cul-de-sac. The situation demands that a vigorous restatement of historic belief emerges which will offer a convincing and credible way out. Evangelical scholarship intends to do this, setting as its main goal nothing less than the recapturing of leadership in theological research. Indeed, more than that,

7

it aims to hold out a healing word to a world whose culture and theology are alike dying.

These are high aims, but nothing less than this will be equal to the situation nor will it reflect the uncompromising truth claims of biblical faith. For evangelical faith seeks to conform itself to biblical faith, and biblical faith is that which Christ Himself taught. Consequently, Evangelicals insist that there must be theological identity between present Christian understanding and the corpus of apostolic teaching contained in Scripture. There is, indeed, an apostolic succession but it is realized *doctrinally* and not ecclesiastically. Christian theology today must maintain uncompromisingly, as the apostles did in their day, "the truth" (2 Th. 2:13; 2 Ti. 2:18, 25), "the preaching" (Ro. 16:25), "the gospel" (Gal. 2:2; Ro. 2:16; 1 Co. 15:1), "the confession" (Heb. 3:1; 4:14; 10:23), "the faith" (Gal. 1:23; Col. 1:27; Eph. 4:5, 1 Tim. 1:19; 5:8; Titus 1:13), and "the word" (1 Th. 1:6; 2 Th. 3:1; 1 Co. 14:36; Gal. 6:6; Phil. 1:14). Our affirmation must reiterate theirs, for central to both is the unchanging Christ.

What is the substance of apostolic and evangelical faith? Reduced to bare propositions, it affirms first, that Scripture provides an authoritative and formal structure within which Christian theology must be conceived; second, that soteriology is central to the understanding of Christian faith, and this soteriology teaches that God's justification of the sinner through the God-Man, Jesus Christ, is entirely un-merited and gratuitous, received under the conditions of repentance and faith. Christianity, to be sure, is greater than these propositions; yet, it will cease to be Christian if it affirms less than these do.

This volume attests an impressive de facto unity on these central Christian dogmas. It commends "mere Christianity." This is perhaps surprising when it is remembered how diverse are the backgrounds, nationalities, denominational preferences and educational careers of the men whose thought is here represented. This is something to be preserved, and without it the resurgence of biblical faith since the war could become dissipated. In a land of cultural, historical and intellectual diversity such as ours is, it is inevitable, even as it is regrettable, that Christian thought will develop along different lines in different places. Movements emerge with distinctive emphases, divinity schools nourish their own special "insights," denominational distinctives are pursued with vigor, and exclusive mentalities become entrenched in the milieux which first produced them. When these exclusive emphases and insights are then looked upon as *de fide,* diversity degenerates into disunity. Disunity undercuts the very base on which the preservation of the gospel depends. The emergence, therefore, of this new unity is something which must be carefully guarded. It will best be protected as we all seek to make the central axioms of Christian faith central and as we see sectarianism for the divisive thing that it is. This, after all, is what Christians in their best moments have always tried to do. John Donne, among many others, is a case in point:

> Nothing becomes a Christian better then sobriety; to make a true difference betweene problematicall, and dogmaticall points, betweene upper buildings, and foundations, betweene collaterall doctrines, and Doctrines in the right line: for fundamentall things, *Sine haesitatione credantur.* They must be beleeved without disputing; for things that are not so, we are to weigh them in two balances, in the balance of Analogy, and in the balance of scandall: we must hold them so, as may be analogall, proportionable, agreeable to the Articles of our Faith, and we must hold them so, as our brother be not justly offended, nor scandalized by them; wee must weigh them with faith, for our own strength, and we must weigh them with charity, for others weknesse.[2]

The purpose of this book is to bring together contributions by leading evangelical scholars which focus on a problem central to their field of study. The aim is not to survey the several divisions of theological work, but to indicate where the decisive action is taking place and to move toward a constructive, evangelical proposal. We hope the volume will be an anticipation of greater things to come and will serve to point up directions that need to be followed into the future. It is sent forth in the hope that it will serve God's purposes and, as Augustine said, "plentifully dispense unto thy people the flour of thy wheat, the gladness of thy oil and the sober inebriation of thy wine."[3]

DAVID F. WELLS
CLARK H. PINNOCK

FOOTNOTES

1. Cf. Claude Welch, "Theology" in *Religion*, ed. Paul Ramsey (Englewood Cliffs, N.J.: Prentice-Hall, 1965), pp. 274 ff.

2. John Donne, *Sermons on the Psalms and Gospels*, ed. Evelyn M. Simpson (Berkeley and Los Angeles: U. California, 1967), pp. 35-36.

3. Augustine, *The Confessions of Saint Augustine*, trans. Edward Pusey (New York: Collier Books, 1969), pp. 76-77.

PERSEPECTIVE ON OLD TESTAMENT STUDY

by R.K. Harrison

During the last century in particular, the Old Testament has been under constant investigation by people of widely differing interests and standpoints. The protagonists in the protracted discussion on the merits of organic evolution as against divine creation used and abused the Genesis narratives by turn. The positivist historians, following Comte, denied the importance of metaphysics or theological speculation in their attempts to explain Hebrew history in terms of verifiable laws of succession. The earlier students of Old Testament religion employed evolutionary and naturalistic approaches as they compared the phenomena of the Hebrew faith with the data of primitive religious experience. Equally industrious, European scholars were engaging in a minute dissection of Old Testament writings in an attempt to isolate alleged underlying literary sources. To add to these groups were a great many disparate individuals who looked to the Old Testament for the kind of evidence which would either justify their fondest hopes or confirm their worst fears.

11

All these people, whether they were aware of the fact or not, had one thing in common. They were applying some sort of method, however haphazardly and unconsciously, to the subject matter of their inquiry. For many of the earlier students of the Old Testament, method was much more to the forefront than factual evidence itself, and this was certainly the case for the exponents of literary criticism. Much of the reason for this was undoubtedly emotional in character. The last century of Old Testament study received its initial impetus from a time when "evolution" was the key concept in all interpretative processes. The idea of a continuous and progressive development from rudimentary to much more highly differentiated forms was borrowed from biology and applied quite uncritically to other disciplines, including that of Old Testament study. This tendency reached its classic expression in the writings of Wellhausen, an erudite German scholar who, under the avowed influence of Hegelian thought, formulated a detailed developmental theory of Pentateuchal origins which placed that body among the latest of Old Testament writings while at the same time he applied analagous principles to Hebrew history and religion. [1]

Because this latter method of Old Testament study has received such acclaim until recent years, it is worthwhile to glance at the most important criteria by which it became established. As far as the developmental hypothesis of the Pentateuch was concerned, the work of Wellhausen merely incorporated, in a somewhat rearranged fashion, the literary-critical speculations of earlier writers such as Astruc, Eichhorn, Geddes and de Wette. The principal criteria for source analysis which they had adopted were the presence of "duplicate"[2] narratives in Genesis and the incidence of two specific names, YHWH and *Elohim,* as designations of Deity. With an uncritical innocence which bordered on complete naïveté, European scholars proceeded to divide the Pentateuch into "documents" which were thought to underlie the finished composition. Had they but taken the trouble to test the validity of this method by applying it to the Koran, a comparable though later body of Semitic literature,[3] as was their wont with certain other kinds of evidence, they would have seen at once that the number and incidence of the divine names in that work entirely precluded the use of such criteria for purposes of serious literary analysis.

What was even worse than the completely arbitrary and oft-challenged method of arriving at the content of "documentary" sources, however, were the a priori philosophical presuppositions by which this kind of study was motivated. A priori reasoning deduces consequences from assumed principles or formulated definitions and, as a strictly philosophical term, describes reasoning which proceeds from the mere examination of ideas without any resort to the substance of experience for purposes of practical testing.

In the case of the literary-analytical school, the theoretical principles from which they commenced their deductions were those of a unilinear view of Hebrew history which had much in common with the skeptical and positivistic approach of Hegelian philosophy on the one hand and with the biological theories of Darwin and Wallace on the other.[4] Thus, under Wellhausen, Hebrew history emerged, not from the developed cultures of the ancient Near East, but from primitive phases reminiscent of the Old Stone Age, and finally progressed to a climax in the postexilic period. Hebrew religion, similarly, was depicted as moving slowly from the crudities of animism and totemism to the complex ritual worship of what the literary-critical school called the "priestly code," a source which they generally assigned to the later postexilic period.

This method could only portray a progressive movement of culture and faith at the expense of some awkward but objective facts. Needless to say, objectivity has seldom been the concern of a priori speculators in any field, and to this principle the literary-analytical school proved no exception. Once Wellhausen had formulated his theoretical position, he employed every possible means to prove his case. If particular verses stood in the way of his hypothesis they were pronounced as "corrupt," "additions by a later hand," "editorial redactions," and so on, thereby being removed from the scene. If some late Arabic practice could be adduced in support of his position, it was paraded with great confidence, regardless of whether it had originated in the Old Testament period. All social, historical and religious phenomena were made to conform to a predetermined pattern, and those which did not were savagely and unashamedly reconstructed to the point where they did.

What is so astonishing in the light of modern knowledge are the supreme arrogance and peremptoriness with which Wellhausen and his followers promoted their findings. Without regard to anything other than the interests of a priori speculation they described their findings as "demonstrating conclusively," "showing incontrovertibly" or constituting the "most assured results of biblical scholarship." The fact that their pronouncements rested generally upon the flimsiest of what could charitably be called "evidence" did not seem to deter or disturb the enthusiastic investigators for one moment.

It is now evident that the work of this school suffered from some devastating weaknesses, one of which was that it was constructed artificially upon the insecure foundations of a biological theory of origins which at that period had not been examined critically.[5] Another deficiency, consistent with the attitudes of a priori speculators, was the appalling indifference which was exhibited toward the objective evidence being furnished increasingly by archeological discoveries. This resulted, among other things, in the amazing assumption that writing was only utilized about the time of King David, thus positively precluding Mosaic composition of the Pentateuch. [6] Such a view could only be maintained by turning away resolutely from such enormously important discoveries as the Tell el-Amarna tablets, found in 1887 and subsequently published by Winckler in a critical edition, to say nothing of the ancient literary materials excavated in the nineteenth century from Nineveh, Nimrud, Erech, Larse and elsewhere. Perhaps the worst claim that could be made for a method which, without recourse to any significant objective evidence, found the Old Testament full of confused repetitions of events, gross historical and geographical inaccuracies, patent textual errors and worthless chronologies, was that it was an essentially scientific approach to the problems of the Old Testament. To those who have the slightest acquaintance with the methods of modern scientific investigation a more fundamental contradiction of the facts is difficult to imagine, since a priori deductive reasoning is the very antithesis of what ought to take place in the formulating of a scientific hypothesis.

Within recent years fewer members of the literary-critical school have claimed the term *scientific* as a description of their method. Whether this is because they assume that others now take this for granted, or because they wish to spare both themselves and their readers the embarrassment of such a claim, is not easy to determine. Yet, if only because the old a priori, critical legacy is still prized in some quarters, it seems important to assess its antecedent methodology in the light of what is actually involved in the exercise of a genuine modern scientific study of phenomena.

In the popular mind the scientist commences his research by collecting a mass of facts from observation and experiment. On the basis of this material he then arrives at a tentative hypothesis and, if this formulation survives additional testing and experimentation, the scientist is then able to promulgate a new theory or law of nature. If this

15

were actually what happened in real life, the procedure would, of course, guarantee the impartiality and objectivity of scientific method.

However, this picture of the modern scientist at work amid the disinterested and factual environment of the laboratory is, unfortunately, entirely mythical. The fact of the matter is that, whatever field he even considers, the scientist is immediately engulfed by an avalanche of data to the point where, if he followed the advice of Huxley and sat down before the facts as a little child, letting them lead him where they would, he himself would be completely overwhelmed and prevented from making any real beginning. As Schiller showed some years ago, scientific endeavor is selective in a twofold sense: the scientist is directed by the selection of a problem because of native interest, and after he has begun his observations he must of necessity choose his hypothesis from among many rival hypotheses, a procedure in which factors of inclination and training have an important place.[7]

While disinterestedness may well be an *ideal* of science, it still remains true that in practice the scientist is always necessarily biased. He is impelled to approach his task with some sort of direction in mind which will enable him to select all those facts which are relevant to his particular research problem. Without some tentative idea in terms of which he can organize specific facts, the work of the scientist would be endless, since it is physically impossible for a person to observe all the available data.[8] The process of selection furnishes a context which helps him to interpret the data with which he deals, and sets the stage for the next phase, namely, the elevation of a working hypothesis to the level of a theory. If at any time the observed facts militate against the hypothesis which the investigator has formulated, he has several choices at his disposal. He can either modify or extend his theory to account for the new findings; he can abandon his original hypothesis and replace it by a newer and more satisfactory one; or, if no acceptable substitute is in sight, he can retain it on a tentative basis until a more inclusive hypothesis can be formulated in the light of additional experimentation.

It is important for the nonscientist to be aware of the correct usage of terms in a scientific experimental situation. The hypothesis represents the lowest level of factual interpretation and, when additional supporting evidence has been accumulated and tested, the hypothesis is elevated to the status of a theory. When the theory can be regarded as capable of explaining coherently all those instances which it exemplifies, it may then be regarded as a scientific law. It goes without saying that even though human purpose and interest are inevitably present even in the most objective of scientific enterprises, the work of description, classification and experimentation must be accurately planned, rigorously controlled, and honestly reported. Since the primary concern of scientific method is with objective reality, it is of paramount importance that the data of the investigator should be able to be verified by any other competent scientist.

This process of sifting and sorting, reviewing and relating, revising and formulating, is sometimes described as "inductive generalization" because it involves a procedure of argumentation from particular instances to a general conclusion.[9] It is in fact the a posteriori or inductive method of investigation which derives propositions from the observation of factual data. As in a priori speculation, there are certain perils implicit in the process of reasoning by induction, but in the case of the latter they can be avoided easily by a careful checking of the objective evidence.

A good working hypothesis will be able to explain, organize and integrate a body of data in the form of a theory, and perhaps even a possible law of nature, and do so in a manner which will account for the known facts in the simplest and most natural way possible. [10] Of equal importance is the requirement that a good hypothesis must be consistent with the principles and previously verified facts in the particular area of investigation. If these criteria cannot be met, the hypothesis must be regarded as at best an inadequate explanation of the data, and in the end may only prove useful because it has pointed the way to a better and more inclusive hypothesis.

From the foregoing remarks it will be evident that the way in which the literary-critical school of the nineteenth century addressed itself to the task of Old Testament analysis was the very antithesis of all that could be called truly scientific. The members of this school commenced their labors, as has been observed previously, with an avowed a priori theoretical position and then, with an efficient combination of industry and ingenuity, they set about making all available material conform to their views. However much they may have imagined that what they were doing was in the tradition of scientific study, the inescapable fact remains that none of those who crystallized the developmental theories had the slightest acquaintance with anything approaching modern scientific method.

This situation stands in stark contrast with the brilliant discoveries of the nineteenth-century Russian chemist Mendeléeff, who prior to 1870 had been working for some time on the problem of classifying elements into "families" which possessed similar properties. By 1871, six years before Wellhausen published his book on the composition of the Hexateuch, Mendeléeff had employed the inductive scientific approach to the point where he was able to arrange the elements in a table according to their atomic weights, and also to group them into families, provided that certain gaps were left in the periodic table. On the basis of his studies he felt confident enough to predict not merely that elements unknown in his day would be found to occupy the vacant spaces in the table, but he also forecast with

18

remarkable accuracy many of the properties of those undiscovered elements now familiar to modern chemists. What had previously been rather in the nature of accident had suddenly become scientifically predictable through the application of an inductive method which arrived at a hypothesis as the result of experimentation. As a result, the periodic table of elements is one of the cornerstones of chemical theory, formulating as it does a principle which has received striking confirmation since the time of Mendeléeff.

However well intentioned any hypothesis may purport to be, it cannot begin to lay serious claim to the description "scientific" until it is first firmly grounded in all the relevant evidence. The tragedy of the approach fostered by de Wette, Graf and others, and brought by Wellhausen to what appeared to be its logical conclusion, was that so much of what even in those days constituted factual relevant evidence was sacrificed callously to the demands of a priori theorizing. To give but one example, the accumulated corpus of archeological knowledge which had been initiated in 1765 when Carsten Niebuhr copied out some trilingual inscriptions from Persepolis had already reached enormous proportions by the time Wellhausen was ready to publish his theories. [11] Yet this fundamentally important corpus of objective evidence was ignored in the formulation of the Wellhausenian hypotheses of origins and growth, so that as a result they bore little or no real relationship to the facts of the situation.

There can hardly be any doubt that, had Wellhausen weighed the available relevant data carefully, his developmental theories would have seen the light of day in a very different form indeed, if, in fact, they had emerged at all. But to the author of a grand schema who was already convinced that his purely arbitrary and subjective method was "scientific," and who managed to persuade his followers of this with very little effort, such considerations were

19

entirely coincidental to the formulation of the master plan and could therefore be dismissed out of hand without the slightest concern or recrimination.

It is thus small wonder that objections to the literary-analytical position such as those advanced by the so-called Uppsala school should relate so pertinently to the methodological deficiencies of the Wellhausenian approach. To furnish but one example of this tendency, at the time that Pedersen was writing, it was uniformly held by those who employed the documentary method of Pentateuchal analysis that Genesis 34 had been compiled from two irreconcilable sources, a situation which was deemed to be the obvious explanation of the large number of apparent contradictions in that particular chapter. Yet Pedersen firmly maintained that this was an entirely erroneous view, based upon a false conception of the relationship in ancient Israel between the individual and the community. [12] Because the criteria by which this passage had been analyzed into supposedly conflicting "sources" could be explained quite adequately simply by reference to the sociological background, the method of analysis itself was immediately laid under suspicion.

Another criticism of the approach followed by the adherents of the Wellhausenian theories has emerged from the form-historical studies of Gunkel. Form criticism as a literary discipline had been applied for nearly a century previously to German folk literature, and grew out of the principle that "folk memory" operated in terms of small units such as poetic couplets. Because these emerged from some life situation such as a wedding, they were held to be rooted in the behavior and attitudes of people. If such oral units could be detected in the Old Testament narratives it would be possible to recover the original sources in terms of the oral sagas associated with a particular person or occasion rather than some "document" which for them represented a comparatively late stage in the development of the tradition. This kind of method was applied by Gunkel and others to the study of Genesis and the Psalter. Although the approach was intended to grasp the spiritual values which for Gunkel had been largely obscured by the Wellhausen school, it too suffered from some serious deficiencies which are noted subsequently.

Criticisms of this kind are not so much petulant reactions against a virtually invulnerable theoretical position on the part of a small minority of dissidents made insecure by the presence of greatness, but rather, they represent valid objections to the use of a method which simply does not possess an adequate critical basis, and whose procedural canons are therefore unable to claim the authority and credence of genuine scientific method. They are even more potent in the light of the vast amount of information about the ancient Near East which has become available to the Old Testament scholar as the result of findings in archeology, comparative religious studies, history, linguistics, and other disciplines. This accumulation of data is the result of honest scholarship over several decades, and it is impossible to ignore it any longer out of deference to, or support for, an inadequate and incorrect nineteenth-century methodological approach to the Old Testament.

Those who still profess adherence to the literary-critical methods of Wellhausen find themselves in an unfortunately embarrassing position for at least two distinct reasons. First, the staggering increase of knowledge which has characterized every field of learning in the past two decades has had a direct effect on Old Testament studies also, furnishing for the investigator a wealth of objective data which challenges and confutes the literary-critical theorists in many vital areas. Second, the traditional liberal critic of the Old Testament is faced with the fact that what he had been led to believe was a scientific method of investigation now proves to be the very antithesis of the a posteriori approach characteristic of the descriptive sciences. [13] It is possible, of course, for a teacher or a writer to ignore the great accumulation of relevant material in his field, and to cling tenaciously to an outworn hypothesis or methodological procedure. But if he does so, he can hardly expect to have his findings taken at all seriously, [14] and if he persists in the claim that his approach is "scientific" he will invite criticism and derision from those who have a firmer acquaintance with modern scientific procedures.

In view of the great resources of knowledge which have a direct bearing upon biblical studies, the time has come for the Old Testament scholar to adopt a proper method in his work so that the results will reflect a truly scientific approach. This procedure need not be as difficult to achieve as some may imagine, because the groundwork has already been laid by the activities of Near Eastern scholars. These men, unhampered by a priori hypotheses of the kind foisted on Old Testament scholarship by the speculations of the Wellhausen school, have for several decades been sifting the data presented by archeology and other disciplines related to their task, and on the basis of the objective evidence have been endeavoring to formulate hypotheses in the way that the modern scientist does. [15]

An accredited methodology for Old Testament studies will necessarily commence with relevant facts from the ancient Near Eastern world, which is, of course, the cultural milieu of the Old Testament. In the light of the scholar's particular interest, this material will then be examined carefully in order to discern the direction in which the facts clearly point. [16] At this stage absolute primacy will be given to the testimony of the objective, tangible evidence. Facts will control theoretical speculation at every phase in the process, and a posteriori induction will be followed rigorously. The investigator will, of course, be sufficiently familiar with his field to detect the occurrence of special tendencies in the evidence, such as the Egyptian custom of presenting propaganda as though it were history. But unless indications of this kind are clearly apparent, he will assume that the statements in his sources are broadly reliable in character. Although he will almost certainly encounter some discrepancies in extant sources, it will be his responsibility to try to establish the basic harmony which is generally the case with ancient Near Eastern records. This not infrequently involves an attempt to determine why the scribe concerned wrote his material in the way he did, a procedure which may even uncover the presence of inadvertent error in one of the scholar's primary sources.

An approach of this kind, which is essentially holistic, is the direct opposite of the atomizing tendencies of the literary-analytical school since it seeks to determine the total picture and to interpret specific items of evidence against this larger background. The Old Testament scholar who is prepared to follow the rigorous procedures of modern scientific method must be aware of the fact that there are a great many gaps in existing knowledge of ancient Near Eastern life. Extant cuneiform tablets, for example, have been thought to represent only 1 percent of similar material still in the ground. [17] Artifacts may or may not be recovered in the future to supplement present sources of information and clarify many of the current problems; but, regardless of this, the serious investigator must commit himself to the task of sifting and evaluating the relevant material at hand, and by critical scrutiny must proceed from factual evidence to some sort of tentative explanation of the data. If the latter survives repeated testing through the application of related data, it can then be advanced with great caution as a hypothesis on the understanding that, whenever relevant factual material requires it, the appropriate changes in the hypothesis will be made.

An excellent example of the application of the kind of critical scientific methodology being commended for future use by Old Testament scholars can be seen in the work of E. R. Thiele. Up to 1951, when he published his definitive treatment of the chronology of the divided monarchy, [18] that particular subject had been one of the most troublesome in the whole of Old Testament study. [19] Although one or two investigators had purported to discern some kind of patternism in the lists of kings, the vast majority of literary-analytical scholars had dismissed the chronologies in Kings and Chronicles as having no validity whatever for purposes of historical reckoning.

Thiele's approach was based upon the most rigid scholarly application of scientific method to relevant data, a point which W. A. Irwin, himself one of the more radical of Old Testament critics, was gracious to concede in his introduction to the book. [20] In the original preface Thiele stated that his early work was of an exploratory and experimental nature, unmarred by a priori decisions, and that only when the objective data provided by the Hebrew text had been assessed critically did he feel able to suggest a tentative pattern.

In private conversation with the present writer, Thiele stated that he was determined to allow the evidence of the Hebrew to speak for itself without being hampered by literary-critical presuppositions, and that he worked many hours daily for over three years before he achieved his first real insights into the type of patternism employed. His developed explanation demonstrates clearly the various types of scribal compilations underlying the text, and shows without question the essential trustworthiness and historical reliability of the material once it is understood from the standpoint of the compilers. Consequently it is now evident that the Hebrew scribes were every bit as responsible as their pagan counterparts, and that, so far from compiling and transmitting a corrupt and worthless text, they had actually recorded their observations with the scrupulous care which is now known to characterize both Hittite and Hebrew historiography.

The great advantage of such an approach is that the

ancient Hebrew Scriptures were permitted to give evidence on their own behalf without being laughed out of court, as was not infrequently the case in liberal circles, because investigators had brought to the lists of kings the a priori presuppositions which they expected to find reflected in the passages in question. Because the procedures of Thiele were grounded in a properly scientific Near Eastern methodology, they produced results which at once solved virtually every problem connected with the chronology of the divided monarchy, related these historical sequences realistically to other dates in ancient Near Eastern history, and demonstrated the high degree of trustworthiness inherent in the Hebrew text.

However, not all methods which purport to be based on an understanding of the Near Eastern background are effective instruments for investigation, and this is due to the fact that a rigorous a posteriori approach is not being followed consistently. Mention was made earlier of the form-critical studies associated with Gunkel which, in some quarters, have been hailed as "the only ones that can be applied" to ancient Near Eastern studies.[21] What is not generally appreciated is that, while the procedure itself has some merit, it was applied originally with characteristic German zeal to writings such as the Psalter to such an extent that Gunkel was compelled almost to rewrite certain psalms so that they would conform to his method. To say nothing else, this kind of approach unfortunately stands in the worst tradition of the literary-critical school, whose ravaging of spiritual values Gunkel was supposed to be protesting against so vigorously.

When the method is scrutinized more carefully, some crucial questions arise as to its objectivity and suitability for general use in Old Testament study. The first is as to the warrant by which it can be transported from the area of Germanic lore and applied to biblical material written, not in an Indo-European language, but in a Semitic one. In reply to this, the most that can be said at present is that there is no authenticating evidence that form criticism can be applied so rigorously to the literature of a language such as biblical Hebrew unless due attention is paid to the divergences between German and Semitic culture, a situation which immediately points to theoretical weaknesses in the methodological approach. The second casts doubt on the validity of the criteria employed to identify the supposed form-critical units, particularly in those instances where they comprise a few words at the most. [22] It seems difficult to escape the conclusion that such units are essentially subjective in character, and that they can only approach objective reality when they correspond specifically in form to such demonstrable entities as cuneiform tablets. [23]

Additional objections to the subjectivity of form-critical presuppositions have been raised by Freedman, [24] who pointed out that terms such as *myth* and *legend,* which are used in the method, are in fact more of a judgment of value than an objective description. Another drawback is the circularity of the method, since the cultural context is reconstructed in terms of material which purports to depict a certain kind of setting, and then this reconstruction is employed to reinterpret the contents of the narrative or related material. Quite clearly, therefore, a method which is at once subjective and circular is of extremely limited value in modern Old Testament study.

Another approach which raises methodological questions is that of the oral traditionists, which is featured mostly in the writings of the Uppsala school. According to the exponents of this procedure, the prophetic corpus passed through a lengthy period of oral transmission before being recorded in written form. One unfortunate corollary of this view is that the scholar can never be absolutely sure of being able to recover the *ipsissima verba* of the spiritual masters, but at best must be satisfied with handling the tradition about what was said.

The basic weakness of this method lies in the inadequacy of the term *oral transmission* as an interpretation of the way in which information was circulated in the ancient Near East. Members of the Uppsala group have followed Gunkel in drawing parallels, not from ancient Oriental literature as such, but principally from different cultural and historical sources such as those of Old Iceland, Islam and Hindu India.[25] What was being overlooked in the process was that, whereas the European nations in particular were almost wholly illiterate during the biblical period, those of the ancient Near East enjoyed an advanced degree of literacy. It was the tradition of these latter peoples to make a written account of any event of importance at the time of its occurrence or shortly afterward. But at this juncture the Near Eastern scholar becomes aware of a difference between the concepts of oral dissemination and oral transmission of such material. Insofar as information about the particular event was circulated by word of mouth in contemporary society, it was being disseminated orally. Only in those instances where a spoken description of the occurrence was handed down to posterity can it be considered to have been transmitted orally, and always in the context of an earlier written account.

In the Orient the practice of committing events to written form followed as a matter of course, and literary sources from all walks of life demonstrate amply that, as Kitchen has remarked, neither national traditions nor the repute of individuals was left to the care of campfire bards in the ancient Near East.[26] By contrast, in a virtually illiterate culture such as could be found frequently in Europe, oral dissemination was the only means available for perpetuating local and national traditions. But to assume without any warrant that what transpired in early Scandinavia was also the norm for ancient Near Eastern methods of communication is a gross travesty of scientific method, to say nothing of the sheer inadequacy of knowledge of the an-

27

cient Near East which is reflected by such a premise. As far as actual proof is concerned, the oral traditionists have failed completely to demonstrate that oral tradition as defined above existed alone in the ancient Orient without a parallel written form from the earliest period of the particular circumstance under study. It therefore seems inadvisable for the term *scientific* to be applied to this method also, since it obviously rests upon unproved assumptions which, following the pattern of the ancient Greek philosophers, have analogy rather than a critical scrutiny of the objective evidence as their motivating feature.

One of the tragedies of the nineteenth-century literary-critical method was that it beguiled its adherents to the point where they made embarrassing mistakes in their attempts to sustain and promote its use. This unfortunate tendency can be illustrated at considerable length, but for the purposes of this chapter, three instances can be adduced as examples, all of them, rather coincidentally, having to do with the book of Daniel. This composition came at one time under the scrutiny of the late H. H. Rowley, who though by no means extreme in his views was nevertheless a lifelong adherent of the Wellhausen theories. Like others of that persuasion he felt it his duty to attempt to present an authoritative basis for assigning the composition of Daniel to the Maccabean period. He began by using inferior translations of the Nabonidus Chronicle to establish the identity of the Gobryas mentioned in the texts, [27] finally depicting this individual as a composite of the Gubaru and Ugbaru of the cuneiform references, the Gobryas mentioned by Xenophon and Herodotus, and the Gaubaruva identified in the Behistun Inscription as the "son of Mardonius a Persian." [28] Having set up such a man of straw, it was not difficult for Rowley to demolish it by stating that such a Gobryas could not possibly be identified with Darius the Mede, and thus he rejected by implication the historicity of Darius the Mede himself.

Had Rowley worked from the cuneiform, instead of from inferior translations, he would have become aware of the fact that the Nabonidus Chronicle mentioned two distinct persons, Gubaru and Ugbaru,[29] who took an active part in the overthrowing of Babylon on October 12, 539 B.C. However, Ugbaru, who had been governor of Gutium, died three weeks after the successful attack on Babylon, perhaps from wounds. Gubaru was placed in charge of Babylonia by Cyrus, and he in turn appointed subordinates to control the conquered territory while still retaining his own title of "Governor of Babylon and the Regions Beyond the River" for at least fourteen years. In contrast with the earlier attempts of Rowley, when J. C. Whitcomb argued inductively from the cuneiform sources,[30] he was able to distinguish clearly between the two men and make a positive contribution toward elucidating the problems connected with the identity of Darius the Mede. Unfortunately for Rowley, the error which he committed as the result of employing an improper a priori approach was as elementary as it was devastating.

Literary-critical studies of the book of Daniel have been gravely hampered by the fact that the opinions of Porphyry have been perpetuated with monotonous regularity and equally little imagination, even when they have been shown to be completely inadequate on various grounds. Porphyry, it will be recalled, lived in the third century A.D. and was one of the chief exponents of Neoplatonist philosophy. He was the first to assign the composition of Daniel to the period of Antiochus IV Epiphanes, and he did so on the entirely a priori assumption that, since Daniel could not possibly have predicted the future with such minute precision, the work obviously must have been a roughly contemporary Maccabean record. Conclusions of this kind were in complete harmony with the theorizing of the Wellhausen school, so it was hardly surprising that they were accepted so avidly.

Unfortunately, literary-critical orthodoxy still demands of its followers an adherence to a Maccabean dating for Daniel, all other evidence to the contrary, and this fact has placed some of its exponents in an extremely embarrassing position. Thus, in his book on the history of Israel, John Bright was lured into making the astonishing statement that, whereas the apocryphal additions to Daniel could be dated about 170 B.C., the composition of Daniel proper was to be assigned to 166 B.C. [31] Just how additions can be written before the main body of a work has been compiled is not at all clear and, as the present writer has remarked elsewhere,[32] it would be most instructive to know precisely how this literary feat was accomplished.

In this general connection a curious piece of literary-critical ambivalence concerning the date of Daniel might well be noticed at this point. Many scholars are quite satisfied to allow the validity of evidence from the writings of Josephus concerning the fact that Jaddua was high priest in Jerusalem during the time of Alexander the Great (*Antiquities.* 6, 7, 2; 11, 8, 5), and on this basis to assign a date of between 350 and 250 B.C. for the work of the chronicler. Yet these very same scholars are adamant in their refusal to allow, from the very same literary source, the historical correctness of the testimony which makes it quite clear that the scroll of Daniel was in its completed form by 330 B.C. (*Antiquities,* 11, 8, 5). Unfortunately for those who are the victims, however unwillingly, of the a priori method, no amount of critical legerdemain has yet been able to resolve this curiously contradictory evaluation of a specific historical situation.

Commitment in the past to the a priori approach has stultified a great deal of what otherwise would have been creative endeavor in scholarship, and has forced those writers who wished to maintain literary-analytical respectability to promulgate a dogma whose pronouncements were as outmoded as its methodology. This tendency has received one of its most unfortunate expressions in a recent commentary on Daniel by N. W. Porteous, originally written for the *Alte Testament Deutsch* series in 1962, and published subsequently in English.[33] The book itself is a surprisingly slim volume which rests heavily in crucial areas upon the work of other liberal scholars. In harmony with the traditions of a bygone age of criticism, the author enunciated his position with supreme confidence. And although a great many of his statements are open to serious question, his propositions were stated with the kind of peremptoriness which must have afforded his original German audience a great deal of satisfaction.

Despite the existence of a great amount of material on the book of Daniel written from standpoints widely different from that adopted by Porteous, all positions other than the one which he espoused were ignored in the interests of a consistent a priori approach, and the reader who is unacquainted with the field would never imagine for one moment the complexity of the issues which the writer was able to dismiss in a few flat words. Characteristic of the approach which Wellhausen adopted toward external evidence was the highly selective way in which the materials from Qumran were handled, all of which were made to serve the attempt to establish a Maccabean date for Daniel. The result of all this activity was a commentary of such academic and spiritual inadequacy as might well cause considerable embarrassment in liberal circles, and perhaps excite derision in others.

If, by contrast, an a posteriori methodology had been employed, the first step would have been to assess the available objective evidence. Here the manuscripts and fragments found at Qumran would have been of prime importance. Although Porteous mentioned material such as the Habakkuk commentary and the Prayer of Nabonidus, he never once came to grips with the implications for the dating of the book of those fragments of Daniel recovered from the first Qumran cave, and which are related palaeographically to the large Isaiah manuscript. To have done this would have been to raise a fundamental challenge to the a priori presuppositions involving the date of Daniel. All biblical materials recovered from Qumran are copies, not originals, and since the brotherhood which lived there was itself Maccabean in origin, it follows that the manuscripts from which the Qumran copies were made must have emerged from an earlier period, a situation which places the original autographs still further away from the Maccabean era.

On the basis of this manuscript evidence Millar Burrows was able to discuss the relation between the original book of Isaiah and the large copy recovered from Qumran, and to conclude: "The Book of Isaiah certainly comes from a time several centuries before the earliest date to which this manuscript can be assigned on any grounds." [34] In that event precisely the same conditions ought to apply to the Daniel fragments which, as observed above, are related palaeographically. Even in the highly unlikely circumstance that such a relationship should be definitely disproved, the Daniel material would still demand a date for the autograph considerably earlier than the age of the Maccabees since if the usual procedure was followed there would have been insufficient time for Maccabean compositions to have been circulated, venerated, and finally accepted as canonical by a Maccabean sect.

A second century B.C. fragmentary copy of the Psalter (4QPsa^a) shows clearly that the collection of canonical psalms was already fixed by the time of the Maccabees, and this source alone has persuaded scholars to assign to the Persian period, without undue fanfare, psalms which once were confidently acclaimed in literary-critical circles as being Maccabean in origin. [35] If such a radical step can be taken for the so-called Maccabean psalms, it is far from easy to see why, on the same factual evidence, the Maccabean dating of Daniel should not also be abandoned in favor of placing the work in the historical setting from which it purports to have emerged, namely, that of the Chaldean period. Needless to say, objective evidence of this kind not merely cuts across the methodology of Porteous but demolishes his entire theoretical position. The simple fact is that, whatever may be thought about the ability of Daniel to predict in detail, the manuscript evidence from Qumran absolutely precludes a date of composition in the Maccabean period, but does point to one in the Neo-Babylonian era (626-539 B.C.), and all future treatises on Daniel will have to take note of this consideration.

The data from Qumran bears directly upon other internal evidence in Daniel which might be adduced in favor of a late date, and demands that it, too, be reassessed in the light of the archeological picture. The linguistic character of the book is obviously important in this connection, and here Porteous characteristically described the Hebrew as "late" and assigned the Aramaic sections to a time not earlier than the third century B.C., and perhaps even the second century. [36] This bald statement, for which not the slightest degree of argument or supporting evidence is furnished, disregards the vast amount of research undertaken in connection with Aramaic since the days of Wellhausen. [37]

The term *Aramaic* actually describes a group of Semitic dialects closely related to one another and also to biblical Hebrew. Aramaic has a lengthy prehistory, with an early form evidently being spoken in the Patriarchal period ("proto-Aramaic"), and the earliest extant texts in the Aramaic language proper emerging from the tenth and ninth centuries B.C. The Aramaic of Daniel is part of Imperial Aramaic, which was already being used early in the Assyrian period (*c.* 1100-605 B.C.), and by the fifth century B.C., or earlier, almost all the Aramaic words in Daniel were in general use.

Even allowing for ancient Near Eastern scribal practices, including changes in spelling and gramatical forms, there is nothing in the Aramaic to preclude on dogmatic grounds a sixth or fifth century B.C. date for the book. Equally true is the fact that there is nothing which demonstrates conclusively that the Aramaic of Daniel comes specifically from the second century B.C. The linguistic evidence, in fact, can no longer be adduced to support a given date as such, but it can be used to point to a period of composition in advance of 300 B.C. rather than after that time. [38] So far from the Hebrew being "late," it is now known that the words listed by Driver as *rare* or *absent* in earlier Old Testament literature were in use prior to the Greek period. [39] As W. J. Martin has concluded, there is therefore nothing about the Hebrew of Daniel which would be out of the ordinary for a bilingual person of the sixth century B.C. [40]

Any supposedly "late" factors in the linguistic picture of Daniel will have to be accounted for by means other than those employed at present if only to accommodate the upward revision of the date of Daniel which the manuscript evidence from Qumran now demands. The very phenomenon of "lateness," so usefully employed in some quarters, is just one concept which will require substantial critical reappraisal in the light of current Near Eastern linguistic knowledge if it is to be utilized with any confidence in a scientific approach to Old Testament literature. To furnish but one example from Daniel, the Aramaic word *shpr* ("please" or "appear acceptable") was regarded by Wellhausen and his school as rare and generally late in incidence. But with the discovery of tangible written sources from properly attested sites in the ancient Near East, it now becomes clear that this word occurs in the fifth century B.C. Ahiqar papyrus, on the Sefiré stele from the middle of the eighth century B.C., and even in a list of slaves named in one of the Brooklyn papyri. [41]

As the present gaps in the Aramaic linguistic picture are filled in by the discovery and critical appraisal of additional literary sources, it will become increasingly possible to survey the development of the language holistically, and place the study of individual words on a properly accredited basis of linguistic science.[42] But regardless of future developments in this area, scholars can now be sure of one thing. The sheer fact that biblical manuscripts were discovered at Qumran has made it abundantly evident on objective grounds that no component of the Old Testament canon could possibly have been compiled as late as the second century B.C. This consideration, of course, applies to the book of Daniel just as cogently as it does to what were once considered "Maccabean" psalms.

Thus, whatever the difficulties involved, the objective evidence must be confronted squarely as the first step in any scientific methodological procedure. In the light of the enormous accumulation of relevant factual data now at hand, the scholarship of the future must adopt a proper a posteriori inductive approach if it is to discharge its functions in a responsible manner. Authoritarian a priori pronouncements which either ignore objective data or manipulate the facts to suit theoretical exigencies must no longer be allowed to masquerade under the guise of scholarship.

There have been those, such as the late H. H. Rowley, who have professed complete willingness to abandon current Old Testament developmental theories, provided that adequate replacements can be found.[43] In the view of the present writer this response is as faulty as the methodology from which it has emerged. What future Old Testament scholarship needs is not another all-embracing theory of origins or growth so much as the consistent application of a properly accredited scientific method to the data on hand.

Instead of coming to the Old Testament with the view that it is replete with error, full of internal contradictions, characterized by the presence of unhistorical material, marred hopelessly by textual corruptions, etc., the scholar of the coming decades will be convinced of the urgent need for the application of a correct methodology to his task of examining the Hebrew against what is known of the complexity of life in the ancient Near East from at least the third millennium B.C. That this is already being attempted is reflected by the statement of Orlinsky, who wrote: "More and more the older view that the Biblical data were suspect, and even likely to be false, unless corroborated by extra-biblical facts, is giving way to one which holds that, by and large, the Biblical accounts are more likely to be true than false, unless clear-cut evidence from sources outside the Bible demonstrates the reverse." [44]

In the light of all the relevant information currently available it is quite legitimate to scrap such time-honored formulations as the Graf-Wellhausen theory of Pentateuchal origins because of their gross methodological inadequacies. This is not to say that such theories, however extreme in some areas, have had no value for scholarship despite their faulty nature, for the fact is that Old Testament studies would have been infinitely poorer without them. They have served their purpose, however, in that they have pointed the way to a better and more scientific approach to an examination of the Old Testament.

The future labors of scholars must, if they are to be truly productive, be controlled by the most rigorous application of the a posteriori method to the task of evaluating the cultural setting from which the various elements of the canonical Hebrew literature emerged. Instead of formulating or condoning a priori speculation, scholars must lend themselves openly and willingly to the exercise, not of a more moderate form of classical literary criticism, but of an accredited and balanced inductive investigation of all the appropriate objective elements. By this means they will encounter living personalities of the past, and will be able to hear what God had to say to His ancient people, and through them to the world.

FOOTNOTES

1. For an outline of this process see R. K. Harrison, *Introduction to the Old Testament* (Grand Rapids: Eerdmans, 1969), pp. 14-32; 500-9.
2. The narratives in question are not, of course, duplicated since there are significant divergences in matters of detail. Form criticism has shown that repetition with variations was an accredited part of ancient Near Eastern narration. Cf. J. Pedersen, *Israel, Its Life and Culture, I-II* (London: Oxford U., 1946), p. 123.
3. As exemplified by R. D. Wilson, "The Use of 'God' and 'Lord' in the Koran," *Princeton Theological Review* 17 (1919): 644 ff.
4. Cf. W. F. Albright, *History, Archaeology and Christian Humanism* (New York: McGraw-Hill, 1964), pp. 136-37.
5. Darwin's self-developing schema of "natural selection" has been shown to be fallacious. Leo Berg *(Nomogenesis* [London: Constable, 1926], pp. 19 ff. has demonstrated the paroxysmal nature of evolution, while J. B. S. Haldane *(The Causes of Evolution* [New York: Harper, 1932], p. 167) has pointed out that the normal pattern followed by an evolving line has been that of degeneration.
6. Thus, for example, H. Schultz, *Old Testament Theology* (Edinburgh: T & T. Clark, 1893), 1: 25.
7. F. C. S. Schiller, *Logic for Use* (New York: Harcourt, Brace, 1929), p. 410.
8. H. L. Searles, *Logic and Scientific Methods* (New York: Ronald, 1956), p. 210.
9. So L. H. Cragg and R. P. Graham, *An Introduction to the Principles of Chemistry* (Toronto: Clarke, Irwin, 1954), p. 6. This procedure had already been outlined admirably in 1864 by J. A. Froude, *Short Studies on Great Subjects* (London & Glasgow: Collins, n.d.), pp. 11, 16.
10. This latter is the so-called "principle of parsimony," which emphasizes simplicity and economy in the choice of hypotheses.
11. See Harrison, p. 510.
12. Pedersen, pp. 521-22.
13. This term is used in a nonpejorative sense to differentiate the concrete or material disciplines such as the physical, life, psycho-physical and social sciences from both the formal (or abstract) sciences such as mathematics and logic, and the

normative disciplines such as ethics and aesthetics.

14. On these grounds C. A. Simpson's book *The Early Traditions of Israel* (Oxford: Clarendon Press, 1948) was criticized, among others by H. H. Rowley, *The Society for Old Testament Study Book List* (1949), p. 34. Reprinted in H. H. Rowley, *Eleven Years of Bible Bibliography* (Indian Hill, Colo.: Falcon's Wings, 1957), p. 198.

15. For comments on the contrast between Old Testament and Near Eastern methodology see K. A. Kitchen, *Ancient Orient and Old Testament* (London: Tyndale, 1966), pp. 20-28.

16. As emphasized, for example, by C. H. Gordon, "Higher Critics and Forbidden Fruit," *Christianity Today* 4, no. 4 (1959): 3-6.

17. E. Chiera, *They Wrote on Clay* (Cambridge: U. Press, 1939), p. 233.

18. E. R. Thiele, *The Mysterious Numbers of the Hebrew Kings* (Chicago: U. Chicago, 1951). A revised edition (Grand Rapids: Eerdmans) was issued in 1965.

19. For the major earlier studies see Harrison, p. 733, n. 29.

20. Thiele, p. xxi.

21. So Albright, *From the Stone Age to Christianity* (New York: Doubleday, 1957), p. 77.

22. As, for example, in the work of G. von Rad, *Studies in Deuteronomy* (London: SCM, 1953), pp. 26 ff., and B.S. Childs, *Memory and Tradition in Israel* (London: SCM, 1962), p. 34.

23. For the view, first suggested by Naville, that the bulk of Genesis comprises sources in the form of eleven tablets, see Harrison, pp. 542-51.

24. D. N. Freedman, "The Interpretation of Scripture," *Interpretation* 17 (1963): pp. 308-18.

25. So especially E. Nielsen, *Oral Tradition* (London: SCM, 1954), pp. 21 passim.

26. Kitchen, p. 136.

27. Rowley, *Darius the Mede and the Four World Empires in the Book of Daniel* (Cardiff: U. Wales, 1935), pp. 20 ff.

28. Probably the Gobryas of Xenophon was Ugbaru (cf. *Cyropaedia*, 4, 6, 1 ff.), while that of Herodotus was evidently the Behistun Gaubaruva (cf. *The Persian Wars*, 3:70).

29. Cf. col. 3, lines 20, 22, of the Nabonidus Chronicle.

30. J. C. Whitcomb, Jr., *Darius the Mede* (Grand Rapids: Eerd-

mans, 1959), pp. 10 ff.

31. J. Bright, *A History of Israel* (Philadelphia: Westminster, 1960), p. 418.
32. Harrison, *Archaeology of the Old Testament* (London: English Universities, 1962), p. 156, n. 99.
33. N. W. Porteous, *Daniel: A Commentary* (Philadelphia: Westminster, 1965).
34. M. Burrows, *The Dead Sea Scrolls* (New York: Viking, 1955), p. 109.
35. Cf. P. Hyatt, "The Dead Sea Discoveries: Retrospect and Challenge," *Journal of Biblical Literature* 76 (1957): 5; F. M. Cross, Jr., *The Ancient Library of Qumran and Modern Biblical Studies* (New York: Doubleday, 1961), p. 165.
36. Porteous, p. 13.
37. For a careful summary see Kitchen in D. J. Wiseman et al., *Notes on Some Problems in the Book of Daniel* (London: Tyndale, 1965), pp. 31-79.
38. Cf. E. G. Kraeling, *The Brooklyn Aramaic Papyri* (New Haven: Yale U., 1953), p. 7; J. J. Koopmans, *Aramäische Chrestomathie*, 2 vols. (Leiden: Nederlandse Instituut Voor Het Nabije Oosten, 1962), 1:154.
39. S. R. Driver, *Introduction to the Literature of the Old Testament* (New York: Scribner, 1913), p. 508.
40. W. J. Martin in Wiseman et al., p. 30.
41. For the latter see Albright, "North-West Semitic Names in a List of Egyptian Slaves from the Eighteenth Century B.C.," *Journal of the American Oriental Society* 74 (1954): 229.
42. For an outline of Near Eastern linguistic procedures see Kitchen, pp. 141 ff.
43. For example, in *The Growth of the Old Testament* (London: Hutchinson's U. Library, 1950), p. 46.
44. H. M. Orlinsky, *Ancient Israel* (New York: Cornell U., 1954), p. 8.

TRADITION OF
THE SAYINGS OF JESUS:
A CRUX INTERPRETUM

by Everett F. Harrison

Ever since the rise of form criticism, students of the New Testament have been reminded over and over again that a long interval of several decades separates the ministry of Jesus from the origin of the gospel records. In that interval, the church was preaching, teaching and growing despite opposition. Form criticism has tended to insist that during this time the tradition was so largely determined by the interests and needs of the Christian community that the gospels actually reflect the faith and life of the church to a greater extent than they do the teaching of our Lord. Much has been altered and much has been added. The presumption is that the church saw no harm in attributing to Jesus what it had experienced and been taught through the ministry of the Spirit. It is asserted that the distinction between the earthly Jesus speaking to His contemporaries and that of the heavenly Lord speaking to His people through the Spirit was hardly felt and was not insisted on.

The problem would be lessened if the remainder of the New Testament recorded a substantial number of Jesus' sayings which could then be compared with the sayings in the gospels. But the number of sayings available for this purpose is exceedingly small. It is this circumstance which has led some scholars to question the existence of any extensive body of teaching from Jesus' lips which could have been utilized by the evangelists. Howard M. Teeple has gone so far as to write an article with the title, "The Oral Tradition that Never Existed." [1] The alternative to a carefully preserved oral tradition is the creation of sayings by the church which are credited to Jesus, though few, if any, are so hardy in their attitude as to claim that none of His sayings is authentic.

A valiant attempt to salvage the recorded utterances of Jesus by grounding their genuineness on faithful transmission has been made by the Swedish scholars Riesenfeld and Gerhardsson. [2] They have stressed the importance of the Jewish milieu in which our Lord worked, and have likened His relationship to His disciples to that of rabbis who required their pupils to memorize their teaching in order to profit by it and be able to communicate it to others. This approach, which seemed to offer real help, has not been widely accepted. Riesenfeld's endeavor to explain the absence of Jesus' words from the missionary preaching of the church on the ground that this was a "holy" tradition not designed or suitable for the public, still leaves unanswered the problem of the scarcity of such material in the epistles.

Other objections have been raised. It is anachronistic to treat Pharisaic Judaism on the basis of rabbinic Judaism of a later time; further, it is unwarranted to create the impression that Jesus was really a rabbi and His disciples were pupils. [3] The element of immediacy, the freedom and extempore character of Jesus' utterances "is such as to exclude conscious concern with mnemonics, catechetical purpose or halakic procedure." [4] Also the theory does not seem to square with the presence of variations in the reporting of Jesus' sayings by the evangelists. Yet, the presentation is by no means a total failure, for it has served to remind us that we cannot sever Jesus and His movement from the Jewish milieu in which He lived and served. Although W. D. Davies is critical of some features of the view of the two Swedish scholars, he feels obliged to say:

> They have made it far more historically probable and reasonably credible, over against the scepticism of much form-criticism, that in the Gospels we are within hearing of the authentic voice and within sight of the authentic activity of Jesus of Nazareth, however much muffled and obscured these may be by the process of transmission. [5]

A far different approach to the task of recovering the teaching of Jesus is that of Bultmann.

> We can only count on possessing a genuine similitude of Jesus where, on the one hand, expression is given to the contrast between Jewish morality and piety and the distinctive eschatological temper which characterized the preaching of Jesus; and where on the other hand we find no specifically Christian features. [6]

This methodology, based on contrast, can be expected to yield only minimal results, for the criteria are restricted and negative in character. No account is taken of the possibility of common ground between Jesus and the Jewish background or between Him and the church He established. Nevertheless, the results achieved by the application of these guidelines can be expected to receive general recognition and should be gratefully acknowledged. For example, the studies of Jeremias on the word *Amen*[7] as an introductory formula to some of Jesus' utterances and on His use of *Abba*[8] have won wide acceptance. However, Bultmann's insistence on trying to distinguish between the contribution of the Hebrew-Christian church and that of the Hellenistic-Christian communities is a dubious refinement. Our sources represent the latter segment as dependent on and in accord with the former. Jerusalem remained for some time the center of the church's influence because of the presence of the apostles. Without ruling out completely the possibility of the *Gemeindetheologie* explanation for some sayings attributed to Jesus, it behooves us to examine the gospels to see whether they encourage us to hope for a solution along this line.

THE GOSPELS

All will agree that, according to the gospels, teaching was one of the major activities of the Master and that His teaching made a profound impression on those who heard it (Mk. 1:22; cf. Jn. 7:46). To have a tradition *that* Jesus taught, without a tradition of *what* He taught, would be strange indeed and quite incomprehensible, since the tradition *that* He taught includes the report of the impact of His words. It would be strange also, on the assumption that the church rather than Jesus has authored or doctored the greater part of the corpus of instruction in the gospels, that the statement of His uniqueness in this area should be retained, "You are not to be called rabbi, for you have one teacher" (Mt. 23:8, RSV; cf. Mk. 1:27).

According to the prologue of Luke's gospel, from the very beginning of the public ministry of Jesus He was attended by "eyewitnesses and ministers of the word" (Lk. 1:2, RSV). The term *eyewitnesses* evidently has reference to the things which Jesus did, whereas *ministers of the word* bears on the spoken ministry of our Lord. We are not suggesting that two groups are in view here, but only that the two phrases seem designed to cover the two major aspects of the mission, namely, His deeds and His words. *Ministers of the Word* suggests more than hearers. At the very least it means that these people passed on what they heard, which is explicitly affirmed in *paredosan*—"they handed down." Luke's words are strongly opposed to the notion of the church as a community which created sayings and attributed them to Jesus. Rather, the church is pictured as the recipient of a tradition of Jesus' deeds and words transmitted by an accredited group who were with the Lord from the beginning of His work. We have an echo of this duality of content (deeds and words) in the testimony of Peter and John to the Sanhedrin: "We cannot but speak of what we have seen and heard" (Ac. 4:20, RSV).

Literary criticism has insisted that one of the sources utilized by Matthew and Luke was Q, basically a collection of the sayings of Jesus. To be sure, strenuous efforts have been put forth here and there to eliminate the necessity for Q, especially on the assumption that Luke derived his non-Markan material from Matthew.[9] But this cannot be successfully demonstrated. As C. S. C. Williams remarks, "A close study of sections in a Synopsis where Matthew has a fuller account than Mark and where Luke also uses Mark shows that Luke did not use Matthew but Mark as a source; this point, which should have received consideration in any attempt to dispense with Q, makes it impossible to set Q aside on the theory that Luke depended on Matthew."[10] Other matters remain debatable, such as the precise contents of Q and the question whether it is to be regarded as a written or an oral source, but all that concerns us at the moment is the likelihood that such a collection was in existence and was regarded so highly by two gospel writers as to be drawn upon in reporting the sayings of Jesus. Kümmel observes that, although Matthew made changes at various points in the content of Mark, he almost never altered the sayings of Jesus recorded there.[11]

One of the most easily recognized forms of Jesus' teaching which has been isolated by the form-critical school is the pronouncement story. It is obvious that the story was preserved for the sake of the pronouncement that marks the climax and gives point to the whole episode. Examples are the Zaccheus incident, culminating in the saying, "For the Son of man came to seek and to save the lost," and the story of the tribute money, concluding with the telling remark, "Render to Caesar the things that are Caesar's, and to God the things that are God's." Pronouncement stories testify to the high regard accorded Jesus' teaching.

Another readily detectable form is the parable, which is used to set forth a considerable portion of His instruction to the people. That the church created these units is highly improbable, seeing that there is no evidence that in its own instruction parables were spawned. No attempt was made to imitate the Master in this area, where His genius was inimitable. The same respect was shown toward the Son of man sayings.

The stamp of Jesus is on the Lord's Prayer, which was clearly intended to be used, and in this process it would become fixed in the memory. It is important to observe that no distinctly Christian (post-Easter) elements intrude here, even though Matthew and Luke differ at places in the wording, possibly reflecting differing church settings. Nothing hinders our acceptance of it as reflecting the words of the Master.

Here and there statements of Jesus are cited in which the use of His words by His followers in a permanent way is implied. "He who hears you hears me" (Lk. 10:16, RSV) seems to indicate a very close relationship between the words of Christ and the words of those who go forth to represent Him. In saying, "My words will not pass away" (Mt. 24:35, RSV) He makes a prediction which could only be realized as His words were retained and transmitted. Even if one were to hold that such a statement was put in His mouth by the evangelist, at the very least this would reflect a sense of the enduring worth of His sayings, which in turn argues for a real effort to preserve them.

The same can be said of certain statements in the gospel according to John: "The words that I have spoken to you are spirit and life" (Jn. 6:63, RSV). "He who rejects me and does not receive my sayings has a judge; the word that I have spoken will be his judge on the last day" (Jn. 12:48, RSV). "If you abide in me, and my words abide in you, ask

46

whatever you will, and it shall be done for you" (Jn. 15:7, RSV).

Doubtless, some attention should be paid to the possibility that the church may have regarded the function of the Spirit as teacher as operating in a way which did not demand absolute recall and strict fidelity in transmission. Yet the promise of the Savior is put in very precise language: "He will teach you all things, and bring to your remembrance all that I have said to you" (Jn. 14:26, RSV). This does not exclude further sayings through the Spirit (Rev. 2-3). If the church at the time of the writing of the fourth gospel had as a church abandoned the idea of a faithful transmission of the words of Jesus, John's emphasis is strangely anachronistic.

Jesus' words are sometimes intimately related to events. Nowhere is this relationship more striking than in the matter of His death. Here we grasp the firm texture of historic fact. We can start with the circumstances which on the human side determined how His career would come to a close. It was not only the high claims He made for Himself that excited opposition but also there was the offense created by His words, those stinging utterances directed toward the scribes and Pharisees which laid bare their hypocrisy. The decision to effect the death of the Prophet of Nazareth reflects the genuineness of these statements.

But the gospels do not stop here. They also represent Jesus as foreseeing and predicting His death. Bultmann and other extreme advocates of the form-critical approach regard these sayings as prophecies stemming from the event and hence not prophecies at all, but utterances put in Jesus' mouth by the church. Yet even so radical a critic as Maurice Goguel is not prepared to dismiss all such sayings cavalierly. While he sees the hand of the church in the three formulations predicting the Passion in Mark and Matthew, he feels obliged to accept the genuineness of Luke 17:25, which follows a saying regarding the coming of the Son of man and reads thus: "But first he must suffer many things and be rejected by this generation" (RSV). Goguel's comment is, "This saying cannot have been invented by tradition, for it does not mention death or resurrection." [12] There is widespread agreement that Jesus could and did predict His death, although opinions differ as to whether or not all the details of the predictions were spoken by Him or in some cases were supplied by the Christian community in the light of the cross event.

A very positive and satisfying statement has been made on this issue by Goppelt:

> Jesus' own view of the conclusion of His earthly ministry should be briefly explained here. At the end of His career He did not simply expect the dawn of judgment and salvation as did the prophets until John the Baptist. He proclaimed not only the coming of the kingdom of God with its concomitant judgment upon all evil (Mt. 4:17), but also the coming of the Son of man as judge of the world (Lk. 12:8) as well as the rejection and the exaltation of the Son of man (Mk. 8:31; 9:12; Lk. 17:25). At first glance it is surprising that these three pronouncements are never tied together to each other but always appear separately. This observation has prompted Bultmann's school to conclude that only the proclamation of the kingdom is genuine with Jesus and that the assertions about the Son of man represent constructions of the early church. This is, they think, especially true of the passion predictions, all of which then are *vaticinia ex eventu*. On the contrary, the observation that the three strands remain separate can be explained only if all of them genuinely do arise from the situation of Jesus' earthly ministry. Jesus could not unite the future coming of the Son of man as judge of the world with the coming of the kingdom of God because both of them do not coincide. It is now in the present that "the kingdom of God has come upon you" (Mt. 12:28)! By the same token He could hardly say that the Son of man must be rejected, rise again, and come as the judge of the world. Such a combination would have contradicted the sense of both pronouncements. Each is addressed to a different audience. The pronouncement that the Son of man as judge of the world will acknowledge those as His own who here have acknowledged Jesus is a public call to repentance. It makes clear to all that their response to Jesus determines their eternal destiny. The

passion predictions, on the other hand, are always addressed to the disciples. Only to them do they make any sense. If we look at the original components of these predictions we see that they interpret Jesus' journey to Jerusalem for the disciples and promise them the concealed resurrection of Jesus. The resurrected Lord did indeed appear only to them. The passion predictions are surely much more than predictions about Jesus' own fate. They "teach" what "must" happen to the promised One according to God's redemptive plan proclaimed in the scriptures (cf. Lk. 24:25ff.). They thus announce the conclusion of Jesus' ministry, and it is only from this conclusion that the entire ministry can be made meaningful. [13]

With respect to the possibility of prophecy on the part of Jesus, Johannes Munck, a New Testament scholar of rank, has protested the rigid exclusion which criticism has imposed. He writes,

If you have not seen this difference between us and the better position of the OT scholars I can give you an example. It is a thing which for many years has puzzled me. Namely, that in the NT discipline a prophecy of Jesus about, let us say, the destruction of Jerusalem must be a *vaticinium ex eventu*, a prophecy invented after the event. When Jerusalem had been destroyed these words were attributed to Jesus by the church. But in the OT discipline when a prophet had predicted the destruction of Jerusalem our OT colleagues will say: as Jerusalem was destroyed the year so and so, this prophecy must have been spoken some years before. [14]

Goppelt's comments about the predictions of Jesus include a reference to His audience. This subject has been made the theme of a study by J. Arthur Baird, who feels he has established a definite correlation between wording and audience in the teaching of Jesus, with the result that at certain points, at least, it is possible to be reasonably sure that we have His *ipsissima verba*. "One must probably say that audience was an important part of the wording of a particular logion; that is, wording and audience were equally important to the editors, and far more important than historical, literary, or geographical factors." [15]

49

Before leaving the gospels to explore the remainder of the New Testament, we propose to look at the Great Commission in Matthew 28:19-20. This passage has been challenged on the ground that the trinitarian phrasing of the application of baptism is not reflected in the book of Acts and must therefore reflect later church usage. We cannot turn aside to discuss this problem except to say that Matthew's report presupposes a Gentile setting, whereas Acts speaks of Jews who become Christians. We must concentrate, rather, on the words attributed to Jesus: "teaching them to observe all that I have commanded you." This injunction follows the command to go and disciple all nations. The objection raised at this point is that the church could hardly have received such a command in the light of its failure to move out to the nations until it was obliged to do so under the pressure of persecution or special revelation (Peter in Ac. 10-11). We do not have the data to interpret the thinking of the Jerusalem church about its worldwide obligation in this early period. No time schedule was attached to the program of witnessing, whether in Matthew 28:19-20 or in Acts 1:8. The success of the church in Jerusalem and Judea may well have been a factor in hindering more remote operations. One should not overlook the possibility that some of the converts who had lived abroad returned after a time to the country of their birth and evangelized there. The founding of the Roman church in this fashion is a distinct possibility. But looking beyond this question, even if we were to grant that the church could have put the Great Commission into the mouth of the risen Lord, we think it extremely unlikely that it would have elected to make Him say that the disciples were to teach Gentile as well as Jewish converts all that He had taught them *if they did not possess those words and cherish them.* Actually, it is not necessary to concede that the words of the commission were supplied by the church, since examination of Matthew discloses that the motif of reaching the Gentiles already had a secure place in the ministry of Jesus (8:5-13; 13:38; 15:21-28; 24:14; 26:13). Now that redemption has been achieved in the cross and resurrection, the charge to carry the message to all nations is the natural and climactic sequel.

THE ACTS

We have sampled some of the data in the gospels relating to the teaching of Jesus. Space forbids further investigation of this area. We turn next to the book of Acts. It must be admitted at the outset that there is an almost complete lack of reference to the teaching of Jesus here, for Luke is intent on setting forth the proclamation, the kerygma, as that which accounts for the growth of the church. It is tantalizing to find references indicating that the church was taught by its leaders and yet be given no information as to the content of the teaching. This is true, for example, of Acts 2:42, where we read concerning the converts at Pentecost that "they devoted themselves to the apostles' teaching." Bo Reicke's comment is helpful:

> Acts 2:42, where the instruction given by the twelve apostles is mentioned, indicates that the apostles acted as teachers of the Jerusalem congregation. Considering the fact that according to Acts 1:21-22 every apostle had to be an eyewitness of the life of Jesus, one may postulate that the actions and sayings of the Lord were an important subject of this teaching.[16]

One might add that special attention would likely be given to the fulfillment of Old Testament prophecy concerning the mission of the Messiah, going into more detail than Peter had been able to include in his Pentecost sermon. In this connection we do well to recall Philip's use of Isaiah 53 with the Ethiopian eunuch (Ac. 8:32-35).

In Acts 11:26 it is stated that for a whole year Barnabas and Saul conducted a teaching ministry in the Antioch church, and in 13:1 other teachers are named. If teaching is noted as a prominent element in the life of the two leading congregations of the early church, it is reasonable to conclude that this practice prevailed in other centers as well. F. F. Bruce comments:

> As the number of converts increased, especially in the course of the Gentile mission, "schools" for the training of instructors would have become almost a necessity, and digests of the teaching of Jesus would inevitably have been drawn up, orally if not in writing. We may envisage such a life-setting for the "sayings collection" on which Matthew and Luke drew, and at a later date the Matthean Gospel itself has been viewed as taking place in such a school. [17]

In the light of the passages we have noted from Acts, it is hazardous to assume, as some have done, that the church did not need to have the teaching of Jesus conveyed to it in a didactic form, since it had prophets ministering to its needs spontaneously from time to time. It is fairly evident from Acts 13:1-2 that prophets functioned along with teachers in the life of the church. Both were needed. But the ministry of prophets did not make unnecessary the instruction provided by apostles and teachers who labored under their direction. It is sufficient here to point to the characteristic way in which believers are described in Acts, namely, as disciples (learners).

But so far we have not found any explicit reference to Jesus' teaching in the Acts. However, there is a passage of this nature, a statement by Paul in the course of his message to the Ephesian elders (20:35, RSV): "In all things I have shown you that by so toiling one must help the weak, remembering the words of the Lord Jesus, how he said, 'It is more blessed to give than to receive.' " In this sentence the antecedent of "remembering" is not Paul but is general in its reference and includes the elders. From this we can deduce that Paul must have taught them this saying. Further, it is noteworthy that the emphatic pronoun *autos* occurs here with reference to Jesus. He Himself said this. No one put these words in His mouth. Again, the word "blessed" *(makarion)* is a word which according to our gospels was frequently used by Jesus, for example in the Beatitudes. Also, the saying before us accords with Jesus' counsel about inviting those to dinner who will be unable to repay the favor (Lk. 14:12-14), so it has the ring of genuineness. To conjecture that Luke has put these words in the mouth of Paul is faulty procedure, for on this occasion Luke was present as a companion of the apostle. Would he introduce into Paul's message a statement which does not appear in his gospel any more than in Mark or Matthew? As a matter of fact, the speech as a whole reflects Pauline ideas and language to a remarkable degree, as Percy Gardner has shown. 18 Paul does not appeal to a documentary source but to an oral tradition—"the words of the Lord Jesus." This passage indicates that the early church was in possession of a tradition of Jesus' sayings. The silence of Acts is not total. In fact, we are warranted in concluding that if a saying not found in our gospels was current in the church, those which are included in these documents must have been widely known in order to command a place in the record.

THE EPISTLES

There is still need to continue our quest, which now reaches into the epistles. Acts 20:35 affords an easy transition to the writings of Paul.

That Paul had ample opportunity to consult people who were close to the tradition of Jesus' sayings is easily demonstrated. During his postconversion days in Damascus he could have learned much from believers who had come from the Jerusalem church. His first visit to Jerusalem as a Christian brought him into contact with Peter for a period of two weeks. The language suggests that he was Peter's houseguest. Can we possibly imagine Paul not making the best use of this time by questioning this leading apostle about the words and deeds of Jesus? There was opportunity to consult with James also (Gal. 1:19). It seems that Paul was especially close to Barnabas (Ac. 9:27), who may well have been connected with the Jerusalem church from the very beginning and was an important source of information. The year they spent together at Antioch and their period of joint missionary endeavor (Ac. 11:26; 13:1—14:28) provided more advantages for learning and discussion about the topic dearest to them both. John Mark was still another contact with the early Jerusalem church (Ac. 13:5). Several trips to Jerusalem brought Paul into touch with the elders of the mother church, men who would be familiar with the patterns of instruction given to new converts. Other possible sources of information were Silas (Ac. 15:22, 40), Andronicus and Junias (Ro. 16:7), Philip the evangelist (Ac. 18:22; 21:8), and Mnason (Ac. 21:16). Besides these there must have been many unnamed persons available to Paul who had listened to the Savior during His public ministry.

Probably the earliest of Paul's letters is First Thessalonians. Two passages are worthy of note. The first (2:13-16) has been made the subject of a special study by R. Schippers. [19] When Paul refers to the word of God which he proclaimed at Thessalonica he has in mind oral communication rather than Scripture. In fact, he makes use of the technical term for oral transmission *(paralabontes)*. The general theme of the passage is persecution, including a parallel drawn between the situation of the Thessalonian believers and Christians in Judea who have suffered at the hands of their fellow countrymen. These unbelieving Jews had hindered Paul wherever he had gone, seeking to prevent his ministry to the Gentiles. The language may be reminiscent of Jesus' words to the Pharisees, charging them not only with refusal to enter the kingdom of heaven but also with not allowing others to enter (Mt. 23:13). More striking is the occurrence of several words in the Pauline passage which are identical or nearly so with terms used in Matthew 23: *apokteinō, prophētai, ekdiōkō* (Matthew has *diōkō),* and *anaplēroō (Matthew has plēroō).* While the ending of the Pauline passage is not verbally in agreement with Matthew 23, the relationship in thought is very close: "But God's wrath has come upon them at last," and "Behold, your house is forsaken and desolate." The conclusion to which one naturally comes is that Paul was familiar with Jesus' teaching in this matter of Jewish opposition to God's message and messengers. No written gospels were yet available, but much was preserved in oral tradition that Paul could draw upon, material that was to find its way into written form.

In 1 Thessalonians 5:2-3 Paul uses the figure of the thief in the night when warning about the unexpectedness of the Lord's return and the need for watchfulness. Jesus used the same figure in relation to the same subject (Mt. 24:43).

The apostle's first letter to the Corinthians is unusually rich in apparent allusions to the teaching of Christ. Paul's observation that celibacy involves special qualifications (7:7) may well be an echo of the Master's teaching contained in Matthew 19:12, even though the language is quite different. In 7:10 the apostle appeals to the teaching of the Lord to the effect that a wife is not to separate from her husband (cf. Mt. 19:3-9). Here we are not left in doubt. Paul knows what Jesus taught on this subject. Gerhardsson appears to be justified in saying, "One who argues in this way, and considers the commandments of Jesus, the Lord, as binding doctrine and precept, must regard it as his duty to gain access to as much as possible of what Jesus said and taught." [20]

In the same chapter the apostle seeks to show the advantage for the single woman over the married woman in terms of undistracted devotion to the Lord (1 Co. 7:34-35). The words *euparedron tō kuriō aperispastōs* tally so closely with the description of Mary in contrast to Martha (Lk.

10:38-42) as to lead C. F. D. Moule to remark, "One cannot help wondering, therefore, whether this story, which St. Luke was later to include in his gospel, was not already current, perhaps orally, and whether St. Paul was not mentally drawing upon it to illustrate his ethical teaching."[21]

Farther on, Paul touches the right of an apostle to receive financial support and declares, "The Lord commanded that those who proclaim the gospel should get their living by the gospel" (1 Co. 9:14, RSV). Here also Paul may have become familiar with the saying later incorporated by Luke, "The laborer deserves his wages" (Lk. 10:7, RSV). The theme is the same in both passages.

Paul's words on the institution of the Lord's Supper involve tradition, since the technical terms "received" and "delivered" occur here (1 Co. 11:23; cf. 15:3). But here the situation is somewhat complicated in that he states that he received this information from the Lord, in contrast to 15:3, where the Jerusalem church is the mediating factor, judging by the contents of the paragraph. The usual explanation for the phrase "from the Lord" is that Paul has in mind the ultimate source of the tradition, namely, the one who instituted the supper. Cullmann thinks we are able to go beyond this explanation:

> The designation *Kyrios* can be understood as not only pointing to the historical Jesus as the chronological beginning and the first link of the chain of tradition, but to the exalted Lord as the real author of the whole tradition developing itself within the apostolic Church. This hypothesis best explains St. Paul's direct identification of the apostolic *paradosis* with *Kyrios*: the Lord himself is at work in the transmission of his words and deeds by the Church; he works through the Church.[22]

This insight may be correct, although it is possible to maintain that Paul could apply the title "Lord" to the earthly Jesus, just as Luke does on occasion (e.g., Lk. 10:39-41). Note especially a passage already considered (1 Co. 9:14), where Paul couples "Lord" with a past tense ("commanded").

The apostle's word about mountain-moving faith (1 Co. 13:2) may depend on the Lord's use of similar language as reported in two passages (Mt. 17:20; 21:21), although the possibility that this had already become a proverbial expression before Jesus used it should be borne in mind. Turning to Romans, a cluster of sayings is found in the paraenetic portions of the epistle that seem to depend on a knowledge of the sayings of Jesus. "Bless those who persecute you; bless and do not curse them" (12:14, RSV) is not verbally identical with "Love your enemies and pray for those who persecute you" (Mt. 5:44, RSV) but conveys much the same sentiment. A similar situation is seen in Paul's word, "Repay no one evil for evil" (12:17, RSV) when compared with "Do not resist one who is evil" (Mt. 5:39, RSV). Although the apostle's statement about paying one's obligations to the state (Ro. 13:7) is couched in terminology that differs somewhat from that of Jesus in a more restricted area (Mt. 22:15-22), the key word *apodote* occurs in both and reveals a similar approach to the whole issue. There is considerable resemblance between Paul's warning against placing a stumbling block or hindrance in the way of a brother (Ro. 14:13) and the stern utterance of Jesus about those who cause the little ones who believe in him to stumble (Mt. 18:5-6). The following verse has something for us also: "I know and am persuaded in the Lord Jesus that nothing is unclean in itself" (14:14). This language invites comparison with the episode in which Jesus, in defiance of Jewish tradition, declared all foods clean (Mk. 7:18-19). Of special interest is the fact that Paul finds his certainty on this point "in the Lord Jesus." While it may be possible to assign this simply to the apostle's Christian experience,[23] greater probability lies in the judgment that he is referring to our Lord's teaching. "It may be thought that this style [the solemn tone of the verse] is due to the fact that Paul intends to be understood as referring to a teaching of Jesus. This is confirmed by the mention of the name of Jesus itself, for everywhere else he speaks of the Lord only."[24]

One other passage from Paul should be examined: "Let the word of Christ dwell in you richly" (Col. 3:16). The phrase, "the word of Christ," does not occur elsewhere. Although the construction could be an objective genitive (the word about Christ), the parallel with "the peace of Christ" in the preceding verse suggests otherwise. Just as the peace of Christ surely means the peace that comes from Christ, so the word of Christ is best taken as the word or teaching that proceeds from Him. Since Paul goes on to urge his readers to teach and admonish one another on the basis of this word, it is not presuming too much to suppose that he has in mind a body of teaching emanating from the Savior which he has given out during his teaching sessions at the hall of Tyrannus in Ephesus, which in turn has been passed on by Epaphras to these believers in Colossae.

The very structure of Paul's eschatological thought is probably derived from Jesus, since the terminology of the two ages, the present one and the one to come, is not found in the Old Testament. G. E. Ladd writes:

> We must recognize the possibility that this terminology existed in rabbinic Judaism and that Paul brought it into the Christian tradition. However, for this there is no proof. It is more likely, in view of the appearance of the terminology in our sources, that it came into the Christian tradition through Jesus' teaching, and Paul uses this same terminology which was also emerging simultaneously in rabbinic idiom.[25]

It is plausible also that the apostle's frequent references to suffering with Christ as an aspect of Christian life stem from his familiarity with the precross teaching of the Master on the necessity of bearing the cross as part of the obligation of discipleship.

One finds it hard to accept the notion that a man who in

his early days had steeped himself not only in the law (Phil. 3:5-6) but also in the traditions of the fathers (Gal. 1:13-14), and then turned to faith in Jesus of Nazareth, would be indifferent to what was available to him concerning the teaching that the Master had committed to His followers. Nevertheless, the sum total of the apostle's dependence on the sayings of Jesus in his letters is admittedly small. How can this be explained? It may be helpful to reflect that Paul has almost nothing to say either about the deeds of Jesus or the events of His earthly life. The great exception is his preoccupation with the death and resurrection of the Savior. To him the importance of Jesus' redemptive achievement was so great, so overwhelming, that it almost eclipsed what had gone before. The life and the ministry were viewed as basically preparation for the climax.

When founding churches, Paul was in essentially the same position as his predecessors. His converts required teaching. As we have seen, the great congregations at Jerusalem and Antioch were faithfully and regularly taught, and we cannot imagine that this ministry was carried out apart from reference to the content of Jesus' teaching. The virtual silence of Acts on that content is to a considerable degree matched in Paul's letters. Yet the instruction must have been given. Instead of approaching the problem simply from the side of Paul, we should put ourselves in the place of his congregations. To suppose that there was no curiosity or demand to learn of what preceded the cross and the resurrection is to close one's eyes to human nature. As surely as the gospels were needed to satisfy such a desire, the spoken word of the servant of Christ must have been called on to meet the need in the period before the gospels were written.

The habit of epistolary writers in general (here we are anticipating somewhat the brief comments on James and 1 Peter to follow) of giving the substance of Jesus' teaching rather than quoting Him directly may be due to the fact that the use of quotations was ordinarily reserved in the church for referring to the Old Testament, at least at this early period.

It is not expedient to examine thoroughly the general epistles. Regarding James, it has been well said, "James says less about the Master than any other writer in the NT, but his speech is more like that of the Master than the speech of any one of them."[26] We shall make use of only one instance, probably the most striking of all the echoes of Jesus' speech in his epistle. "But above all, my brethren, do not swear, either by heaven or by earth or with any other oath, but let your yes be yes and your no be no, that you may not fall under condemnation" (Ja. 5:12, RSV). Examination of Matthew 5:34-37 shows that James has reproduced the essence of the teaching recorded there, including the reference to heaven and earth as well as the injunction to be restricted to yes and no.

First Peter is famous for its inclusion of *verba Christi*.[27] We shall restrict ourselves to one example: "Maintain good conduct among the Gentiles, so that in case they speak against you as wrongdoers, they may see your good deeds and glorify God on the day of visitation" (2:12, RSV). The counterpart in Jesus' words is this: "Let your light so shine before men, that they may see your good works and give glory to your Father who is in heaven" (Mt. 5:16, RSV).

It is true of these writers as of Paul that almost all of the dominical material appears in hortatory passages. This may help to explain why there is no attribution to Jesus. "It is not the nature of paraenesis to include direct quotation."[28]

CONCLUSION

In conclusion, it is fairly obvious that we have been dealing with a difficult problem. Sparse indeed are the references to the words of Jesus in the Acts and the epistles, though they are abundant in the gospels. Some scholars believe that the only way to tackle the problem is through the form-critical approach. Norman Perrin says:

> In our attempts to reconstruct the teaching of Jesus, then, we must first seek to write a history of the tradition with which we are concerned and to arrive at the earliest form of the saying in the tradition, or the earliest form of the saying we can reconstruct from the tradition. What next? Well, clearly, we have to ask ourselves the question as to whether this saying should now be attributed to the early Church or to the historical Jesus, *and the nature of the synoptic tradition is such that the burden of proof will be upon the claim to authenticity.* 29

This is an extreme approach that can hope to yield only meager results. Great areas of Jesus' teaching, on such a basis, must remain under the critic's suspicion without real justification.

If a person faces a dark screen, punctuated only by occasional gleams of light, he will be wise to conclude that the other side of the screen is ablaze with light. As the student looks at the Acts and the epistles, he is facing such a screen. He can reasonably conclude that there is a far larger corpus of tradition of the sayings of Jesus behind the screen, on which the evangelists have drawn for their gospel accounts.

FOOTNOTES

1. Howard M. Teeple, "The Oral Tradition that Never Existed," *Journal of Biblical Literature*, 1970.

2. Harald Riesenfeld, "The Gospel Tradition and Its Beginnings," *Studia Evangelica* (Berlin, 1959), pp. 43-65; Birger Gerhardsson, *Memory and Manuscript*, trans. Eric Sharpe (Uppsala: C. W. K. Gleer, 1961); and *Tradition and Transmission in Early Christianity*, trans. Eric Sharpe (Lund: C. W. K. Gleer, 1964).

3. Morton Smith, "A Comparison of Early Christian and Early Rabbinic Tradition," *Journal of Biblical Literature* 82 (June, 1963): 171-72. Cf. T. W. Manson, *The Teaching of Jesus* (Cambridge: U. Press, 1939), pp. 239-40.

4. A. N. Wilder, "Form-history and the Oldest Tradition," *Neotestamentica et Patristica* (Leiden: Brill, 1962), p. 8.

5. W. D. Davies, "Reflections on a Scandinavian Approach to 'the Gospel Tradition,' " *Neotestamentica et Partristica*, p. 34.

6. R. Bultmann, The History of the Synoptic Tradition, trans. John Marsh (Oxford: Blackwell, 1963), p. 205.

7. J. Jeremias, "Kennzeichen der ipsissima vox Jesu" in the Alfred Wikenhauser Festschrift, *Synoptische Studien* (Munchen: Zink, 1953), pp. 86-93.

8. Jeremias, *The Central Message of the New Testament* (New York: Scribner, 1965), pp. 9-30.

9. E.g., A. M. Farrer, "On Dispensing with Q" in *Studies in the Gospels*, ed. D. E. Nineham (Oxford: Blackwell, 1955), pp. 55-86; and W. R. Farmer, *The Synoptic Problem* (New York: Macmillan, 1964).

10. C. S. C. Williams, "Luke-Acts in Recent Study," *The Expository Times* (Feb., 1962), p. 134.

11. W. G. Kümmel, *Introduction to the New Testament*, trans. A. J. Mattill (Nashville: Abingdon, 1966).

12. Maurice Goguel, *The Life of Jesus*, trans. Olive Wyon (New York: Macmillan, 1949), p. 390.

13. L. Goppelt, *Jesus, Paul, and Judaism*, trans. and ed. Edward Schroeder (New York: Nelson, 1964), pp. 91-92.

14. Johannes Munck, "Pauline Research Since Schweitzer" in *The Bible in Modern Scholarship*, ed. James Philip (Nashville: Abingdon, 1965), p. 177.

15. J. Arthur Baird, *Audience Criticism and the Historical Jesus* (Philadelphia: Westminster, 1969), p. 62.

16. Bo Reicke, *The Gospels Reconsidered* (Oxford: Blackwell, 1960), p. 111.

17. G. C. D. Howley et al., eds., *A New Testament Commentary* (Grand Rapids: Zondervan, 1969), p. 95.

18. Percy Gardiner, "The Speeches of St. Paul in Acts" in *Essays on Some Biblical Questions of the Day by the Members of the University of Cambridge*, ed. H. B. Swete (London: Macmillan, 1909), p. 402.

19. R. Schippers, "Pre-Synoptic Tradition in I Thessalonians 2:13-16," *Novum Testamentum* 8 (1966): 223-34.

20. Gerhardsson, *Memory and Manuscript*, p. 320.

21. C. F. D. Moule, "Uses of Parables and Sayings as Illustrative Material in Early Christian Catechesis," *Journal of Theological Studies* 3 (Apr., 1952): 76.

22. O. Cullmann, *The Early Church*, ed. A. J. B. Higgins (Philadelphia: Westminster, 1956), p. 62.

23. C. H. Dodd, *The Epistle of Paul to the Romans* (New York: R. Long and R. R. Smith, 1932), p. 215.

24. F. J. Leenhardt, *The Epistle to the Romans*, trans. Harold Knight (London: Lutterworth, 1961), p. 352.

25. G. E. Ladd, *Jesus and the Kingdom* (New York: Harper & Row, 1964), p. 111, n. 24.

26. D. A. Hayes, "James, Epistle of," *The International Standard Bible Encyclopaedia*, ed. James Orr et al., 5 vols. (Grand Rapids: Eerdmans, 1939), 3:1964.

27. See Robert H. Gundry, "Verba Christi in I Peter," *New Testament Studies* 13 (July, 1967): 336-50.

28. Gerhardsson, *Memory and Manuscript*, p. 305, n. 2.

29. Norman Perrin, *Rediscovering the Teaching of Jesus* (New York: Harper & Row, 1967), pp. 38-39.

THE OUTLOOK FOR BIBLICAL THEOLOGY

by Palmer Robertson

Generally biblical theology is regarded today as a rather recent-born discipline. Indeed, the debate continues to rage fiercely over the fundamental question of the nature and task of "biblical theology."[1] Yet the address of J. P. Gabler in 1787 is still generally recognized as the launching point of this field of inquiry.[2]

Gabler's work did have the effect of declaring biblical theology to be liberated from the stranglehold of dogmatics. Yet it may be somewhat presumptuous for nineteenth- and twentieth-century scholarship to attribute to itself the creation of something "new under the sun."[3] As a matter of fact, the eighteenth-century beginning of biblical theology should be regarded as just one further effort of the church to solve the complex problem of the "unity in diversity" represented by the Christian Scriptures.[4]

To speak of the "Christian" Scriptures is not to deny the claim of Judaism and other religions to various portions of the Old and New Testaments. It is only to limit the scope of this study to a more carefully defined concept of the task of biblical theology from the outset. Such a limitation rests on the firm conviction that the entirety of the Bible binds itself together as a unified revelation which relates to Jesus the Christ. Either of the Testaments may be understood in the final sense only as it relates to this Christ of the Scriptures.

The question of the Christian's treatment of the total message of the two Testaments always has been a source of problems. These problems have been multiplied by the sophistication of biblical studies since the Reformation. Now questions of documentary analysis, form criticism, and *Religionsgeschichte* complicate the already difficult task of deciphering the unique message of the Bible.

Yet at the same time it should be acknowledged that the study of biblical theology would not have advanced to its position of significance today had it not been for these modern catalysts. The fires of scholarly scrutiny have done much toward purifying theological analysis of the Scriptures. [5] Yet the principal question still is being debated: What *is* biblical theology?

WHAT IS BIBLICAL THEOLOGY?

DISTINCTIVE NATURE OF THE DISCIPLINE

Out of the clamor of voices proclaiming their discovery of the essential character of biblical theology arise several features of a distinctive discipline which may merit the ascription of "biblical theology."

First, biblical theology may be regarded as an historical discipline. [6] As historical, biblical theology must concern itself with the progression of revelation as it has occurred over the ages in which the Scriptures were produced.

It is at this point that the distinctiveness of biblical theology over against systematic theology must be maintained. Systematic theology should be no less "biblical" in orientation than "biblical theology." Yet the manner of the treatment of the scriptural material by these two disciplines diverges quite widely. While systematic theology may present the sum total of scriptural truth on the doctrine of man, God, sin or salvation, biblical theology cuts across the grain to expose the particular stage of maturation of God's revelation to men in the time of the patriarchs, of Moses, of Christ.

Second, biblical theology concentrates on the organic wholeness of Scripture. Organic wholeness suggests both the concepts of germination and coherence. The beginning stages of the revelational process should be understood as possessing in seed form all that which manifests itself more fully at later stages. At the same time, while something resembling the "husk" of the kernel may be shed in the process of maturation of biblical truth, the emphasis of scriptural development must be on the concept of coherence.[7] The form of the truth of revelation may vary, but the substance will remain in harmonious relationship. In other words, the principle of continuity rather than discontinuity must dominate the work of the biblical theologian. No rejection factor may be conveniently introduced to dispose of the more difficult elements appearing at various points throughout the history of the biblical revelation. Israel's *cherem* warfare, the psalmists' imprecatory prayers, God's command to Abraham to sacrifice his own son must be seen as organically related to the totality of the history of redemption.

Third, biblical theology must see the totality of the movement of scriptural revelation as progressing toward a goal. In particular, no point in the history of redemption may be understood aright until its precise relationship to the consummation of the movement has been perceived. It is at this point that the Christian biblical theologian must acknowledge that he regards Jesus Christ to be the consummation of the entire process of biblical history. No advantage will be achieved by the Christian believer repudiating his commitment in this regard. If the cause of biblical theology is to be served, the tasks of the Old Testament and of the New Testament biblical theologian must be seen as complementary. From the Old Testament perspective, the historical process of the biblical revelation must be seen in terms of its consummation in Christ. From the New Testament perspective, the consummation which is Christ must be seen in terms of the historical process which anticipated it.

Such an approach to the Scriptures is indeed cluttered with difficulties. Too often the superimposition of the New Testament onto the Old muzzles the historical distinctiveness of the Old Testament. Nevertheless, the question must be asked: how can the Christian biblical theologian stop short of indicating the significance of the Old Testament truth in the newfound light of its consummation in the new covenant? Great exegetical advantage will be gained by reading the Old Testament from the historical perspective of the original authors. But this perspective must be only a temporary stance for the Christian exegete. He cannot be content to speak finally as an ancient Israelite, or he will deny in practice the faith which initially brought him to the study of the Scriptures. [8]

While other characteristics may be of significance, these three elements set apart the particular discipline of biblical theology to its own domain. Biblical theology is historically progressive; biblical theology is organic in nature; biblical theology centers on the consummation. Accordingly, biblical theology may be defined as the study of the progressive unfolding of the revelation of God in terms of its consummation in the new covenant. [9]

METHODOLOGICAL CONSIDERATIONS

Before indicating something of the perspective of biblical theology for days to come, it may be appropriate to rehearse basic methodological considerations which should play a vital role in the continuing development of an aggressive biblical theology for today.

Since a primary distinctive of biblical theology involves its historical approach to the truth of Scripture, an early effort must be made to mark out the historical epochs of God's revelation. [10] Such partitioning of scriptural periods cannot be carried to extremes, but should give recognition to that which is inherent in Scripture itself.

Clearly the most basic division lies between Old and New Testaments, between anticipation and realization. Christ gave clear expression to His recognition of this line of division in His grouping of all history into two periods: the period "until John (the Baptist)," and the period thereafter (Mt. 11:13). The apostle Paul equally recognizes this primary division of redemptive history in his note concerning the "fulness of time" and the period of bondage which preceded it (Gal. 4:3-4). A second basic division, recognized in particular by Paul, is the period before and after "law," here meaning the formal inscribing of the will of God at Sinai (Gal. 3:17). Similarly, the New Testament recognizes an inherent time division between the period of Christ's personal earth ministry, and the period of His ministry through the Spirit (Ac. 2:32-33).

Other historical divisions of the periods of God's revelation certainly are inherent in Scripture. Let the recognition of these basic divisions suffice to show that an essential element in the analysis of the historical progress of the biblical revelation will be the discovery of those great epochs of time recognized by Scripture itself.

Once the theological place in history of a portion of Scripture has been ascertained, the biblical theologian may proceed to apply the best traditions of grammatico-historical exegesis. Needless to say, the task of treating with exegetical caution all the portions of Scripture belonging to one particular biblical epoch looms large. Yet such an effort must be made before anything resembling an appropriate characterization of a particular epoch may be attempted.

A final note on methodology for biblical-theological study may be offered. Rather than superimposing the standard categories of systematic theology on the various epochs, a much more inductive method would involve letting the emphasis of the period itself become the emphasis of the presentation. Instead of inquiring into the particular view of God, man, sin and salvation which was found, for instance, in the patriarchal period, a more appropriate methodology would be to analyze the significance of the nomadic way of life of the patriarchs for Israel's later theological development. [11] At every point, the goal of the biblical theologian must be to allow the emphases of Scripture to be heard.

Having dealt with the more basic questions of an introductory nature, it is possible to treat the primary question at hand as it applies to Old Testament and New Testament studies: Whither biblical theology?

WHITHER BIBLICAL THEOLOGY?

It would be futile at this point to attempt to predict future developments in the field of biblical theology. Instead, some suggestions will be made as to the directions in which biblical theology could move constructively in days to come.

BIBLICAL PERSPECTIVES FOR OLD TESTAMENT THEOLOGY

With respect to Old Testament studies, primary attention must be centered on the historical character of Old Testament theology. While much conversation has centered about the role of history in Israel's theology, more still remains to be done in terms of actual exploitation of the Scripture's own intentions in presenting its theology from an historical perspective. [12]

In particular, full recognition must be given to the fact that Israel's history presents itself as redemptive history. Israel did not simply think of God as being active in its external history; God was active in a redeeming sense in Israel. Their redemption pertained to the deliverance of the total man, and his reconciliation to God. In this history, God was actively at work redeeming a people for Himself. God acted in the vertical as well as the horizontal realm to deliver Israel from Egypt, to bear them through the wilderness, to establish them in the land of Canaan, to give them priests, prophets and kings. It is only by giving full weight to the uniquely redemptive character of Israel's history that positive progress will be made in the field of Old Testament theology. [13]

A second distinctiveness of Israel's history needing development is the revelational character of Old Testament history. Geerhardus Vos says, "The process of revelation is not only concomitant with history, but it becomes incarnate in history. The facts of history themselves acquire a revealing significance." [14]

Perhaps the profound significance of this suggestion concerning the distinctiveness of Old Testament history may be clarified by a biblical illustration. The night of the Passover came to Israel amid all the vitalities and unforeseeable options of the movement of history. Later, this experience of Israel was introduced into their cultic ceremonies and became an annual festival.

Unless the student of Scripture wholly naturalizes this aspect of Israel's life, the Passover celebration foreshadowed by God's intention the manner by which God would redeem His people. This assertion may be made equally of the first in-time-and-history experience of the Passover, and of the subsequent cultic rehearsals.

Yet, observe the radical difference in the two occurrences. The later celebrations of the Passover were static, controlled performances. It is comparably easy to assert that such celebrations were designed to depict revelationally the truth concerning man's redemption.

The first Passover is another matter. The dynamics and

vitalities of the historical process are at work. With all the freedoms and contingencies of the created order involved, this history nonetheless embodies revelational truth. The in-time-and-history offering of the Passover lamb unveils the principle of a blood-shedding substitute as the way of man's redemption from death.

Not only was this historical event revelational to Israel of this particular truth concerning the way of man's redemption before God. It was prophetic truth, pointing beyond itself to the substitutionary and sacrificial death of Jesus Christ the Lamb of God (1 Co. 5:7; cf. Jn. 1:29). In other words, this event of Old Testament history was so guided and controlled by God as to embody and thereby to reveal redemptive truth.

Can this be said of any history other than Old Testament history? Can it be said that the events of Dunkirk or of Washington's crossing the Delaware were so arranged by God as to reveal truth concerning the way of man's redemption? Indeed, it cannot be said.

It must be concluded that Old Testament history is unique in its revelatory character. While all history reveals something of the nature of God and His relation to men, only biblical history embodies by the appointment of God the truths of the way of redemption.

How extensively does Old Testament history embody in itself revelational truth in this manner? Only the careful and patient study of Scripture will answer that question. But even a cursory study of the New Testament's employment of the Old Testament demands a serious scrutiny of the greater bulk of Old Testament historical materials. [15]

A third dimension of Old Testament history requiring full investigation is the consummative character of this history. With all its greatness as redemptive and revelational history, the discovery of the full significance of Old Testament history is contingent upon the manifestation of that which it promises. This provisional nature of Old Testament history says something about the proper methodology to be followed. Since the provisional now has been replaced by the actual, it is necessary to interpret the provisional consistently in the light of the actual. Those events occurring to Israel in the process of its historical experience cannot be interpreted as ends in themselves, but may be understood properly only as their relation to the consummate kingdom is uncovered. What is the ultimate significance of the election of national Israel? What is the meaning in the fullest sense of Israel's establishment of a kingship? How is the psalter's interpretation of Israel's kingship to be related to the New Testament assumption of this material for its own experience? In what sense does Israel's experience as the suffering servant of God relate to the New Testament enlargement and application of this concept to Jesus Christ? [16]

If the whole unfolding process of biblical theology involves movement toward consummation in the new covenant, some self-consciousness must be developed in the analysis of the various phases of the Old Testament revelation as they relate to Christ. At this point, the whole question of prophecy, typology, analogy, symbolism and allegory comes to the fore. [17]

As the various approaches to the question of the precise relation of Old Testament anticipation to New Testament realization are evaluated, one cannot but be struck with the earnest longing on the part of all for some valid basis by which Christ may be seen in all the Scriptures. The frightening barrenness in terms of "religious" worth of the earlier rationalistic criticism explains in part the determination to produce something of lasting value.

Yet it may be said quite definitely at this point that the success of these endeavors has proven to be extremely dubious. No two approaches agree, either as to methodology or as to results, on how the Old Testament is to be understood as progressing toward the New. [18]

73

It may be that this process of interchange is essential for progress. It may be that the confusion of opinions represents movement toward a solution. One may suspect, however, that a more recent evaluation of the fruit of these endeavors may be correct.

> The hope for a vital rebirth of the Bible has for years been invested in the biblical theologian. The biblical theologian would overcome, it was expected, the historicism and rationalism of biblical research and allow the biblical revelation to come alive for our contemporary situation. This hope has now collapsed. [19]

There can be no doubt that the "collapse" of modern biblical theology hinges on the failure of everyone concerned to achieve some acceptable basis for relating the two Testaments.

In the complex situation of alternatives, the infinite variety of possible methods by which the Old Testament progresses toward the New must be recognized. Typological relations do exist. These types may be historically dynamic or symbolically static. The "historically dynamic" type embodies by God's intention a principle of redemptive history which foreshadows some aspect of the realized consummation. By God's intentional guiding of Old Testament history, a shadowed form anticipates the unveiled reality. The brazen serpent anticipates the cursed Deliverer of God's people (Num. 21:9; Jn. 3:14-15; Deu. 21:23; Gal. 3:13). The "symbolically static" type, although inevitably a part of Israel's history, relates more directly to the ritualistic ceremonies of Israel. The annually repeated "day of atonement" in Israel anticipates the "once-ness" of Christ's atoning sacrifice (Lev. 16:34; Zec. 3:1-10; Heb. 9:24-28).

While the typological relation between the Testaments assumes the God-intended purpose to embody revelational truth in the type, the relationship of analogy suggests more simply a correspondence of circumstances. This likeness of circumstances generally should be understood as finding its root in principles of God's redemptive working which remain essentially constant, or at least comparably related in the various stages of God's manifestation of redemptive truth. The leaf remains in the same basic relationship to its stem, although gradually unfolding its ultimate shape. Likewise, brothers betray the innocent for material gain in the case of Joseph (Gen. 37:27-28), in the days of Amos (Amos 2:6), and in the experience of Jesus Christ (Mt. 26:14-16). It may not be desirable to assert a typological relationship in each of these instances. Yet a single principle of redemptive history manifests itself in each case.

Some clarity of understanding in the treatment of these categories of relationships between the Testaments may be provided by considering typology and analogy as they relate to prophecy. Essential to typology is the concept of prophecy.[20] While the type does have significance for the present, its concentration of direction is toward the future. By God's appointment, it testifies to a greater than itself yet to come. The flow of typology is from Old Testament to New Testament.

Analogous relations of the Testaments are somewhat different. The Old Testament member of the analogous construction does not speak in and of itself of something yet to come. Only after the New Testament member of the analogy has arisen does the possibility of a relationship suggest itself. While typology demands expectation, analogy recognizes the validity of a subsequent comparison.

While discussing the prophetic dimension of typology, it should be recognized that prophecy as a category is quite larger than typology. Typology may be regarded as one aspect of prophecy—prophecy enacted. Verbal prophecy represents another dimension of this category. In this case, a verbalized conception anticipates the future con- summation of some aspect of God's redemptive purposes.

Having made this distinction, it should be noted immediately that the greatest possible disservice to Old Testament prophecy may be rendered by isolating prophetic proof texts which are supposed to pinpoint futuristic events. Recognition of Isaiah 7:14 as a verbally prophetic text should be accompanied by the exposure of its relation to the threat to the Davidic line implicit in the historical context of the Syro-Ephraimite war. Only in the context of the typical role of the Davidic line as ideal king-Messiah in Israel may this promise of a virgin-born Immanuel properly be appreciated. Such a method of evaluation holds true equally for Messianic psalms (cf. Ps. 2, 110), for the suffering Servant of Israel (Is. 53), for the promised Bethlehemite (Mic. 5:2).

Of an entirely different category is the allegorical method of exegesis. If a proper role for the typological is to be provided, the allegorical must be restricted to its own domain. To achieve this confinement, an allegory may best be defined as an artificial and accidental relationship, in contrast with the actual and intentional correspondence of typology, or the substantial correspondence of analogy. [21] If this restriction of allegory can be maintained, much progress may be made in the proper understanding of the movement of the Old Testament toward its consummation in the New. That movement is not artificial or accidental; it is actual and intentional. It must not be spoiled by man's fanciful imaginations, but must be uncovered by the patient and cautious exploration of the intention of Old Testament Scripture.

In this regard, it may be admitted that a full assertion that Old Testament history is God-directed in its movement toward the Messiah continues to be essential. Not man's subsequent structuring, but God's original purposing must provide the foundation for the analysis of the progress of redemptive revelation.

The Evangelical in particular should be encouraged as he considers what may be ahead in the field of New Testament biblical theology. This encouragement should be directed toward the open-ended needs still outstanding in the field. The time is ripe for creative, constructive contributions toward the formation of a contemporary evangelical theology of the New Testament. Particularly significant needs for the present are as follows:

First, a comprehensive analysis of the special problem of New Testament biblical theology as distinguished from Old Testament biblical theology is needed. If the primary distinctiveness of the discipline of biblical theology from systematic theology lies in the recognition of the historically progressive character of the revelation, New Testament biblical theology cannot lose sight of this distinctiveness without obliterating itself.

The special problem of New Testament theology relates to the compactness of the period in which a progression must be maintained. While the revelation of Old Testament theology covered a period of approximately one thousand years, New Testament theology contracts to a period of merely one hundred years or less. Can progressiveness within this scope of time be noted meaningfully? [22] Does the New Testament itself suggest that a genuine progression of significance occurred?

A further complicating factor in New Testament theology which marks the distinctiveness of its progression arises when it is noted that the consummation of all revelation, which is Christ Himself, appears very early in the process of New Testament revelation. If all the truth of God is summed up in Christ, how can revelation progress beyond the point of the manifestation of Christ in history?

These factors in themselves might seem sufficient to discourage the pursuit of a biblical-theological arrangement of New Testament material. However, indications within the New Testament itself suggest the presence of an inherently progressive character of the revelation. John the Baptist speaks of one coming after him who will advance the revelation (Mt. 3:11). In complementary fashion, Jesus indicates that John consummated the entire process of Old Testament revelation, and notes a definite epochal break by the use of the phrase "until John" (Mt. 11:10-14). Near the end of His own revelational ministry, Jesus stated that He still had many things to say to His disciples, which had to wait the further development involved in the sending of the Spirit (Jn. 16:12-14). The content of the Spirit's revelation would be related to what has preceded, for He would speak of the things of Christ. Yet the material of His revelation surely would progress beyond the revelation involved in Christ's earthly ministry.

An interesting note suggesting progression within the period of New Testament theology arises from the apostolic evaluation of the significance of Christ's resurrection appearances. According to Acts 10:40 – 41, God gave Christ to be made manifest (*emphanē* — clearly a revelation term) at the time of His appearances. The disciples definitely entered a new stage of revelational reception by the appearance of Christ in resurrected form.

Still further "stages" of the progress of New Testament revelation may be seen in the establishment of the offices of apostle and prophet in the New Testament church, the inspired inscripturation of an authoritative New Testament literature (cf. the apparently early references to such in 2 Th. 2:15; 3:14), and the apocalyptic visions of John.

The presence of these and other indications of a progressiveness in New Testament theology do encourage the student to persist in seeking out the progressive aspects of New Testament theology. The need still remains for a full exploration of the distinctiveness of the New Testament progression of revelation, and the effect of this distinctiveness on New Testament theology.

Second, the current scene in New Testament biblical theology magnifies the need for an evangelical work that will arrange its material in an historically progressive manner. Much of the appeal of Rudolf Bultmann's *Theology of the New Testament*[23] lies not just in the mastery of such a bulk of material, or in the comprehensive application of current form-critical studies to the entirety of the New Testament. Its appeal lies also in the organization of the material in an historically progressive fashion. Disagreement may be registered against the refined development of a period of the "Hellenistic church aside from Paul,"[24] into which most of the wealth of New Testament theology is deposited without adequate substantiation of sources. But the virileness of Bultmann's work arises from his historical structuration of the progress of New Testament theology. The same word of appreciation may be said for Ethelbert Stauffer's always fresh *New Testament Theology,*[25] and the more recent work of Hans Conzelmann.[26] Likewise, although Oscar Cullmann arranges his principal work on New Testament theology topically by the titles assigned to Christ, nonetheless he quite consciously treats each title in an historically progressive fashion.[27]

The need presses on evangelical Christianity today to produce a New Testament theology which gives full recognition to the progressive character of the New Testament revelation. Will Evangelicals demonstrate a willingness to proceed delicately with a believing and disciplined scholarship which will produce a New Testament theology truly sympathetic to the sense of progression found in the New Testament itself? Dare evangelical New Testament scholarship risk the extraction of a theology of Jesus from the theological framework of the gospel writers, or a theology of the earliest Christian confessions from the later theology of the epistles? If a vital

New Testament theology is to be developed, which presents some picture of the progressive growth of a New Testament theology, some such method must be pursued. New Testament theology needs this type of presentation of the progressive character of the substance of New Testament thought patterns.

A third significant area in the field of New Testament theology today involves the need for a unifying theme for New Testament theology. In many respects, the gap between Jesus and Paul remains unspanned. Jesus teaches about the kingdom, hardly mentioning the church. Paul concentrates on ecclesiology, confining his remarks concerning the kingdom quite rigidly. How may these two areas of concentration be seen as a whole? What will bring these two teachings into a unity, while at the same time acknowledging diversity? [28] Such a problem must be given significant priority in the continuing work of New Testament theology.

Cullmann perhaps has come closest to unifying New Testament theology by his employment of the Christological theme. However, his use of the titles attributed to Christ as an organizing principle cannot fail to hamper the achievement of a comprehensive picture. More devastatingly, his modalistic view of Christ distorts the balance of New Testament evidence. [29] The Evangelical, with his sympathetic appreciation for the centrality of the person of Jesus in His earthly manifestation and in His resurrection status, has an unsurpassed opportunity to unify the whole of New Testament theology about the person of Christ. May a new day give birth to fresh exaltation of the unique Son of God.

A fourth significant need concerns the consolidation of gains in the appreciation of the New Testament as understandable only in the light of the Old Testament. A healthy and undiminishing flow of material in this area has added greatly to the general comprehension of the formative influence of the Old Testament on the thought patterns of the New Testament theologians.[30] Yet no comprehensive picture of this whole new scene has been completed. It is to be doubted that a New Testament theology truly in tune with the perspectives of the New Testament itself ever will be developed apart from a total appreciation of the influence of Old Testament theology on the New Testament. The never ending debate concerning the sources of New Testament theology will be put in proper perspective only after the full weight of the Old Testament's influences on the New has been apprehended.

A fifth need in the study of New Testament biblical theology concerns the translation of the formal material of biblical theology into categories significant for the modern day. It has been suggested that the problem may be reduced to the difficult task of making significant for the current age the thought patterns of a past age.[31]

However, it is not at all clear that the task of the biblical theologian is to translate abiding values from a naïvely superstitious biblical context to a modern framework in which man at last has come of age. For on the one hand, much more of mysticism and naïve superstition exists today than modern sophisticates would like to admit. Bultmann's researches into gnosticism may prove of great value for analyzing contemporary occultism. On the other hand, much less of naïve believism characterizes New Testament theologians than is often suggested. First Corinthians 15:3-8 still stands as one of the earliest summations of apostolic faith. Written into the rubric of the whole is Paul's insistent citation of historical witnesses to the resurrection of Jesus. Far from playing on the gullibility of his contemporaries, Paul appeals to the objectivity of God's supernatural intervention into time and history.

While contemporary hermeneutic attempts to bypass the positive demand for faith in the resurrection of Christ in time and history for faith in the "recurrent event of language," [32] the great challenge of New Testament theology is to make unavoidable a confrontation with the essence of New Testament claims concerning Jesus. Only a compulsory decision in face of the genuine Christ will serve to "make relevant" the message of the gospel for today.

A sixth and final need facing the field of New Testament theology concerns the directing of the resources of New Testament theology toward the specific problems confronting the church today. Among the most crucial areas are:

1. *The doctrine of the church.* The ecumenical impetus of the twentieth century continues to swell in magnitude. Where shall formative direction for this movement be found? If the traditional dogmas concerning the sacraments and order of the church do not prove to be adequately flexible to sustain the momentum of today's impatient church scene, can biblical theology provide assistance? Is there a vital dimension to the understanding of the nature and mission of the church which may be provided by biblical theology? The church today needs to hear from the living resources of biblical theology as it confronts these crucial questions. [33]

2. *The role of ethnic Israel in New Testament theology.* As international forces gather again about the rim of the Middle East, the Christian world must be helped by a biblical perspective on the role of ethnic Israel in the purposes of God. The real possibility not only of a third world holocaust, but also of revived Christian Crusades, this time on behalf of ethnic Israel, may well be written into the annals of current history. The tools of New Testament theology, with its historically conditioned orientation, must supply light to the confusing situation of today.[34]

3. *The renewal of the phenomena of "prophetic utterances" and the gift of tongue-speaking in the church today.* No denominational grouping may extricate itself from the demand to resolve this question as it faces the

church. A professedly unobtrusive phenomenon threatens to shake the foundations of church structures and theology as they have been known since the Reformation. What does New Testament biblical theology say to this question? How does the progressive structuring of New Testament theology provide distinctive perspective to this matter? The church today needs the contribution to understanding which biblical theology may provide to this question.

Quite obviously other matters of relevance in the present church scene could be mentioned. But the areas cited should make apparent the need of the church today for a vital New Testament theology. The task ahead is an exciting one indeed.

FOOTNOTES

1. Note the passionate salvos of Walter Eichrodt contra Gerhard von Rad in his *Theology of the Old Testament*, trans. P. M. G. Stalker, 2 vols. (Philadelphia: Westminster, 1961), 1:512 ff. and the answering volleys of von Rad contra Eichrodt in his *Old Testament Theology*, trans. J. A. Baker (New York: Harper, 1962), p. 114, n. 13.

2. Cf. N. W. Porteous, "Old Testament Theology," *The Old Testament and Modern Study*, ed. H. H. Rowley (Oxford: Oxford U., 1951), p. 312; and von Rad, 1:112.

3. Cf. von Rad's characterization of the "theology of the Old Testament" as "indeed . . . one of the youngest of the disciplines of Biblical studies" (Ibid., 1:v).

4. This perspective receives healthy exposure in J. Barton Payne, *Theology of the Older Testament* (Grand Rapids: Zondervan, 1962), pp. 25 ff., in which he begins his sketch of Old Testament theology with the church Fathers.

5. At the same time it must be said with regret that many believers in the truth of God have been turned aside by the general tenor of disbelief which has enveloped these labors.

6. This was the point in particular which was made by Gabler in his address referred to in the opening paragraph of the present study.

7. Cf. G. Vos, *Biblical Theology* (Grand Rapids: Eerdmans, 1959), pp. 15 ff. Vos' treatment of the organic character of the progression of God's revelation emphasizes the unified character of this type of progression in contradistinction to a naturalistic nonorganic concept of progression.

8. The precaution cited by F. F. Bruce, *The New Testament Development of Old Testament Themes* (Grand Rapids: Eerdmans, 1968), p. 11, to the effect that the Old Testament theologian should never allow himself the luxury of taking advantage of the New Testament's exegesis of an Old Testament text may be balanced by a remark such as that of H. W. Wolff, "The Understanding of History in the Old Testament Prophets" in *Essays on Old Testament Interpretation*, ed. Claus Westermann (London: SCM, 1963), pp.

352 ff.: "Our Old Testament theology would be false if alongside the historical distance from the New Testament we ignored the aids to understanding which are supplied in the New Testament analogies and the New Testament completion of God's history with Israel."

9. The precise definition of biblical theology by Vos, p. 13, as "that branch of exegetical theology which deals with the process of the self revelation of God deposited in the Bible" is as fine a definition of this discipline as may be found. It does, however, omit the consummative aspect of biblical theology which is so apparent throughout Vos' own works.

10. Ibid., p. 25. It may be suggested that the basic distinction between this epoch-making approach and the "dispensational" dividing of Scripture resides in the recognition given to the organic relation of the various epochs. Indeed, modern dispensationalism has proven itself anxious to defend its adherence to the organically progressive character of biblical revelation. Cf. in particular the work of C. C. Ryrie, *Dispensationalism Today* (Chicago: Moody, 1965), pp. 33 ff.; *The New Scofield Reference Bible* (New York: Oxford U., 1967), pp. vii, 3. Yet an insistence on a formalistic fulfillment of Old Testament promises for ethnic Israel in contradistinction from their actual fulfillment in the church of Christ cannot fail to rend the organically progressive unity of biblical revelation. Note in this regard the summarizing position on the church in dispensationalism by Ryrie, pp. 154 f.: "If the dispensational emphasis on the distinctiveness of the Church seems to result in a 'dichotomy,' let it stand as long as it is a result of literal interpretation." Ryrie's acceptance of the term *dichotomy*, although conditioned, does seem to indicate a disruption in the orderly realization of the purposes of God.

11. The systematic approach to biblical theology may have been in the mind of B. B. Warfield, "The Idea of Systematic Theology" in *Studies in Theology* (New York: Oxford U., 1932), pp. 67 ff., when he suggested that exegesis was as a recruiter, biblical theology as a squad, and systematic theology as an army. Such a perspective does not appear to give adequate recognition to the distinctiveness of biblical theology. A much more satisfactory distinction among these disciplines may be found in John Murray, "Systematic Theology," *The Westminster Theological Journal* 26 (Nov., 1963): 33-46.

12. Many suggestive hints may be found in von Rad, 2:320 ff. As fruitful as von Rad's suggestions may be, they are severely marred by being placed in a context of "recapitulation" or "actualization." Rather than seeking the God-originating revelation embodied in biblical history, von Rad offers hints useful for the act of reproclamation of the biblical faith, which his existentialism assumes to be the key to the discipline of Old Testament theology.

13. An excellent example of an effort to deny the redemptive distinctiveness of biblical history may be found in Alan Richardson, *History, Sacred and Profane* (Philadelphia: Westminster, 1964), pp. 224 ff. The author speaks of an event of Israel's history such as the exodus as a "disclosure situation," which he defines as an historic moment in which meaning is discerned, evoking a response. Says Richardson: "The disclosure situations attested in the Old Testament are not different in kind from those of other histories . . . . Though rooted in particular predicaments of Israel's actual history, these disclosure situations illuminate the truth concerning the predicament of all nations in every age, the real situation of man as man. Israel's history is not unique, except in the sense that every nation's history is unique; other nations have endured similar vicissitudes." Richardson proceeds with an attempt to parallel Israel's deliverance from Egypt with current British history. The defeat of the Spanish Armada became a "sign," leading John Milton to speak of "God's England." Prosperity led to squalid nationalism (cf. Deu. 6:10-12). In the crisis of 1939-1945 the vision was renewed and moral purpose revived in this vivid "disclosure situation."

It might be suggested, to be consistent with such a view, that men might just as well choose Winston Churchill (or Adolf Hitler) as savior in place of the Passover Lamb who was slain. In Richardson's own reconstruction of modern British history, the fatal omission of any reference to a reconciliation to God tells the tale. Indeed, it would be presumptuous to interpret any event in modern British history as propitiating for Britain's sin before God. If any argument is needed to convince of the absolute distinctiveness of biblical history, it is supplied by Richardson's argument of its nondistinctiveness.

14. Vos. p. 15.

15. Although assuming a basically different attitude from the one just enunciated, an extensive development of the possibilities of Old Testament history as it relates to New Testament redemptive truth may be found in L. Goppelt, *Typos. Die typologische Deutung des Alten Testaments im Neuen* (Gütersloh: C. Barthelsmann, 1939).

16. Cf. one suggestive development of this dimension ot Israel's history as it relates to the servant concept of Isaiah in O.T. Allis, *The Unity of Isaiah* (Philadelphia: Presbyterian & Reformed, 1950), pp. 81 ff. On p. 85 Allis relates even the Cyrus-servant passages to the Messiah: "We may see in him a type of the Messiah. For he freed Israel from a grievous bondage which was the penalty and punishment of sin."

17. The most helpful collection of interchanges on this subject as it relates to the current scene in biblical-theological studies may be found in Claus Westermann, ed., *Essays on Old Testament Interpretation*, James Luther Mays, Eng. ed. (London: SCM, 1963).

18. Comparison of any number of the methodologies being recommended, and more particularly of results achieved, leads inevitably to this conclusion. Von Rad, "Typological Interpretation of the Old Testament" in *Essays on Old Testament Hermeneutics*, p. 38, suggests that the typological interpretation of Old Testament texts must take place "in the freedom of the Holy Spirit," and can be subjected to "no pedagogical norm." James P. Smart, *The Interpretation of Scripture* (Philadelphia: Westminster, 1961), p. 129, asserts that there is "no basis in the New Testament for validating either a typological or an allegorical form of exegesis." On p. 127 Smart illustrates Karl Barth's flair for typology by noting Barth's suggestion that "Adam and Eve were naked and yet not ashamed because Jesus and his people are utterly humbled before each other and yet are not ashamed."

19. J. Christian Beker, "Reflections on Biblical Theology," *Interpretation* 24 (July, 1970): 303.

20. Cf. Walter Eichrodt, "Is Typological Exegesis an Appropriate Method?" in *Essays on Old Testament Hermeneutics*, p. 234. Says Eichrodt, "Thus typology belongs in principle to prophecy."

21. A classic example of the contrast between allegorical and typological interpretation may be found in Philo's and Paul's interpretations of the triangle of Abraham, Sarah and Hagar. In exegeting the Genesis passages which relate the story of the marriages and sons of Abraham, Philo finds an astounding significance. Abraham represents the elect-father of wisdom, while Sarah signifies the virtue which is to rule over the soul. But Abraham's marriage to Sarah is barren until he first weds Hagar, who is from Egypt, the land of the sciences, and who represents knowledge acquired from the disciplines of the educational system of the day. Then Abraham returns to Sarah, and divine virtue brings forth fruit. As a result, the rudimentary disciplines of education (typified in Ishmael) must be permanently cast out. See, for this presentation of Philo's material, John Eadie, *Commentary on the Epistle to the Galatians* (London: T. & T. Clark, 1894), pp. 361 ff. Paul's interpretation is found in the much-discussed passage in Galatians 4:21-31. Rather than quibbling over Paul's use of the word *allegoroumena* , a late Greek term misleadingly transliterated rather than translated into English, discussion on this passage should center about what Paul has done with the Genesis history. He has introduced his discussion with as authoritative an appeal as he can muster (v. 22: *gegraptai*). He has built at minimum on analagous circumstances in which the fleshly conjured Ishmael's persecution of the promise-provided Isaac is seen to parallel the fleshly trusting Judaizers' persecution of the promise-trusting believers of Galatia. At maximum, he is asserting that God intended to embody in this history of Abraham revelation concerning principles of redemptive history which would have authoritative significance for subsequent ages. By no stretch of the imagination has he built on an artificial and accidental resemblance, for the heart of the comparison resides in the organic unity of the two instances.

22. B. B. Warfield, "The Person of Christ According to the New Testament" in *The Person and Work of Christ*, ed. Samuel G. Craig (Philadelphia: Presbyterian & Reformed, 1950), pp. 37 ff., notes the brevity of time lapse in the New Testament period and concludes: "In its fundamental teaching, the New Testament lends itself, therefore, more readily to what is called dogmatic than to what is called genetic treatment."

23. Rudolf Bultmann, *Theology of the New Testament*, trans. Kendrick Grobel, 2 vols. (New York: Scribner, 1951, 1955).

24. Ibid., 1:63-184.

25. Ethelbert Stauffer, *New Testament Theology*, trans. John March (London: SCM, 1963). While Stauffer's work is not strictly historical in its arrangement of material, it manifests a thoroughgoing appreciation of the historical character of the New Testament revelation throughout.

26. Hans Conzelmann, *An Outline of the Theology of the New Testament*, trans. John Bowden (London: SCM, 1969).

27. Oscar Cullmann, *Christology of the New Testament*, trans. Shirley C. Guthrie and Charles A. Hall (Philadelphia: Westminster, 1959).

28. H. N. Ridderbos, *Paul and Jesus*, trans. David H. Freeman (Philadelphia: Presbyterian & Reformed, 1957) has done much to relieve the tension felt because of the diversity of the New Testament witness. Ridderbos traces the source of Pauline theology to Jesus Himself, and explains Paul's paucity of reference to the historical Jesus by noting that Paul quite naturally concentrated on discussing the Jesus he knew, which was the resurrected Christ (pp. 43 ff.). But explaining the differences between Paul and Jesus is not quite the same thing as expounding the unity of Paul and Jesus.

29. This revived modalism is announced at the beginning of Cullmann's *Christology of the New Testament*, p. 3, and plays a vital role in his conclusion (p. 326: "Functional Christology is the only kind which exists"). It is seen most particularly in his treatment of the title "Son of God." In dealing with 1 Co. 15:28, Cullmann asserts that Paul speaks of the unity of Father and Son "only in the closest connection with *Heilsgeschichte*" (p. 293). More explicitly, he says, *"It is only meaningful to speak of the Son in view of God's revelatory action, not in view of his being"* (p. 293, Cullmann's emphasis).

It may be suggested that Cullmann has erred in his basic approach to this passage in 1 Co. 15 by subsuming his discussion under the title "Son of God." The term "Son" indeed occurs in 1 Co. 15:28. But the quotation from Ps. 8:6 in the immediately preceding verse (1 Co. 15:27) clearly indicates that the sonship involved is that of "Son of man" rather than "Son of God." Even Cullmann himself discusses the quotation of Ps. 8 appearing in Heb. 2 under the "Son of man" title (p. 188).

30. Recent works on the subject include C.H. Dodd, *According to the Scriptures* (London: Nisbet, 1952); F. F. Bruce, *New Testament Development of Old Testament Themes* (Grand Rapids: Eerdmans, 1969); E. E. Ellis, *Paul's Use of the Old Testament* (Edinburgh: Oliver & Boyd, 1959); T. F. Glasson, *Moses in the Fourth Gospel* (London: SCM, 1963); R. P. C. Hanson, *Allegory and Event* (Richmond: John Knox, 1959); G. W. K. Lampe and K. J. Woolcombe, *Essays on Typology* (London: SCM, 1957); B. Lindars, *New Testament Apologetic* (Philadelphia: Westminster, 1961); F. C. Synge, *Hebrews and the Scriptures* (London: SPCK, 1959). Perhaps the fullest exposition of one aspect of the subject is found in Goppelt's *Typos*. Countless articles provide virtually an unlimited source material for this pursuit. Notice in particular the bibliographical sources cited in B. Childs, *Biblical Theology in Crisis* (Philadelphia: Westminster, 1970), pp. 114 ff. Childs bases one of his major hopes for a renewed biblical theology on the analysis of Old Testament quotations in the New Testament.

31. Krister Stendahl, "Biblical Theology" in *Interpreter's Dictionary of the Bible*, ed. George Arthur Buttrick, 4 vols. (New York: Abingdon, 1962), 1:422. Stendahl says the tension between biblical statements and contemporary life now has become clarified as "one between two centuries with drastically different modes of thought." Stendahl's analysis of the problem created by the new hermeneutic is quite helpful. He points in particular to the lack of adequate interest in the descriptive task of biblical theology, which is the "nucleus of all biblical theology" (p. 442).

32. James M. Robinson, "Hermeneutic Since Barth" in *New Frontiers in Theology*, vol. 2: *The New Hermeneutic*, ed. James M. Robinson and John B. Cobb (New York: Harper & Row, 1964), p. 63.

33. Childs, p. 81, cites Erich Dinkler in his 1967 report to the

Commission on Faith and Order of the World Council of Churches to the effect that the enthusiastic hope for the unification of Christendom sparked by the current biblical-theology movement has now disintegrated. This current disappointment should be a mighty spur to the Evangelical to press his advantage. A properly oriented biblical theology can offer hope for the realization of true unity among Christendom.

34. Cf. the recent treatment of Ernst Käsemann, "Paul and Israel" in *New Testament Questions of Today* (London: SCM, 1969), pp. 183-87. Käsemann's otherwise helpful article is marred by confining Israel's role for Paul as one of "exemplary significance."

PROSPECTS FOR SYSTEMATIC THEOLOGY

by Clark Pinnock

INTRODUCTION

An evangelical theology, if it is to be truly valid, must run the risk of displeasing both the conservatives who are content to rehearse thoughtlessly the slogans of the past, and the radicals who seek liberation from biblical norms in order to shape a system to suit their own taste. Theology is a creative activity which cannot rest content with mere reiteration of earlier insights. Men have not yet exhausted the material of divine revelation, nor have they finished the task of translating it into complete and sufficient intelligibility. A theology which seeks only to restate the system of some honored theological forerunner is less than fully biblical. We would best honor Luther and Calvin by going directly to Scripture where they began, rather than by slavishly imitating their systems. Theology has become stagnant and sterile when it is reduced to repetition and imitation. Dogmatic landmarks are useful when charting our course. But there comes a time when our own faith in response to the Word of God must express itself with conviction. It is now time for evangelical thinkers to forsake the unimaginative mimicry of "textbook" theology and forge an expression of biblical faith which will have the power to grip our generation.[1]

A theology of reiteration, arising as it does from a certain nostalgia for the grand theological systems built up in past ages of faith, is not simply sub-biblical in that it fails to record a contemporary interaction with divine truth, it is also an anachronistic activity. Our theology ought to arise out of and relate to the times in which we live. This is not to imply that its subject matter, the pole of divine revelation, is slippery or ambivalent; it is because the world which we address is the historical world of dynamic change which requires of us great flexibility in correlating God's Word to man's situations. As a steward of God's mysteries and a herald of the good news, the theologian has a responsibility to his hearers that they should understand his message. To fulfill this hermeneutical obligation, we must continually revise and redo our theology in relation to contemporary circumstances and cultural moods.

Certainly evangelical theology must not worship timeliness and relevance as liberal theology has done. This has the effect of making the shifting consensus of secular modernity the norm for our theological work. This has created a flood of theological fads and novelties by men who wish above all else to be "with it." The first thrill of excitement in discovery is soon replaced with disillusionment when the public asks "What's next?" and turns to something new. The dizzy gyration from one novelty to another may reflect a deep desire to discover a valid commitment for men in our time, but it is hardly the way to solve the fundamental cognitive question in religion. Evangelical theology has full confidence that the resources of traditional, biblical Christianity are sufficient to provide a firm basis for intelligent commitment in our day, but it does not on that account forfeit its obligation to express itself meaningfully.[2]

94

Because theology is concerned to be bi-polar, that is, faithful to divine revelation and sensitive to the need for effective communication, it must take careful note of the theological and cultural moods of the day. Of great importance is the fact that contemporary theologians feel alienated from the community of faith, themselves as much doubters as believers. In the past it was thought that the theologian was a believer who differed from others only by virtue of his office, which was to clarify and defend the Word of God. However, since the rise of deistic rationalism and biblical criticism, the theologians have come to accept more and more of the premises of their unbelieving opponents which earlier men of their calling had thought it imperative to refute.

One of the distinguishing characteristics of the theological revolution going on all around us today, quite apart from the radicalness of it, is the fact that it is taking place *within* and not only without the churches. Questioning of Christian beliefs has always occurred in the secular world outside the believing community. But now we discover the theologians themselves participating in and sometimes leading radical criticism of traditional concepts, a questioning which does not stay with matters of minor importance, but addresses itself to fundamental issues like the reality of God Himself. [3]

While it is true that the ferment in modern theology is largely due to the breakup of the liberal alternative to orthodoxy, it cannot be ignored by evangelical theology. We do our work in an age when many believe all the old certainties have dissolved and doubt that theology itself has any sure future. Although we reject the judgment as false, the fact that it is widely believed cannot but affect the style and direction of our own theological endeavor. We may not, ostrichlike, bury our heads in the sand and pretend not to notice the radicalness of doubt in modern theology. Evangelicals cannot simply carry on business as usual and continue to add to structures whose very foundations are believed to have shifted. If we would extend the work of eminent Christian thinkers before us, we must do it amid considerable theological confusion and, therefore, take great pains to clarify the bases on which we think it proper and legitimate to proceed in that direction. [4]

The purpose of this essay is to locate the issue of central importance for theology in the days ahead and to offer a constructive proposal toward resolving it. It is already clear what that issue is and the direction which our remarks must take. The question of questions for our time is the very possibility of any theology at all. Other ages could afford to debate subtle points of faith and practice, and engage in discussions which, in the circle of faith, still have a certain relevance today.

However, it would be a begging of the question were we to suggest that all which remains for evangelical theology to do is a tidying up of some loose ends of doctrine and a weaving of them into the largely completed fabric of a theological system. Our calling as servants of God is more painful than that. The only responsible thing to do here is to accept the challenge of modern theology and culture to demonstrate the basis on which and the method by which we propose to construct a theology which has authority and stability.

But before this can be done it is first necessary to uncover the real cause of the present theological ferment so that our evangelical alternative will be clearly seen to be, not preliberal (as if we wished to pretend that nothing of importance had happened in theology since Luther or Calvin!), but postliberal, a proposal which self-consciously turns away from the deficiencies of liberal thought and aligns itself in a fresh way with the historic faith of the church.

Theologians like to tell us the *secularity* is the cause of the present difficulty. Traditional religion is on the decline throughout the world. People are groping for new forms of belief, other symbols with which to thematize their modern consciousness. The day of the secular city is upon us. For the man come of age, only the profane is real. Everything is contingent and transient, and swims in the relativity of time. The secular mood has compelled theologians to abandon ancient loyalties and embark upon a strange and dangerous voyage. This is the picture they would like us to believe. It portrays the radical theologians as gallant knights of faith, dedicated to making the Christian message viable for our time.

As a matter of sociological fact, however, the situation is very different. Indeed, one receives the distinct impression that it is the theologians and not the sociologists who are pushing the secularization hypothesis. Religion, we are told, no longer has the influence it once did. Immediately there are two difficulties with such a generalizing statement. First, a century ago there were no sociologists to do the surveys to supply the comparative data needed for such a judgment. Second, the actual empirical data points in quite the other direction. In a recent study by sociologist Guy E. Swanson it became evident that in a comparison of political and religious knowledge, interest and participation, religion won out over politics in terms of the relevance people believe it has. On the basis of actual data, as distinguished from wishful thinking, the secular city is certainly not yet a reality and probably never will be. This is not to say we can afford to be complacent, or that doing theology today is without difficulties. Our concern is merely to separate the real problems from the spurious ones so that the latter may be faced.[5]

THE MASSIVE INFLUENCE OF
POSITIVISTIC SCIENCE

Theology likes to think itself independent of cultural influences and as arising more or less directly out of divine revelation. The charge we are about to make must come as something of a shock. Nonetheless, it seems quite incontrovertible that the shape of modern theology has been determined more by naturalistic science than by any other single factor. We are not thinking, of course, of the empirical, fact-gathering activity which is genuine science, for which we are all deeply grateful. For no discovery in this field has yet made a single article of the Christian faith invalid or untenable. Rather, we are making reference to positivistic science which is more philosophical than scientific. According to this perspective, the world is entirely self-contained. All natural phenomena and effects are to be rigorously explained in terms of mundane realities, and the transcendent dimension, if there is one, is inaccessible to reason and knowledge. Positivistic science is, in effect, a monism which reduces all reality which is open to investigation to one material principle. It is the assault of this pseudoscientific picture of the world that is primarily responsible for the shift in theology from orthodoxy to the various liberal alternatives.[6]

Rudolf Bultmann provides a clear illustration of our point because his presupposition is permitted such a forceful and deliberate expression. He boldly affirms that his interpretation of the New Testament presupposes a continuum of natural causes in a closed system, and therefore excludes miracle altogether. "The idea of wonder as miracle has become almost impossible for us today because we understand the processes of nature as governed by law. . .the idea of miracle has, therefore, become untenable and must be abandoned."[7] In addition, he has the honesty to admit that his view requires demythologizing the Christ event itself. Nowhere is Bultmann's liberal heritage more clearly visible than in this matter. The idea that scientific modernity necessitates a dismantling of the Christian tradition and the retention of only those elements which could stand side by side with a broad-minded acceptance of "modern thought" is transparently liberal and, before that, rationalistic. The canon of modernity becomes the normative criterion for Christian theology, requiring of it a considerable cognitive adjustment. In practical terms it means that man today should not be expected to believe in such things as the fall of man, the miraculous conception, atoning death, and bodily resurrection of Christ, the existence of Satan, or the second advent.

The genealogy of this curious attitude stretches back into remote history. Sarah who laughed at the promise of God, the disciples who refused to believe Christ was risen, the Athenians who made fun of Paul's preaching—all of these manifest a similar reaction to the mighty acts of God in history as Bultmann does. But it is enough to trace its background in the modern period. There is Spinoza's monistic naturalism which closed his eyes to the Hebraic myths, the fearless rejection of miracles by Reimarus as mere superstition, the efforts of David Hume to discount the value of historical testimony in this matter, the mythical interpretation of the gospels by David Strauss, and the radical desupernaturalizing of atheist Ludwig Feuerbach. The story is a long and dismal one.[8] Seldom amid all the appeals to reason was the obvious fact grasped that this question of miracle was, after all is said and done, a matter of history and not of philosophy.

As far as contemporary theologians are concerned, however, no name is more important than Ernst Troeltsch (1865-1923). His reflections on the nature of historical thinking, especially his principle of "analogy," have done more than almost anything else to precipitate the crisis of twentieth-century theology. In his view, every event is tied in with other events in a closed, coherent system. Everything is to be explained in terms of factors immanent in the natural process. Extraordinary modes of divine activity like miracles are excluded a priori. His shadow, long and dark as it is, lies over modern theology.[9] According to

Van A. Harvey, his influence has made it impossible for a truly modern man to accept biblical Christianity in its traditional, and in most of its modern, forms. One thing is clear: if Troeltsch is only half right, the Christian truth claim is fundamentally mistaken, and the gospel must be prepared to take its place alongside the other religions in the ocean of relativity and flux. [10]

In the providence of God we have been summoned to do theology alongside colleagues who see an irreconcilable opposition between the premises of supernatural theism and the whole direction of our experience and reflection as secular men. The fact that Bultmann had to point out the need for demythologizing is a *testimonium paupertatis* for our theological situation. "The scientific world picture is here to stay and will assert its rights against any theology, however imposing, the conflicts with it." [11] The same author insists at length elsewhere that loyalty to scientific modernity as he understands it cannot be sacrificed, but that our conception of Christianity must be revised in the light of it. [12] As if to confirm this sentiment, Charles I. Glicksberg, at the end of a powerful book showing the impossibility of functioning humanly in an atheistic universe, refuses Christianity because "universal determinism admits of no exceptions" and the "old religious sanctions are anachronistic and absurd." [13] There can be no mistaking what has happened. An understanding of the implications of modern science (we would prefer to call it "scientism") has made it impossible for many modern theologians to believe in the biblical *Heilsgeschichte,* from fall to incarnation, from resurrection to *parousia*, from Trinity to demonology. The entire framework of biblical religion has had to be scrapped—all, they would have us believe, in the interests of intellectual honesty and integrity.

The effect of this new mood upon traditional Christian theology can scarcely be exaggerated. The very historical facts upon which theology formerly sought to rest her claim to divine truth have been declared spurious. The biblical documents, which have from earliest times been regarded as God's written Word and in which these redemptive events are recorded, are judged unreliable and perhaps deceptive. The foundations beneath the thought of the Bible and the creeds have collapsed. The problem for those who accept this style of thinking is to discover what function and what authority, if any, theology has now. Inevitably the liberal theologians were thrown back upon human experiences of religious reality and upon the symbolic systems which have historically arisen out of these encounters. Gone forever is the claim to truth of universal and objective validity.

Because of scientific modernity, then, everything in Scripture which is uncongenial to the mood of modern man is to be scrapped for the simple reason that it is uncongenial. Later we contest the validity of this approach. It is enough, at present, to have shown that it is believed to be scientific and that this belief is largely responsible for the theological revolution of recent times. [14]

THE RELATIVE IS THE REAL

One terribly important consequence of this approach is the relativity of Christian belief, the end of any possibility of claiming absolute truth. Troeltsch's principle of analogy in historical research (as well as Hume's principle of the continuity of human experiencing) has the effect of *leveling* all things. There is no difference between the biblical events and other events. Indeed, there is no possibility of rising above the flux of endless historical change. It is worthwhile pausing to consider the meaning of relativity in the contemporary intellectual climate.

Acute awareness of the relativity of things human is rather recent. Researches into sociology and anthropology have revealed to us the degree to which man's ability to know is affected by his environment and cultural setting.

Kant, for example, did not travel any considerable distance from his home, and was, therefore, not exposed at all to other men and places. In our day of rapid travel the importance of a particular culture for the structure of human consciousness has been made very real to us. This observation can become problematic for religion. There are too many truth claims. Isn't it easier just to explain them all in terms of sociological factors? They all seem relative to their historical settings. "Whirl is king, having driven out Zeus" (Aristophanes). All man's time-honored absolutes seem to have been swallowed up by the new historical consciousness. The validity and value of his rational thought may be doubted. Only conflicting human authorities remain. The awareness of relativity is certainly responsible for much of the rootlessness and aimlessness in modern society. [15]

Although not sufficiently recognized, the challenge which sociology makes to Christian theology is as strong as any today. This is because sociology tends to regard religious ideals believed to be unique and authoritative as merely the human products of cultural evolution. It dethrones the Christian's fondest convictions about ultimate reality by explaining them in terms of the social consensus and process. The society organizes us in all sorts of ways, and religion is one of them. The relativity of human knowledge is a necessity of our condition as social beings. It has led many to despair of finding the meaning of life and history, and others to opt for the "absolute of decision" which would arbitrarily name absolutes, overcoming relativity by bare choice. Kaufman has constructed an entire theology on the basis of relativity. Christians are those for whom the Jesus story is illuminating of everything else. This is what lends coherence to their experience. Therefore, they call it "revelation." Its validity cannot be measured except pragmatically. Faith must see itself as "tentative and precarious and historically conditioned." It is "idolatrous" to claim finality for any one set of symbols, and quite wrong to attempt to solve the problem of multiplicity in this way. [16]

One curious aspect of this question that should be noted in passing is the double standard employed by the would-be "relativizers." Somehow the past gets relativized, but the present, where the modern man stands, escapes it. But why should modern knowledge be immune from the same treatment? It is difficult to see why a modern belief that miracles do not occur or that angels do not exist should carry with it as much force with people as it does. The modern conviction about such things has little to do with whether there is any reality in such things. God, for example, may exist, despite the inability of some modern men to conceive of it! This point certainly makes Bultmann's jibe that electricity users cannot believe in New Testament Christianity quite absurd. There is good reason to believe that modern man is blind in certain respects to some very real aspects of his existence. Living in modern Germany does not make a person the intellectual superior to the apostle Paul. And how a theologian who lived through the Nazi terrors could emerge from them insisting that modern man can no longer believe myths is quite beyond comprehension. [17]

But this does not get to the heart of the problem of relativity. It does seem as if man is immersed in a process not at all under his control, and his ideas and opinions are to a large extent determined by that social process. In this case, how can man claim transcultural validity for his concepts and judgments? If anything, Scripture supports this reduced evaluation of man's wisdom: "It is not in man who walks to direct his steps" (Jer. 10:23, RSV); "For my thoughts are not your thoughts, neither are your ways my ways, says the LORD" (Is. 55:8, RSV); "The world by wisdom knew not God" (1 Co. 1:21). It actually accepts the human predicament in which finite man cannot rise above his position in the flow of history and gain a perspective over the whole of reality. Human knowledge *is* culturally bound and conditioned.

Therefore, the Bible places all its emphasis upon divine intervention in the historical process, precisely to overcome the problem of relativity. The Word of God comes to man from outside the human situation, vanquishing the despair implicit in relativism and providing the clue to the meaning of it all.

The effect of accepting positivistic science is now clearly visible. By failing to challenge this philosophical dogma parading as science, modern theology has found itself compelled to dismantle the historical structure of the gospel and, in so doing, relinquish the only possible solution to the problem of relativity. Man cannot rise above his situation and deduce the meaning of history by an intellectual achievement. Unless God has invaded the time-space order in an objective self-disclosure within history, there is no alternative. Yet this is precisely the claim which Scripture makes for its message, and one which it is our immense privilege to commend again in our day.[18] J. Rodman Williams expresses the Christian claim neatly when he says:

> All in all Christian faith takes a stance beyond relativism because it attests to the entrance into history of the altogether true, which in its complete historicity addresses every conditioned moment and situation with absoluteness and finality. [19]

THE THEOLOGICAL REVOLUTION

The acceptance of positivistic science required a considerable cognitive adjustment on the part of liberal Protestantism. The glad embracing of modernity was not without a high price. A salvage operation was immediately necessary in order to save something authentically Christian from the acids of historical skepticism. Somehow the real "essence" of Christianity had to be disengaged from the spurious facts on which theologians had always relied previously. This had never been done before. Liberal theology courageously set itself the task of defining Christianity after it had been passed through the sieve of naturalistic science.

As it turned out, the Christian faith was identified with the ideals of the nineteenth century. Schleiermacher related it to man's religious aspirations, and Ritschl to his moral aspirations. Harnack focused upon God's love and the value of the human soul. Evolution was believed to lend support to a religious philosophy of progress.

The moment of truth came when these ideals ceased to captivate the minds of modern men. Liberalism, which had married the spirit of one age, became a widow in the next. What she had salvaged out of biblical religion could no longer be culturally supported. And, as biblical studies developed, it became clear that the liberal conception of religion had little in common with the biblical message. Liberalism, which was essentially a strategy of appeasement in the face of apparent scientific pressures, ended in disarray. Thus the problem of how to be naturalistic and Christian at the same time was not yet solved. Unless a new way can be found, it looks as if the only choice is between orthodoxy and humanism, with no habitable, halfway house in between. [20]

Early in our century, the dialectical theology of Barth and Bultmann came up with a new proposal. The realm of verifiable fact was to be handed over to science, and a ghetto was to be created for religious events and truths. In this way, faith would be saved from attack, and science would be free to do its work unhampered. As a result, theology became a matter of sheer and unsupported kerygmatic proclamation. Neoorthodoxy sought to cope with the challenge of positivistic science by disengaging theological reality from all contact with empirical reality. Such a bifurcation could not satisfy people for long, however. What sense does it make to talk about the "acts of God in history" when these are visible only to the eyes of faith? Why go on talking about the "word of God" when that word can be identified with no extant text? Surely these are pseudo-acts or, at best, the sincere delusions of faith, and this a pseudo-word.

Faced with the dialectical solution, we can only admire the liberal answer more. At least liberal theology sought to be intellectually honest and straightforward. There was no devious beating about the bush in their case. We were told what we could not believe, and offered the residue. But in neoorthodoxy we are asked to regard the absence of any reason to believe a virtue, and the presence of doubts a positive benefit, and then to make a Christian commitment entirely in the dark. Here we have a novel device for segregating religious knowledge from knowledge of any other kind. Theology depends completely on self-authenticating revelation and faith. A person has a right to believe the gospel on such a basis, of course, but there is no reason why he should or would want to. Neoorthodoxy must be judged an epistemological disaster. It offers no help whatsoever to the person who, bothered by nagging doubts about the validity of Christianity, wants to have the matter settled in his mind. [21]

Liberalism and neoorthodoxy react in much the same way to the pressures of positivistic science. Neither makes any serious effort to *contest* the claims of naturalism. Instead, both retreat to religious values, inaccessible to science. Because both suffer from a failure of nerve, they both in their own distinctive way locate the "word of God" in the personal, self-validating encounter of faith. There is little to choose between the authority of religious experience in Schleiermacher and truth-as-encounter in Brunner. In each case, revelation is not objectively given in history and language, but is hidden in the subjectivity of faith. [22]

As soon as this is understood, it becomes clear how the

various radical theologies of our time represent a nemesis to the natural evolution of liberal theology. *If* the charge be true that the religious facts upon which Christianity has traditionally rested are spurious, and *if*, therefore, Christian "truth" has no discernible relationship with what we otherwise know to be the case, then what possible meaning can the gospel now be said to have? Any theology which grants these two premises, as the liberal Troeltsch and the neoorthodox Bultmann do, for example, does not have the strength to repulse the radical invaders. It is indeed a small step to move from the otherness of a God who does not reveal himself unparadoxically, to no God at all![23] Regardless of the fact that the death-of-God thinkers seem to be inconsistent in holding onto the lordship of Jesus after they have pronounced the Deity dead, they have to be congratulated for having exposed clearly the logical resting place of the neoorthodox epistemology. Any theology which rests its entire case upon a subjective, self-validating experience is on shaky ground which can give way any minute. Only orthodoxy has the resources to stem the tide, appealing as it does to empirically verifiable divine activity in history. The death-of-God fad may pass, but the question they asked will not disappear. And thus far the answer of orthodoxy is the only one adequate to satisfy their question.[24]

THE PROBLEM OF STANDPOINT IN MODERN THEOLOGY

In the past, theologians understood quite well what their task was. They knew where to locate God's Word and how to construct an affirmative theology from it. Now it is a very real problem finding that Word (cf. Amos 8:11-12). By its acceptance of naturalistic science and the demythologizing of biblical categories which that entails, theology has found herself sucked into the full ambiguity of the human predicament, the old authorities and certainties being

107

dead.[25] As a result a new phenomenon is emerging, the antitheology, a theology which specializes in not having answers!

Catholic lay-theologian Michael Novak is particularly honest about his viewpoint. He advocates a "theology of the open standpoint." The principle of ultimacy in religion is the drive to ask questions. No single conceptual system or set of religious symbols will suffice. Each symbol is only finite and can be negated. It is the drive to *create* such symbols which is ultimate. Therefore, "a religion whose symbols are open to other forms of cultural expression seems more faithful to the drive to raise questions than are those whose symbols are parochially and irrevocably fixed."[26] No concept is sacred, not even the name or concept of God, because the drive to ask questions is inexhaustible.

For Fritz Buri, religious doctrines are merely *ciphers* (his term for *symbol*, which indicates his respect for the philosophy of Karl Jaspers) which deal with man's existential awareness of an unconditioned responsibility in the world. The Bible contains a mythical expression for man's undefinable relationship to the ultimate horizon of being surrounding him. [27] For Paul Van Buren, doing theology means revising the way a person understands his present circumstances in the light of the biblical story. It is a kind of language game in which one tries to answer the question of meaning from within his relative, time-conditioned situation. [28]

Now that Gilkey has broken with his neoorthodox phase (cf. *Maker of Heaven and Earth*), he has turned to a phenomenological analysis of human experience in order to locate aspects of consciousness which secularity overlooks or fails adequately to thematize By this means he hopes to ground empirically the Christian language game, if he can just show that these symbols make experience more coherent. But even if this is possible, the language in question will remain as mythical and paradoxical as before, and can really assure us nothing of the nature of that ultimate, unconditioned, sacral reality. The results have not been very good. At most he can trace only a "whiff" of ultimacy and transcendence.[29]

A Constructive Evangelical Alternative

The decision to maintain a strictly biblical, supernaturalistic position in the teeth of a cognitively antagonistic world requires no little courage in the face of the heavy pressures to conform to the secular modernity. It means refusing to accept the rules laid down by our cognitive opponents as liberal theology has done, while stubbornly insisting that traditional Christianity has the resources to solve the hermeneutical problem of the twentieth century. As we view the shambles of liberal theology today, the conviction deepens that our alternative is urgently needed, and that, apart from it, there is no way ahead at all. The issue seems quite clear: if liberal theology is correct, the traditional biblical faith as espoused by the vast majority of Christian people for almost two millennia is wrong.

The Achilles' heel of modern theology lies in its decision to accept uncritically the challenge of positivistic science. Therefore, the first requirement of our alternative is to show that this is a philosophical tenet which nothing in genuine science requires us to believe. It is the critical point because all the difficulties flow out of it: the liberals feeling compelled to dismantle the historical-doctrinal structure of the New Testament; the neoorthodox having to create a ghetto for saving history where skepticism cannot touch it; the inability of either to maintain consistently their esteem for the uniqueness of Jesus. What a price to pay for a threadbare dogma of nineteenth-century scientism!

We simply cannot see that the issue has anything to do with "the morality of historical knowledge," or with orthodox belief corroding the delicate machinery of sound judgment.[30] The key to the puzzle is found in two important distinctions which naturalists seem incapable of perceiving: the distinction between genuine science and scientism, and between scientific and historical method. Genuine science is a patient, empirical, organizing activity, undogmatic in mood and open to all the evidence. Scientism is a materialistic "theology" which sets the limits to reality before it examines the data. Scientism cannot be appeased because it is directly anti-Christian, whereas genuine science has come up with nothing that threatens traditional Christian belief.

Insofar as modern theology still accepts the closed-world metaphysic, it is aligned to a pattern of thought calcified a century ago and out of touch with reality. The debate is an ancient one. Paul's question has never been properly answered: "Why is it thought incredible by any of you that God raises the dead?" We are dealing here with a mind-set, not with scientific discovery at all. There is nothing in science which requires us to reject a priori the possibility of supernatural intervention in history. [31] The difficulty comes, not from the informed scientist, who is quite modest in any metaphysical judgments he may make, but from the so-called "man in the street," who knows very little about science and often holds it in quite superstitious regard. Some visit Lourdes, some read horoscopes avidly, some believe miracles cannot happen; is it not possible that positivism is just another modern myth? It is a curious fact that the same theologians who urge men to open their minds to a new possibility of existence carried by the Christian message refuse to have their positivistic presupposition altered even by the gospel. The Hellenistic world had to revise and forsake its closed-fatalistic world view under the pressure of the gospel; why should we not expect modern man to forsake his naturalistic assumption too? The Sadducees ridiculed the idea of resurrection. Their fundamental mistake, as Jesus pointed out, was an ignorance of the power of God (Mk. 12:24). Christianity is a supernatural religion. Modern theology has been tricked into accepting a naturalistic dogma diametrically opposed to it.

The second distinction has to do with the difference between historical and scientific thinking. Science relates itself to data which is subject to repeated experimentation. History, on the other hand, deals in the particular, the unique, and the unrepeatable.[32] The mere fact that no resurrection has occurred within my personal experience is insufficient grounds for denying that the resurrection of Jesus happened. The resurrection is without analogy— precisely! The question of the truth of the *Heilsgeschichte* is entirely a historical, not a philosophical, one. It is a matter of asking after the historical reasons for supposing that divine revelation actually took place. "Regularity" is not a Procrustean bed onto which the evidence can be forced. C. S. Lewis is right to point to the "naturalism in our bones" as the cause of much difficulty in determining whether Christianity is true. If miracles cannot happen, we need not bother to open the text of the New Testament or consider the force of the evidence. It is wise, therefore, to begin by exposing this assumption, or it will be quite futile to proceed further.[33]

We are forced to conclude that liberalism has capitulated to a view of science which is itself premodern. Paradigms in science today are not thought to be unalterable, literal photos of reality. They are criticizable, subject to the constraint of the evidence, and are liable to be replaced with a better hypothesis. Modern theology claims more for science than science claims for itself. It has a shrunken visibility of the possible and the real. Theology's response to naturalistic science was a failure of nerve, a policy of apologetic appeasement designed to attract Christianity's cultured despisers and salvage something authentically Christian in the end. Like an army under attack, it retreated from the plains in order to save the foothills farther back. The result was a surrender of huge tracts of Christian ground to the enemy, and a throwing of the Christian forces into disarray.

CHRIST WITHOUT MYTH

As long as the naturalistic assumption remained unchallenged, modern theology was compelled to disengage itself from history. She was haunted by Lessing's dictum, "accidental truths of history can never become the proof of necessary truths of reason." It became imperative, therefore, to detach faith from the relativities of history. In order to accomplish this, Christianity had to be read as a kind of *gnosis*, unassailable by historical criticism. Thus, in Tillich, Kahler, Barth and Bultmann, historical verity counts for very little. The "saving events" occur on a plane quite inaccessible to science. The manner in which liberalism interprets the gospel in terms of timeless truths, and neoorthodoxy in terms of existential experience, reminds us forcefully of second-century gnosticism. [34] It is alien to the historical shape of the New Testament message, according to which God raised up Jesus in the midst of *profane* history.

If the cost of rescuing Christianity is disengagement from history, the price is too high to pay. "Myths" can be demythologized; events cannot. The deepest intention of Scripture is to affirm the activity of God in time-space history. To "demythologize" the gospel is merely a polite way of denying it. When Christianity is said to be "historical religion," a good deal more is meant by it than that the religion had a beginning and has a history. The gospel is related to history in a unique way. Christ is not the genius who conceived of the ideas in the Christian creed. He is the whole creed! The medium is the message. Salvation depends on knowing Him as risen Lord and Savior. We are called to be "heralds" of good news, announcing to men the mighty acts of God.

Herein lies the reason the New Testament repudiates the category "myth" to qualify its message.[35] Paul takes pains to insist that the gospel is not "myth" (an existentially edifying tale without an historical base) but solid fact (1 Ti. 1:4; 4:7; 2 Ti. 4:4; cf. 2 Pe. 1:16). Even if a modern theologian is unable to regard the gospel in this way, it is still quite improper to handle something as myth which claims to be event. If the event did occur, it is proper to inquire further and ask what it signifies for my life. But if it did not occur, the matter is closed, and the gospel can be placed alongside the Gilgamesh epic. We are not denying that myth is an important mode which primitive man had for grasping reality. We are simply pointing out that biblical religion is self-consciously unmythical, even antimythical, in its self-understanding.[36] If we were to refer to myth in connection with the Christ event, it would only be to observe that here myth became history. The Greek Fathers did some thinking along those lines. Christ is the one in whom the aspirations expressed in the myths of all peoples have found their concrete embodiment.[37]

The New Testament places much store in the factual. The work of Luke, Paul and John was marked by such a concern (Lk. 1:1-4; Ro. 1:4; Ac. 17:31; 1 Co. 15:1-19; Jn. 20:21; 1 Jn. 1:1-3). Whether the redemptive facts actually occurred is by no means set aside scornfully as irrelevant. The word "If Christ has not been raised, your faith is futile and you are still in your sins" has not lost any of its force. Michel says boldly, "If Christ were born in you a thousand times, and never once in history, you would be lost."[38] We owe a debt to Oscar Cullmann for his scholarly insistence that the gospel has to do with datable, factual redemptive events. Seeing correctly the issue to be the validity of the *Heilsgeschichte*, Cullmann has continued to press his case against the neognostic theologians of our day.[39] Wolhart Pannenberg has gone even farther in explaining the relation of historical research and Christian dogmatics. Revelation is not to be understood in terms of religious subjectivity or

113

bare faith encounter, but in terms of a historical process not yet consummated, the meaning of which is made known in the Christ event. Once we have exorcised positivism out of historical research, we can begin to recover the biblical emphasis. "Historical revelation," he insists, "is open to anyone who has eyes to see. It has a universal character."[40] God's mighty acts are so "that men may see and know, may consider and understand together, that the hand of the LORD has done this, the Holy One of Israel has created it" (Is. 41:20, RSV). If some do not perceive it, this implies, not that revelation is visible only to the eyes of faith, but that there is something wrong with man himself (2 Co. 4:4). The revelation itself takes place in the sphere of the tangible and visible, and invites man's response of faith as a reasonable consequence of that fact. The preaching of God's mighty acts brings to man a knowledge from outside the human situation. It becomes a discernment situation in which saving faith can be born and grow.

> This is not to say that faith is made superfluous by the knowledge of God's revelation in the events that demonstrate his deity. Faith has to do with the future. This is the essence of trust. Truth primarily directs itself toward the future, and the future justifies, or disappoints. Thus a person does not come to faith blindly, but by means of an event that can be appropriated as something that can be considered reliable. True faith is not a state of blissful gullibility. The prophets could call Israel to faith in Jahweh's promises and proclaim his prophecy because Israel had experienced the dependability of their God in the course of a long history. The Christian risks his trust, life, and future on the fact of God's having been revealed in the fate of Jesus. This presupposition must be made as certain as possible to him. [41]

The proclamation of the gospel involves setting forth the reliable history about Jesus Christ, and appealing for commitment to Him. The idea that faith is a leap over the dubious historical claims to religious certainty is a monstrosity, biblically and epistemologically.

It is now apparent why theology has fallen upon evil days. The ill-conceived acceptance of the naturalistic presupposition by modern theologians has done away with the only possible and adequate foundation on which the Christian theological structure could be reared. There is no matter so fundamental as the authenticity of the redemptive facts on which the Christian proclamation rests. For the special claims of Christian theology do not rest on any achievement of speculative metaphysics independent of historical fact, but rather upon the act-word revelation of the living God acting in history for man's salvation. [42] Theology cannot survive a successful assault of skepticism upon her historical foundations. The attack must first be repulsed before her work can go on. Modern theology was attempting the impossible when she sought to combine naturalistic humanism and supernatural Christianity in an uneasy dualism. [43] That she has failed to do it is a beneficial fact to be seized upon in formulating the evangelical alternative.

The evangelical insistence that the only criterion and norm which Christian theology can allow to govern her work is the public revelation of God given definitively in the Christ event and closed until the day of His return has relevance also for the new ecumenical dialogue with the Roman Catholic Church since the Second Vatican Council. We can scarcely fail to be impressed with the sincere effort being made on the part of that communion to conform her thought and life to biblical categories. Many old caricatures have had to be discarded as a result, and some of the original questions posed by the Reformation reexamined. Much has been done to remove obstacles to the restoration of a proper Christian unity. Leading Roman Catholic theologians are now openly espousing the view that the Bible is materially sufficient and the *norma normans non normata,* an impressively strong affirmation of the full authority of Scripture. [44] All this is in the right direction. The problems of schism in the church will not be solved until all parties test their opinions on the basis of faithfulness to the scriptural record. Nevertheless, despite the marvelous improvement in personal relations between churchmen and numerous impressive shifts in certain attitudes and emphases, the peculiarly Roman Catholic characteristics which stand in the way of fruitful discussion toward healing the breach, for example, the divine authority of the Petrine office, are precisely those which go far beyond anything explicit or implicit in the Bible. If the Roman Church were to allow the new attitude toward Scripture to work itself out consistently in her thinking, it would become possible for all the children of God to draw closer together, "not in an impoverishing uniformity, but in an enriching diversity of perspectives within which is recognizably the same faith."[45]

CONCLUSION

We have indicated in broad outline where we believe the central issue in modern theology lies. The chaotic ferment in theology today has been brought about by a failure to confront the issue of naturalistic science properly. Instead of recognizing it to be a philosophical antagonist of the gospel, liberal theology sought to draw it into itself, hoping for a peaceful coexistence between faith and secular modernity. The history of recent theology has shown that the effort has failed, leaving behind a disintegrated liberal proposal. The true solution lies, in our opinion, along the lines of defending the fully historical character of the redeeming and revealing activity of God in Jesus Christ. The authority of this event is determinative for human thought, and neither churchly tradition nor the presumptuous claims of secular modernity have any right to challenge it.

Our essay has only pointed to the proper method and perspective for the theological task. An important part of the hermeneutical problem remains to be solved. After we know what we *must* preach, *how* shall we accomplish it? How are we to relate the concepts of the Word of God to modern ears? We may well envy the simple procedure which liberal theology is able to employ. A way out of the dilemma is found by simply passing the gospel through the sieve of the contemporary *Zeitgeist*, casting aside the uncongenial elements, and retaining the residue. Such a simple operation is forbidden to us, because we wish to translate *Christian* content into intelligibility and are not free to conform it to our predilections. Our task is to persuade a skeptical generation that orthodoxy is not only truer as a matter of fact than the alternatives, but it also can be meaningfully applied to human life today. To achieve this will call for a high standard of evangelical theology and preaching. More than an uncritical rehearsal of traditional formulations is required. Our theology will have to spring forth out of a creative encounter with the Word of God, issuing in an impressive, comprehensive grasp of what it means to be human in the light of divine revelation. Ideas which strike men as strange—original sin, the demonic, the atonement—will have to be thought through with deeper biblical profundity and with an eye for sharper contemporary relevance than is customary. The biblical faith must be shown to have a consistency and integrity about it which will command attention and respect from men of our generation. It is difficult to believe that this requirement has already been met by any evangelical work in our day.

Finally, just because we are dealing with the matter of theological prolegomena, the thesis has point also for the task of Christian apologetics. For faith itself rests, where theology does, upon the authenticated truth claim concerning God's redemptive activity in history. For that reason Christian faith escapes the paralyzing relativism to which liberal theology fell heir when it uncritically accepted positivistic science. Resting as it does upon the verified Word received from beyond the human situation, Christian faith is able to keep its poise even in the midst of flux and change. Indeed, it ought to be considered the only appropriate and available solution to the problem of relativism. Montgomery makes a wise observation:

> Man never has sufficient perspective from within the world situation to build an eternal structure of truth and value. Absolute truth and eternal value, if they exist at all, must take their origin from outside the flux of the human situation. . . . The plain consequence is that the only possible answer to modern man's quest for the ultimate meaning of history and for an absolute ethical standard would have to meaning of history and for an absolute ethical standard would have to lie in a revelation from outside the world. If such a revelation does not exist, man will of logical (not merely practical) necessity remain forever bound to his cultural relativities, forever ignorant of life's meaning. But if such a revelation should exist, it would explode the world—turn it, as men said the early Christians did, upside down.[46]

If there were no such Word from God, and relativity were allowed to work itself out, the result would be the destruction of every conviction and standard, of every claim to truth and ethical value. The result would be, and is in part already visible, skepticism, nihilism, and finally barbarism. The joy of traditional theology is to be able to proclaim salvation *from* the Lord in and through a historically attested divine disclosure. It is difficult to imagine, even in theory, what the Christian gospel offers men as a matter of fact. The way ahead for systematic theology is simply to recover the incredible relevance and sheer excitement of revelational Christianity.

FOOTNOTES

1. Karl Rahner has some helpful remarks along this line. *Theological Investigations,* vol. 1: *God, Christ, Mary and Grace,* trans. Cornelius Ernst (Baltimore: Helicon, 1961), pp. 1-5 Barth pauses to give quite a trenchant criticism of the conservative Calvinism found in L. Boettner, *The Reformed Doctrine of Predestination.* See Karl Barth, *Church Dogmatics,* trans. G. T. Thomson et al., 4 vols. (Edinburgh: T. & T. Clark, 1936-69), 2, 2, 13; 36-48.

2. Peter L. Berger has some amusing comments on theological faddists in his *A Rumor of Angels* (New York: Doubleday, 1969, pp. 14 f., 29f. Kenneth Hamilton offers an incisive critical analysis of liberal theology as a "theology of meaningfulness" above all else, in *Revolt Against Heaven. An Enquiry into Anti-Supernaturalism* (Grand Rapids: Eerdmans, 1965).

3. For remarks on the deep division in matters of belief among laymen, see Jeffrey K. Hadden, *The Gathering Storm in the Churches* (New York: Doubleday, 1969).

4. Van A. Harvey has expressed his difficulty lucidly in "The Alienated Theologian," *McCormick Quarterly* 23 (1970): 234-65. For a description of the present ferment in theology, see Langdon Gilkey, *Naming the Whirlwind. The Renewal of God-Language* (New York: Bobbs-Merrill, 1969), pp. 3-29.

5. Guy E. Swanson, "Modern Secularity: Its Meaning, Sources, and Interpretation" in *The Religious Situation: 1968,* ed. Donald R. Cutler (Boston: Beacon, 1968), pp. 801-34; Andrew M. Greeley, *Religion in the Year 2000* (New York: Sheed & Ward, 1969), pp. 15-73.

6. Langdon Gilkey, *Religion and the Scientific Future, Reflections on Myth, Science, and Theology* (New York: Harper, 1970), pp. 3-34.

7. Rudolf Bultmann, "The Question of Wonder" in *Faith and Understanding,* trans. Robert Funk (New York: Harper, 1969), pp. 247, 249. See also his "Is Exegesis Without Presuppositions Possible?" in *Existence and Faith,* ed. Shubert M. Ogden (Cleveland: Meridian, 1960), p. 291; "New

Testament and Mythology" in *Kerygma and Myth. A Theological Debate,* ed. Hans Werner Bartsch (New York: Harper, 1961), pp. 1-16; *Jesus Christ and Mythology* (London: SCM, 1958), pp. 15 f.

8. A valuable book on the centuries-old debate over the miraculous is Ernst Keller and Marie-Louise Keller, *Miracles in Dispute. A Continuing Debate,* trans. Margaret Kohl (Philadelphia: Fortress, 1969).

9. E. Troeltsch, "Historiography," *Encyclopaedia of Religion and Ethics,* ed. James Hastings (Edinburgh: T. & T. Clark, 1913). See Wilhelm Pauck, *Harnack and Troeltsch. Two Historical Theologians* (New York: Oxford U., 1968).

10. Harvey, *The Historian and the Believer* (New York: Macmillan, 1966).

11. Schubert M. Ogden, *The Reality of God* (New York: Harper, 1966), pp. 8, 16 f.

12. Ogden, *Christ Without Myth* (New York: Harper, 1961), pp. 127-38.

13. Charles I. Glicksberg, *Literature and Religion* (Dallas: Southern Methodist U., 1960), pp. 244 f.

14. See the chapter entitled "The Decline and Fall of Christian Dogmatism" in David L. Edwards, *Religion and Change* (New York: Harper, 1969), pp. 158-200.

15. Gordon D. Kaufman, *Relativism, Knowledge and Faith* (Chicago: U. Chicago, 1960); Glicksberg, *Modern Literature and the Death of God* (The Hague: Martinus Nijhoff, 1966).

16. Kaufman, *Systematic Theology. A Historicist Perspective* (New York: Scribner, 1968), pp. xii-xvi.

17. See Berger, chapter entitled "The Perspective of Sociology: Relativizing the Relativizers" in his *Rumor of Angels.*

18. The issue is plainly stated by John Warwick Montgomery in *Where Is History Going?* (Grand Rapids: Zondervan, 1969), pp. 15-36. Wittgenstein understood what was necessary if we were to transcend relativity: "The sense of the world must lie outside the world" *(Tractatus Logico-Philosophicus* [London: Routledge & Kegan Paul, 1922], 6.41-6.421).

19. J. R. Williams, *Contemporary Existentialism and Christian*

Faith (Englewood Cliffs, N. J.: Prentice-Hall, 1965), p. 19

20. One of the most illuminating analyses of the nature of modern theology and the reasons for its current difficulties is Gilkey's *Naming the Whirlwind*, pp. 73-106.

21. For an important study of the early shape of neoorthodox thought, see James D. Smart, *The Divided Mind of Modern Theology, Karl Barth and Rudolf Bultmann 1908-33* (Philadelphia: Westminster, 1967).

22. Our contention is supported by the work of Pannenberg who criticizes both liberal and neoorthodox theologies for locating divine revelation in an inward "epiphany." See his introduction to *Revelation as History*, ed. W. Pannenberg (New York: Macmillan, 1968), pp. 3-21. See also Pannenberg, "The Revelation of God in Jesus of Nazareth" in *Theology as History*, ed. James M. Robinson and John B. Cobb (New York: Harper, 1967).

23. Hamilton made this admission early in his career before he had himself taken that fateful step. *New Essence of Christianity* (New York: Association, 1961), p. 55.

24. Montgomery sets it forth in *The 'Is God Dead?' Controversy* (Grand Rapids: Zondervan, 1966). Gilkey handles the matter well in *Naming the Whirlwind*, pp. 107-78.

25. See Richard L. Rubenstein, *Morality and Eros* (New York: McGraw-Hill, 1970).

26. Michael Novak, "What Is Theology's Standpoint?" *Theology Today* 25 (1967-68): 46. See also his "The New Relativism in American Theology" in *The Religious Situation: 1968*, pp. 197-231; *The Open Church: Vatican II, Act II* (New York: Macmillan, 1964); and *The Experience of Nothingness* (New York: Harper, 1970).

27. F. Buri, *How Can We Still Speak Responsibly of God?* (Philadelphia: Fortress, 1968), pp. 1-40.

28. Van Buren, "On Doing Theology" in *Talk of God* (Royal Institute of Philosophy Lectures), vol. 2, 1967-68 (London: Macmillan, 1969). Experience is definitely back as a formative factor in liberal theology. See Harvey Cox, *Feast of Fools* (Cambridge, Mass: Harvard U., 1969), pp. 165 f.

29. Gilkey, *Religion and the Scientific Future*, p. 64. For his new

121

approach to the validity of religious language, see Part 2 of *Naming the Whirlwind*. Having lost confidence in the Word from outside the human situation, he is now engaged in the liberal quest to locate a dwelling place for the deity within man's capacity for self-understanding. Space for God-talk has to be cleared in the depths of nonreligious experience. Natural theology has completely replaced revealed theology.

30. Harvey, *The Historian* . . ., pp. 102-26.

31. James Kallas, *The Satanward View. A Study in Pauline Theology* (Philadelphia: Westminster, 1966), p. 149; L. Malevez, *The Christian Message and Myth* (London: SCM, 1958), pp. 125 seq.

32. See Richard R. Niebuhr, *Resurrection and Historical Reason* (New York: Scribner, 1957); and A. Richardson, *History Sacred and Profane* (London: SCM, 1964).

33. C. S. Lewis, *Miracles* (London: Fontana, 1960), p. 168. Some of the best thinking on this matter of proper historical method is being done by John Warwick Montogomery. See especially his *Shape of the Past. An Introduction to Philosophical Historiography* (Ann Arbor: Edwards, 1962); "Toward a Christian Philosophy of History" in *Jesus of Nazareth: Saviour and Lord*, ed. C. F. H. Henry (Grand Rapids: Eerdmans, 1966), pp. 227-40; "Clark's Philosophy of History" in *The Philosophy of Gordon H. Clark*, ed. Ronald H. Nash (Philadelphia: Presbyterian & Reformed, 1968), pp. 353-90.

34. W. Rordorf, "The Theology of Rudolf Bultmann and Second-Century Gnosis," *New Testament Studies* 13 (1967), pp. 351-62; G. L. Borchert, "Is Bultmann's Theology a New Gnosticism?" *Evangelical Quarterly* 36 (1964), pp. 222-28.

35. G. Stählin, "Muthos," Gerhard Kittel, ed., *Theological Dictionary of the New Testament*, trans. Geoffrey Bromiley (Grand Rapids: Eerdmans, 1967), 4: 762-95. K. Barth, *Church Dogmatics*, vol. 3, pt. 2, pp. 445-47, 451-54.

36. Brevar S. Childs has shown that where the Old Testament touches mythical material it consistently demythologizes it! *Myth and Reality in the Old Testament* (London: SCM, 1960). See also R. K. Harrison, *Introduction to the Old Testament* (Grand Rapids: Eerdmans, 1969), pp. 450-54.

37. See H. Rahner, *Greek Myths and Christian Mystery*, trans. Brian Buttershaw (London: Burns & Oates, 1963).

38. Otto Michel, "The Event of Salvation and Word in the New Testament," *The Theology of Rudolf Bultmann*, ed. Charles W. Kegley (New York: Harper, 1966), p. 181.

39. O. Cullmann, *Christ and Time*, trans. Floyd V. Filson (London: SCM, 1962); *Salvation in History*, trans. Sidney G. Sowers (New York: Harper, 1967). R. Bultmann reviews *Christ and Time* in his *Existence and Faith*, ed. G. Ogden (Cleveland: World, 1960), pp. 226-40.

40. W. Pannenberg, "Dogmatic Theses on the Doctrine of Revelation," *Revelation as History*, trans. David Granskou (New York: Macmillan, 1968), p. 135. See his "Heilsgeschehen und Geschichte," *Kerygma und Dogma* 5(1959): 218-37.

41. Pannenberg, *Revelation as History*, p. 138. For us the real strength of Pannenberg's position lies in its forthright recognition that divine revelation is mediated factually and historically in the Christ event. It is a recovery, long overdue, of Luther's incarnational emphasis. The weakness of Pannenberg is his reluctance to do justice to the noetic, cognitive content of that revelation. The meaning of the saving events is not self-evident, however, so that greater emphasis needs to be placed on the normative, apostolic interpretation deposited in the God-breathed Scriptures.

42. Schubert M. Ogden can boldly carry through Bultmann's demythologizing program to its consistent end because he is confident that process philosophy is capable of establishing a solid basis for a new-style theism. He deserves credit for at least trying to ground faith in something! The result, however intriguing, is most imprecise in content, and seems not a little like word-magic (as if by calling being-in-process by the name "god" we have really achieved something). See his *The Reality of God*, pp. 44-70. Cf. C. F. H. Henry, "The Reality and Identity of God," *Christianity Today* 13 (Mar. 14 and 28, 1969): 523-26, 580-84.

43. James Orr has some helpful remarks along this line in the preface to B. B. Warfield, *The Right of Systematic Theology* (Edinburgh: T. & T. Clark, 1897), pp. 7-11.

44. See J. R. Geiselmann, *The Meaning of Tradition*, trans. W. J. O'Hara (New York: Herder, 1966); K. Rahner and J. Ratzinger, *Revelation and Tradition*, trans. W. J. O'Hara (New York: Herder, 1966); G. Tavard, *Holy Writ or Holy Church* (London: Burns & Oates, 1959); K. Rahner, *Theological Investigations*, 1:64, 67-93.

45. George A. Lindbeck, *The Future of Roman Catholic Theology* (London: SPCK, 1970), p. 114.

46. John Warwick Montgomery, "The Relevance of Scripture Today," *The Bible, The Living Word of Revelation*, ed. Merrill C. Tenney (Grand Rapids: Zondervan, 1968), pp. 206 f.

PROMISE OF PATRISTIC STUDIES

by Geoffrey W. Bromiley

Patristics is one of the most neglected areas in evangelical theology. This is especially so in American Evangelicalism, for America generally has a certain impatience with the past, the more so the further away it is. Why rummage in remote ages, it is asked, when present problems of thought and practice are so urgent? If historical theology has any importance, should it not begin nearer home, at the Reformation or perhaps even in the eighteenth century, when a full break was made with the past, and most evangelical movements began? A brief survey of all Christian thinking and action might be useful. Some specialists may obviously give fuller attention to the Fathers. But proportionately, it is argued, one should neither spend too much time on them nor expect too much from them. Indeed, the question might be asked whether there is any real place for the Fathers in a review of evangelical prospects and programs.

Oddly enough, the Reformers did not share this view. To be sure, they regarded the Bible as their supreme norm. In this sense they agreed that a dozen Fathers provide no substitute for plain Scripture. Nevertheless, they did not disparage patristics. On the contrary, the Reformers offer fine examples of patristic scholarship. Theirs was, after all, the age when the Renaissance was making available new, exciting texts which lay behind the great figures of scholasticism. Luther and Zwingli were both versed in the Fathers. Oecolampadius of Basel made a special study of patristic texts relating to the Lord's Supper. Cranmer in England collected extracts from the Fathers as well as Scripture on all important issues. Jewel, author of *The Apology*, impaired his health by his assiduous reading of the Fathers, but this enabled him to challenge his Roman Catholic opponents on their own ground. Peter Martyr was also a formidable patristic scholar, and Calvin, even if he particularly favored Augustine, displayed a fine acquaintance with the whole area. [1]

The Reformers had a special reason for devoting time and effort to patristic study. As they understood it, medieval doctrine and practice represented a departure not merely from biblical Christianity but also from early Catholicity. In answer to the common charge that they were introducing a new learning in place of the old, they argued strenuously that theirs was the old learning and Rome's the new.[2] Recent centuries had brought innovations of dogma, religious practice and church government sanctioned only by supposed Roman traditions and not by evidence either from the apostolic writings or the early church. The task of the Reformers themselves was to bring the church back to its beginnings on the New Testament and the first centuries. Calvin, for example, objected violently to prelacy, but episcopacy as practiced in the early period he regarded as a legitimate form of biblical ministry.[3] The Anglican Reformers retained episcopacy on the same premise. As regards practices, Jewel in his famous Paul's cross sermons challenged the Roman party to produce patristic support; if they could he would withdraw his opposition to them.[4] Doctrinally Cranmer in the *Confutation of Unwritten Verities*[5] contrasted the patristic view of authority with the two-source appeal of contemporary traditionalists.

Unlike the Reformers, many evangelical scholars today have become accustomed to a very different reading of the situation. As they seem to see it, the patristic age brought a rapid declension from apostolic Christianity. From at least the early second century, doctrines and practices developed that swept the church into a movement which culminated in the Middle Ages and which still continues in Roman Catholicism. Eastern Orthodoxy, and the Coptic Church. The Reformation represented a return to biblical Christianity but, in the eyes of some, even this was an imperfect return both theologically and practically. Hence the patristic appeal of the Reformers might be construed as a point of weakness rather than of strength. It simply attests to the fact that the Reformers were still children of their own age even though also precursors of the new age. The period from the first to the fifteenth century is, in this view, a long tunnel with only a few shafts of light, such as the basic trinitarian and Christological formulations and isolated movements of reform. The end of the tunnel comes, or is at least in sight, with the Reformation.

Granted this type of interpretation, there is obviously little to be learned from the Fathers. The fixing of the doctrine of God might be studied with profit. The same applies to Christology. The question of anthropology received basic attention in the Pelagian controversy and some useful insights were offered on the atonement. Something is also to be gained from seeing how slight deviations gradually became the monstrous corruptions of the medieval church. Individual works or passages may be enlightening, though what they offer is to be found even more convincingly in Scripture. Patristic commentary can also help to determine the true sense of a biblical word or

127

saying. In particular, study of the biblical text and canon has to find a place for the early postapostolic age. For the rest, however, the patristic period is a kind of wasteland whose chief value is as a warning against defection from the biblical norm.

Liberalism has also contributed in some measure to a negative evaluation of the Fathers. With its historical concern it has, of course, produced some of the finest patristic work of the modern period. Harnack's *History of Dogma* is a monumental piece of scholarship, and a detailed study like Dean Rashdall's *Idea of the Atonement in Christian Theology* offers a fine survey of early soteriology. Yet Harnack's presuppositions are readily enough perceived and Rashdall's bigoted focus on forerunners of his own subjective view as the only real theologians of the early church is apparent on almost every page. The basis of judgment is different here, but the judgment itself is much the same. The early church misinterpreted and obscured the simple message of Jesus, and only with the new and progressive enlightenment of the modern period has it been recaptured. The result of liberalism, then, is to encourage historical investigation, but with tendentious emphases. If authentic Christianity is not now understood, its large-scale forfeiture until the present age is in the main accepted.

One should not overdraw the picture. To take but a few examples, Schaff in his *History of the Christian Church* provides an informed and appreciative account of the patristic period. Augustinian studies have flourished in Reformed theology, B. B. Warfield being an outstanding instance in this regard.[6] Shedd in his *Dogmatic Theology* has a keen sense of the value of the theological contribution of the Fathers. The Anglican Francis Procter wrote the first edition of what became a standard manual of Prayer Book study against the background of the history of worship.[7] Anglicanism in particular produced scholars of distinction who, if they were not distinctively Evangelical, were not pronouncedly Anglo-Catholic nor dogmatically liberal: Henry Gwatkin might be cited as an example.[8] Broadly speaking, however, it is always in churches with a Reformation tradition that evangelical patristic study has continued to flourish. For those of later origin the patristic world is to a large degree unexplored country whose wealth has yet to be assessed and exploited.

PROBLEMS

Some real problems must be stated and tackled before patristic work can be pursued with confidence. The first is that failure to follow up the Reformers' appeal has left the field far too much in nonreforming hands. Roman Catholicism, for example, has used the Fathers in its own defense. It has continued to accord high authority to them. It has pressed patristic statements and developments which lend credence to its own position. It has tried to push back such things as the Roman primacy to the very earliest period. It has been prepared, as with Newman in his *Development of Doctrine*, to subject patristic utterance to a schema of evolution. It has placed Scripture not only under the teaching office but also under the rule of patristic exegesis. It has thus tried to make the Fathers its own preserve, fostering the impression that one will turn to them in vain for any but a Roman Catholic understanding.

Nor has this been done merely by rash assertion. The volume and quality of Roman Catholic work in the field is formidable. The Schoolmen, for example, Lombard and Aquinas, laid the foundation when they adduced patristic evidences for their theses. In the early days of the Reformation Luther could be confronted by a patristic scholar like Eck, who seems to have had the better of the argument at this level. Jewel in his *Defence of the Apology* had to draw on all his resources to meet objections to his conviction that the Reformers are the true catholics. From the Reformation to the present day, Roman Catholicism has more or less dominated the patristic world, so that in the eyes of many the equation of the two seems to be self-evident.

If there is one exception to the rule it is to be found in Anglo-Catholicism. The Tractarians inherited a patristic emphasis which was common both to the Anglican Reformers and also to the high-church Carolines who succeeded them and who still believed that true catholicity lies outside the Roman version. With their desire to bring out again the catholicity and apostolicity of the church, the early leaders of the Oxford Movement jumped back to the first period, avoiding both the Reformation on the one side and Roman Catholicism on the other. Newman and Pusey were both patristic scholars of no mean order. Their successors on into our own century, for example, Gore and Kirk in doctrine, Kidd in church history, and Dix in liturgics, have continued to make notable contribution in the field.

Yet, by and large the emphases of the group have tended to strengthen the view that the Fathers are a "Catholic" preserve which Evangelicals might well abandon in favor of sixteenth-century or more recent studies. After all, it was study of the early church which helped to push Newman back into Roman Catholicism. Pusey resisted this, but with others he could still appeal to the Fathers for practices and ceremonies discarded at the Reformation. Kirk's main attempt in his *Apostolic Ministry* is to establish historically and doctrinally an apostolic succession through the episcopate. Dix's *Shape of the Liturgy* represents a fundamental cleavage from both the structure and also the doctrine of the Anglican Communion Order. Though Anglo-Catholicism undoubtedly distinguishes between true catholicity and Roman Catholic innovation, the fruit of this type of patristic study seems to be an undermining rather than a confirming of evangelical Christianity.

The fact that this is so leads us to what is perhaps the main problem of patristics, namely, the tendency to project back later ideas or disputes into early statements. Scholastic arguing from authorities naturally tended to promote this far-from-historical procedure. Thus, when the doctrine of transubstantiation was developed, early eucharistic language such as that of Irenaeus[4] could be pressed into service as though Irenaeus were already teaching the dogma. Similarly, any reference to the Eucharist as a sacrifice might be taken to imply the doctrine of the propitiatory sacrifice of the mass. [10] Or, to take another example, baptismal regeneration in the medieval sense could be found in Justin. [11] Or again, a hierarchical and sacerdotal ministry could be seen in the reference in *1 Clement* to an orderly structure of high priests, priests, Levites and laity. [12] Or again, any mention of succession in ministry, as in Irenaeus [13] or Tertullian, [14] might seem to offer plain proof that the doctrine of apostolic succession was held and taught in the earliest period.

The Reformers, of course, are not wholly blameless in this regard. In answer to traditionalist arguments they, too, tend to project their own reading back into the primitive texts. Eucharistic references to sacrifice are perhaps overfacilely explained as examples of the *res significata* expressed in terms of the *res significans*. [15] Justin, too, is really speaking of spiritual regeneration when he speaks of being born again in baptism. [16] Indeed, in some cases it is not even necessary to invoke this rule, for the pure offering of the Eucharist might well be the sacrifice or praise and thanksgiving which the Reformers generally teach. [17] What these later theologians hardly stop to do is to ask what precisely the writers themselves, who had never even dreamed of transubstantiation and the debates it caused, were thinking or saying when they used the words they did.

For Evangelicals, however, there is undoubted value in the Reformation (and Anglican High Church) contribution. For it brings to light in a special way the projection process which is so integral a part of the Roman Catholic use of the Fathers. The tragedy is that so many scholars are far too easily misled by the process into thinking that the Fathers do in fact teach, at least incipiently, the developed medieval doctrines. They thus write off patristic theology at these points as an immediate defection from the New Testament. Whether or not the Reformers themselves are right, they do at least show that much of the alleged patristic backing for Roman Catholicism is only of a wooden proof-text variety. The question put to the Fathers is: What do you say about transubstantiation, eucharistic sacrifice, apostolic succession? From the objective historical standpoint, the true answer is probably: Nothing. As Lancelot Andrewes said in his *Responsio ad Apologiam Bellarmini:* "It is perfectly clear that Transubstantiation, which has lately been born in the last four hundred years, never existed in the first four hundred." [18] The Fathers had never heard of such things. They were not discussing them. Any remarks they make are in another context altogether. But these remarks are thought to have a bearing and are thus press-ganged into service. As so often happens with the biblical text, the patristic text is forced to answer a question it never even asks. The Fathers thus become an authority for some other teaching. The impression is left that in germ at least they really teach this too. If opponents of the teaching are deceived by the projection, the question of what the Fathers are really saying will never even be raised. It is to the credit of the Reformers that they in their generation did raise it. Furthermore, their own use of the *res significata / res significans* distinction does at least have the merit of being more an explanation of literary form (figurative usage) than an importing of dogmatic content.

Once the process of projection is understood, many of the supposed problems in the Fathers fall away of themselves. Irenaeus goes too far, no doubt, with his Eve-Mary analogy, but he is not necessarily introducing or fostering Mariology except by way of undesigned influence on others. [19] Ignatius, when he refuses validity to baptisms and eucharists not sanctioned by the bishop, may be just guarding more securely against schismatic or heretical conventicles rather than trying to enforce full-blooded episcopalism. [20] *First Clement,* in depicting succession from the apostles to those appointed by them and then to other approved men, is probably still concerned about due order, not about promoting a new theory of apostolic ministry. [21] In other words, one does not have to accept at face value the interpretations which have been put on patristic statements in the light of later developments or in support of later dogmas. The interpretations may be plausible, but only from the context and situation, insofar as this is known or suggested, can one conclude with certainty what precisely the Father himself is saying.

In this regard, another factor comes into play. The earliest writings in particular are for the most part occasional pieces written for specific purposes. Ignatius, for example, was not writing on all aspects of the ministry nor was Barnabas giving a full account of his understanding of the gospel. If one wishes to know what these Fathers thought about many important things, for example, grace, faith, love, hope, righteousness, the atonement, one can only infer this from incidental references which may well be reliable guides but are scarcely to be treated as comprehensive information. In many instances what is inferred is no doubt quite reliable, but in the absence of any special discussion it can hardly lay claim to finality. No one would wish his full position on a matter to be judged solely by incidental references in a work on another topic.

When all is said, however, ambivalent areas admittedly exist in patristic theology. For one thing, there are in the Fathers many things which do historically provide the basis of later medieval corruptions. The problem of Christian penitence is an example.[22] Though this was not the original intent, the penitential discipline finally turned into Roman Catholic penance. The pleas of confessors for the *lapsi*[23] might also be mentioned; they are a stepping-stone to the intercession of saints. Indeed, the whole matter of post-baptismal sin and its remission seems to move irresistibly toward the medieval complex of absolution, purgatory and so forth. Again, the seeds of *ex opere operato* baptismal regeneration are present in the undeveloped but unguarded understanding of baptism. One might almost say the same about the Eucharist. If transubstantiation has to be projected back, nevertheless patristic sayings offer fertile soil for it. On the other hand, one has to preserve a sense of proportion here. Because one thing follows another, the first is not necessarily responsible for it. Again, one might argue that biblical phrases like the "washing of regen-eration" or "this is my body" are also natural soil for medieval misunderstandings. At the same time, and the more so in the light of the contemporaneous world of Gentile religion, one can hardly contest a certain am-bivalence in some statements, and the same applies to practices too.

Then again the Fathers seem at certain points to take wrong paths. Nygren in his excellent if overdrawn *Agape and Eros* finds a basic mistake in the attempted alliance with philosophy, though twentieth-century theology is in little position to protest too forcefully here. Again, individual Fathers like Origen engage in rather wild flights of fancy,[24] though in fact Origen did not carry the church with him, and he himself, unlike many moderns, perceived a distinction between the essential and the speculative.[25] Again, a fully developed ecclesiasticism emerged in the third century in a writer like Cyprian, and this time, even though Cyprian was addressing specific problems, he stated his position in broad principle and the church largely accepted it.[26] Finally, one might refer to peripheral conjectures, for example, the perpetual virginity of Mary, which Jerome defended with his caustic pen as though they were central doctrines of the faith. Though resisted by some, these gradually established themselves and became part of the legacy of doctrine and piety, in both the East and the West, long before the Middle Ages.

All the same, it is wrong to think that mistakes, however serious in their consequences, invalidate the rich and varied work of a whole period. If this were so, no lessons could ever be learned from the past. The Reformers made mistakes. So did the Anabaptists. So did the Pietists. Modern Evangelicals make mistakes. Indeed, the New Testament records mistakes made by the disciples both before and after Pentecost. The fact that there are problem areas in patristic theology is no more reason to ignore it than the fact that it has been claimed and (mis)used by others. Possibly something is to be gained from the very errors, as many can testify who have tried to guide younger churches abroad. In any case, there is also a positive contribution which surely outweighs the negative.

POSITIVE ASPECTS

Even a purely cursory glance at the history of theology shows that in fact the Fathers laid some solid foundations on which much else is often built almost without thinking. In the present context a brief outline of their work in this regard is all that can be attempted.

First, we owe to the Fathers a full discussion and outworking of the doctrine of the Trinity. [27] To many people this is no great achievement. Indeed, a whole school of thought from the eighteenth century onward has rejected it as simply the confounding of what ought to be simple. [28] Some well-meaning noncreedalists concur on the ground that one should stick to biblical sayings and avoid dogmatic definition. [29] Proponents of relevance, failing to note that the Fathers were in fact using the tools of thought of their time, use their very relevance as a weapon against them, for is not the relevance of today the irrelevance of tomorrow?

In this attack on patristic trinitarianism many important facts are forgotten. It is forgotten that the debates were largely thrust on the Fathers; they were not just indulging in idle speculation. It is forgotten that the views they ruled out are often unwittingly propagated by uninformed non-creedalists. It is forgotten that the definitions adopted were based on an exploration of virtually all possible implications of the biblical statements. It is forgotten that they represent, not a complication, but an attempt at balanced interpretation.

This interpretation, in the judgment of the early church after years of discussion, does most justice to the biblical data. It is not a final explanation of God. The terminology, though convenient, is not canonized. Continued reflection and restatement are by no means excluded. Yet various dead ends have been tried, found wanting, and sealed off. Knowledge of these will save theology and preaching much time and effort that might otherwise have to be devoted to them time and again. In the last resort the glorious mystery of the Godhead remains, so perhaps the finest trinitarian affirmation will always be doxology. But a genuinely biblical doctrine of God will have to build henceforth on this patristic foundation.

What applies to the Trinity applies no less to the person of Christ. The questions are inseparable, though in Christology there is the added dimension of the relation of deity and humanity in the one Christ. Again the Fathers were forced into debate by various errors ranging from early docetism[30] and adoptionism[31] to Arianism, Apollinarianism, Nestorianism and Monophysitism.[32] They had no intention of replacing the biblical doctrine of Christ by involved Hellenic or Hellenistic speculation. If they laboriously shaped a vocabulary of their own—and the task was complicated by the need to fix exact Greek and Latin equivalents[33]—this was partly for the sake of definition and partly because it was natural, perhaps even inevitable, that they should state the truth in contemporary philosophical jargon.

Nor was their interest purely philosophical. Even before the Arian controversy Athanasius [34] had seen that Christology and soteriology are indissolubly united. The true heart of the Nicene confession is thus "for us men and for our salvation." The Tome of Leo expressly makes the same connection. [35] If the Chalcedonian Definition (451) is involved almost to the point of tediousness, it, too, includes the basic soteriological point that Christ is the true Mediator because He is of one substance with God as touching His deity and of one substance with us as touching His humanity.

Chalcedon again is a guide to all future work. The false paths which had been followed are here blocked off, for example, by the famous adverbs. There is no claim that the last word has been said. But these erroneous ways will yield no positive benefit and hence there is no sense in wasting time on them. In the one person, very God and very man, we have the essential foundation both of Christ's person and also of His work. Chalcedon does not forbid us to work through all this again, to try to develop its implications or to understand its mystery, to seek modern words in place of the older and, by this time, technical vocabulary, or to attempt to put it all back in purely biblical words. But there can be no question of going back on the patristic doctrine. To do so can only cause new confusion. Similarly, to ignore it can only mean in the long run that the whole tedious work of exploration will have to be repeated. A grasp of Chalcedon, an understanding of the biblical relationship, and an ability to attempt restatement are prerequisites in any future Christology which is to be worthy of the name.

The Fathers also did some at least of the basic thinking in respect of the atonement. It is perhaps unfortunate that the fancifully expanded ransom theory (the ransom paid to the devil)[36] and the outwitting of the devil by the divine humanity (picturesquely if crudely illustrated by the fishhook and the mousetrap)[37] tended to establish themselves as the orthodox teaching and quite naturally attract the attention of students. In fact, however, the patristic doctrine was far richer than this. Almost every possible understanding of Christ's work was presented somewhere. Thus in Irenaeus alone one finds the concepts of recapitulation,[38] exchange,[39] and liberation.[40] Tertullian speaks of substitution and satisfaction.[41] Later Cyril of Alexandria, stressing the idea of equivalent payment,[42] again describes this as a punishment.[43] The thought of Christ's death as a sacrifice also runs through patristic theology.[44] But reconciliation is also revelation; this is a key thought in Clement of Alexandria[45] and it is also one of the two main approaches in Athanasius.[46] Finally, the death of Christ is an example of obedience[47] and a moving demonstration of love[48] which has power to evoke a response of love in us.[49]

One thing above all is clear. For the Fathers the atonement was basically objective *(for* us) as well as subjective *(in* us). This means, of course, that it is primarily and predominantly God's act. As already noted, it is God's act in and by the incarnate Son. The Fathers avoided the foolish controversy of whether one should focus on the incarnation or the atonement. As they saw it, to focus on the one is to focus on the other. There is much wisdom in consulting the Fathers in this and in much else. Certainly some of the more grotesque features of their presentation are to be avoided. Yet, with them we are surely to stress the objective character of the atonement, to find a due place for the subjective side as well, to appreciate the great wealth of Christ's atoning work, and to bring out the essential link with the incarnation. Future work on the doctrine might do much worse than start with these presuppositions.

Finally, the Fathers made a solid and lasting contribution to anthropology. Not all their work in this field is of equal significance. The discussion of the bipartite or tripartite nature of man will not command too much attention, and if modern studies have hardly carried us further, the solutions to the soul's origin (creationism, traducianism, or preexistence) have something of an abstract ring. On the other hand, the early Fathers saw from the very first the need to maintain human freedom over against determinism or necessity, [50] and Augustine himself fully shares this view. [51] This is an important point, for there has sometimes been a tendency to confuse predestination and determinism.

Along with freedom, Augustine in particular made it his business to establish the theological bondage of the will in the decisive Pelagian controversy of the early fifth century. At issue here were the solidarity of the race in sin, the inability of man to achieve self-righteousness, the initiative of God in salvation, the divine election, and the true nature of freedom as freedom only to do the will of God. [52] During the course of the controversy all the issues and implications were explored and every conceivable view was represented from the extremes of Pelagius and Augustine to the semi-Pelagianism of Arles and the semi-Augustianism of Orange. [53] If no definitive answer to the ultimate problem was given, it is almost impossible to think that any fruitful work can be done in the area without considering the patristic contribution. One might, of course, begin with the sixteenth- or seventeenth-century debates, but these in turn take us back to the earlier controversy. One might go back to the biblical data, but reflection at once raises again the Augustinian-Pelagian issues. One might jump to psychological study, but the moment the relation to God enters the picture the familiar problems of sin, guilt, racial solidarity, the limits of moral freedom, the purpose and work of God, and the liberating ministry of the Spirit all come crowding back. If the Fathers offer no full enlightenment, they do provide the essential materials and insights for informed and intelligent discussion. Even Barth in his attempt at a radically new statement sees it necessary to master and interact with the whole range of historical treatment from the Fathers onward. [54]

REFORMATION EXAMPLES

In addition to the positive contribution of the Fathers, there is much in patristic theology which has been used helpfully and constructively at a later time, particularly by the Reformers. A few instances have been briefly mentioned already to show how the Reformers could find their own understanding rather than that of the Schoolmen in the simple patristic terms or sayings. But beyond that, the Reformers with their vast store of patristic knowledge could often take things written by earlier authors and develop and apply them to their own time. In some instances they might be saying little more than what the Fathers were also saying. In others they might be drawing out implications in relation to their own situation. Either way they offer an instructive illustration of the use to which the theology of the early period may be constructively and yet not illegitimately put.

Thus, in the critical matter of authority, confident appeal is made to the Fathers in support of the supreme position of Holy Scripture. Certainly Irenaeus and Tertullian cite the rule of faith, the traditional message of the apostolic churches, alongside Scripture. Yet, in their case the question seems to be fairly obviously a hermeneutical one. When different conclusions are drawn from Scripture, those that are to be accepted are those which are compatible with the quintessential New Testament doctrines that are handed down from one age to the next in the apostolic rule. There is no challenging of the unique inspiration and authority of Scripture as such, for in fact the Fathers consistently point to Scripture as the ultimate norm.

Cranmer makes this point with great force in the

collection of patristic quotations later published in *The Confutation of Unwritten Verities*. As he saw it, the Fathers would not allow anything to be taught as necessary unless it had scriptural sanction. [55] They spoke strongly of the sole sufficiency of the Bible. [56] They exalted Scripture as the norm for the preacher. [57] They claimed that the Bible is essentially perspicuous and that "testimonies of places certain" should be studied "to take away the doubt of the uncertain sentences. [58] Even the writings of other Fathers were to be tested by the biblical canon. As Augustine rightly said, "For I do not account Cyprian's writings as canonical, but weigh them by the canonical scripture; and that in them which agreeth with canonical I allow to his praise; but that that agreeth not, by his favour I refuse." [59] Similar quotations could easily be adduced to show that the appeal to the Fathers is in itself finally an appeal to the absolute normativeness of Scripture—one of the basic concerns of Reformation theology in its opposition to medieval abuse.

The related understanding of succession is also pertinent. In the second century the rise of unauthorized Gnostic teachers led to a great stress (1) on the properly ordained ministry, [60] and (2) on the tradition preserved by this ministry in the apostolic churches. [61] Out of this, as may be seen, there could and did arise the doctrine of apostolic succession: [62] (1) that only ordination deriving from the apostles is valid, (2) that this succession guarantees orthodoxy, and (3) that it confers the grace of orders.[63] Now the Reformation, though in fact it did maintain episcopal succession in England and Sweden, and presbyteral succession in other lands, had no interest in the doctrine of succession as thus taught. Yet, it did not renounce the concept of succession. Jewel in his *Apology* insisted that succession is vital. Truly understood, however, it is not a doctrine of succession, but succession in doctrine.[64] The real point of the patristic appeal is that the orthodox churches were handing on, not orders, but the basic teaching received from the apostles. Mere succession in orders is of little account. It carries no automatic guarantee of orthodoxy. If a church appeals to Irenaeus or Tertullian on succession, when in fact it no longer conforms to the apostolic norm, this is a sham. Thus the medieval church no doubt maintained sequence of ordination, but its innovations in doctrine and practice broke the sequence of apostolic truth. Yet, the only reason the Fathers were concerned about the former was because they were so concerned about the latter: sequence of ordination was meant to perpetuate sequence of apostolic doctrine. [65] Once it failed to do this, it lost its *raison d'être*, having no intrinsic merit or purpose of its own.

A valuable point here is that Jewel's concept yields what was surely the original dynamic tradition and not just a fixed and static tradition. Tradition is more than a deposit handed down; it is also the handing down. In turn, this brings reconciliation rather than conflict between the authority of Scripture and that of tradition, for these are but two forms (the written form and the oral) of one and the same thing. Scripture, being written, has ultimate normativeness. Nor did the Fathers dispute this, for even when they used, for example, the creed to check wild misinterpretation, they viewed the creed as an epitome of the biblical message. In comparison with Scripture, tradition is the preaching and teaching of the biblical message by the ordained ministry. Ideally, as in the earliest period, succession in doctrine coincides with succession in ministry; but if, as in the Reformation period, this is no longer so, then succession in doctrine must take precedence. This has been finely brought out by Karl Barth in *Church Dogmatics*, where it is argued that apostolicity, that is, abiding by the apostolic rule and truth of Holy Scripture, is alone the focus and guarantee of the church's unity, holiness, and catholicity. [66]

As a final illustration, one might refer to the vexed issue of the Lord's Supper. On the face of it, the patristic evidence seems to run in favor of medieval developments. The Eucharist was commonly seen as a fulfillment of the pure offering of Malachi 1:10, 14. [67]. Against Gnostic dualism, Irenaeus found a convincing answer in the fact that "the eucharist becomes the body of Christ, from which things the substance of our flesh is increased and supported." [68] Sacerdotalism then developed in the third century, [69] and from this it was a more or less logical step to the medieval ideas of transubstantiation and the eucharistic sacrifice.

Nevertheless, the Reformation saw a fundamental break in the chain. An important influence in some circles was Ratramn, who in his *Christ's Body and Blood,* a reply to *The Lord's Body and Blood* by his colleague Radbert, assembled as array of patristic as well as biblical testimonies against incipient transubstantiation. [70] Ridley, who helped Cranmer on this matter, stated that Ratramn (betram) was the author who was chiefly instrumental in leading him to a new biblical and patristic understanding of the eucharistic presence: "real" in the general sense of the term but not in the technical sense. [71] Now already Zwingli had appealed to Augustine's famous dictum: "Believe and thou hast eaten," [72] along with many other references more fully and systematically compiled by Oecolampadius of Basel. As the issue came to a head around 1550, that formidable trio of patristic scholars, Peter Martyr, Cranmer and Jewel, then took in hand the thoroughgoing scholarly investigation which underlies the principle of *res significans / res significata* in interpreting earlier texts. The final key, however, was found in the Christological analogy developed especially in the early church by Theodoret and Hilary. Cranmer in his *Defence of the True and Catholic Doctrine* (amplified in the monumental *Answer*) works this out in comparison with baptism to give a common sacramental understanding. As regards presence, in both baptism and the Lord's Supper, Christ is present as both God and man, yet according to the mode of the period between the ascension and the coming again, that is, by the Holy Spirit, so that there is no identity of the bread and the body. As regards efficacy, the sacrament has a twofold nature analogous to that of Christ, the great error of transubstantiation being that of a sacramental denial of the two natures which the Fathers had seen to be vital to a proper understanding of the sacrament.[73] The points made by Cranmer are well summed up by Lancelot Andrewes in his *Responsio ad Apologiam Bellarmini*: "We believe no less than you that the presence is real. Concerning the method of the presence, we define nothing rashly. . . .It is perfectly clear that transubstantiation, which has lately been born in the last four hundred years, never existed in the first four hundred. . . .There is that kind of union between the visible sacrament and the invisible reality of the sacrament which there is between the manhood and the Godhead of Christ, where, unless you want to smack of Eutyches, the manhood is not transubstantiated into the Godhead."[74]

Now it is true that for those who see no middle ground between transubstantiation and symbolism this interpretation is of little worth. The point is, however, that there has been middle ground historically. The realism of the early statements is, in fact, possible without the slightest commitment to the medieval dogma. The medieval dogma is not necessarily a development, or at any rate a legitimate development, of the patristic teaching. It is an attempt to explain the mode of the presence (Andrewes' "method"). The attempt made the mistake of relevance, in other words, of putting the doctrine in the favored Aristotelian categories of the day rather than in biblical terms. The church then made the even more serious mistake of canonizing the explanation as a dogma. The genius of Cranmer, along with Martyr and Jewel, was to use the Fathers themselves to make a break with the false development and to bring about a return to the biblical teaching. It is no small testimony to Cranmer's success that when at his trial he offered to state his teaching only in the words of Scripture and the Fathers [75] his "catholic" judges found this totally unacceptable. Newman might justify their attitude by the development of dogma. Möhler might claim more frankly and influentially that the church's interpretation is just as authoritative as the biblical (or patristic) saying. But this only shows that intrinsically the early Fathers give more support to evangelical eucharistic teaching than they do to Roman (and Eastern) [76] sacramentalism.

More incidentally, one might point out that in many respects patristic practice offers a corrective to many unhappy corruptions which came into the church later. Since this is a vast subject, a few instances must suffice. Thus the earliest period affords little evidence for any Roman supremacy, except perhaps in dignity. Similarly, there is no evidence of a single administration of the whole church whether under the Roman see or any other agency. Furthermore, the dioceses of the early church were mostly small and the bishops, far from being prelates, devoted themselves predominantly to their spiritual office. One also finds no support for the enforced celibacy of clergy, denial of the cup to the laity, masses for the dead, private confession to priests, pilgrimages, or the veneration of images. Some abuses undoubtedly made their first entry during the patristic age. This one might expect, for no church can claim immunity from mistakes. The deeper one digs, however, the sparser is the support for nonapostolic customs. In this respect the "always" and "by all" of the Vincentian canon act as a sharp and effective razor. [77] The "everywhere" usually completes the destruction of hopeful appeals to patristic authority for enforcement of practices which are no less unbiblical than unwritten.

PROPOSALS

If patristic study has been a useful ally of biblical theology in the past, there is every reason why this should still be true today. Far from avoiding investigation of the Fathers, the church is better advised to pursue this vigorously, not just out of curiosity, but with a view to contemporary application.

The pertinence of this branch of study is nowhere more plain than in the current debate with liberalism. The first mortal threats the church faced, namely, from rationalists, gnostics and Jews, have a great deal in common with the liberal challenge in its rich and varied forms. Celsus reminds us of many a modern in his rejection of the virgin birth, [78] the incarnation, [79] and the resurrection. [80] The Marcionite Apelles is as forthright as anyone today in his rejection of the historicity of the ark, and he goes on to draw the appropriate conclusion: "It is clear that the story is false; but if this be so, it is clear that this scripture is not from God." [81] Trypho anticipates the view that Old Testament predictions do not really find fulfillment in Christ. [82] The speculativeness of liberal theology may rival but it can hardly surpass that of gnosticism. Even in obscurity Basilides is a match for any modern. [83] In content, gnostic ideas, and some of those of Origen, [84] are so audacious as to seem fantastic. Yet there are detailed points of contact (as in universalism), [85] and above all, these theologies share with liberalism the common principle of emancipation from any objective control.

A first proposal, then, is that the response of especially Western theology to gnosticism be reexamined and reassessed with a view to the restoration of objective theological control. The issue as seen by Irenaeus and Tertullian is surely not whether one appeals to Scripture, tradition, or succession. It is simply that Christian truth is by nature objective. Tertullian puts this well when he notes that theology is not a continuing quest or, as one might say, an exploration into God. The Christian has found Christ: "We want no inquisition after receiving the gospel." [86] The task of theology is to consider, develop and apply what is already known. Basically this is known in Scripture. But since the Bible can be expounded arbitrarily, the biblical epitome of the rule of faith serves as a hermeneutical principle which alone establishes exposition as true and not false. This is the ground of what might otherwise seem to be the outrageous claim that heretics "have acquired no right to the Christian Scriptures." [87]

Now one might not wish to adopt Tertullian's hermeneutical principle, but this is not the real point. What finally counts is that patristic theology brings to light the essential distinction between the two approaches to theology, that of gnosticism and liberalism on the one side, that of the Reformation and Evangelicalism on the other. Liberalism, of course, is well aware of the issue. It has even suggested that the Irenaeus-Tertullian type was not really orthodox but, due to various forces, it was the type to survive the second-century turmoil and thus to establish itself as orthodox. Here we are indeed at the very heart of the modern theological debate. The very beginnings of patristic theology offer the occasion for thinking out afresh what theology really is, what is the key to sound hermeneutics, what is the absolute and what the relative in a Christian understanding, and ultimately who the God is with whom we have to do: our own idea of God, or the living God self-revealed in Jesus Christ according to the Scriptures.

The matters dividing Roman Catholic and Evangelical are also just as pertinent today as ever. Indeed, the renewal movement in Roman Catholicism has given them a new urgency. Roman Catholicism itself has opened up in a fresh way many things on which it seemed there could only be endless repetition. Thus, the relation of Scripture to tradition is no longer as fixed as it seemed at Trent. Mariology is the focus of a lively and crucial debate. Papacy and apostolicity stand in need of theological and practical reappraisal. Wide adoption of the principle of husk and kernel, of the current statement enclosing the essential content, has made possible a wholly new attitude to apparently inflexible dogmas, for example, justification [88] and transubstantiation. Even time-honored customs are under scrutiny and are no longer held to be, at least in principle, definitive.

The final impulse behind this great movement is, of course, biblical study. It is no small tribute to the new expositors and biblical theologians of the Roman world that they have been able to press their work to the point of candid self-scrutiny. Yet, as at the Reformation, the new look at the Bible makes possible and indeed requires a new look at the Fathers. Do they really support or underlie the medieval and later developments? Did the Reformers have after all a better grasp of both Scripture and Fathers on many central issues? Will not the biblical work have to be accompanied by extensive and intensive historical work?

A second proposal is, then, that a new patristic investigation of these themes be pursued, if possible in friendly dialogue with Roman Catholic theologians. This should not be just a restatement of the Reformation interpretation as distinct from the Tridentine, although obviously the fine work of the Reformers in this field will demand attention. In other words, the task is not simply that of complacently claiming victory. What is needed is that evangelical and Roman Catholic theologians, preferably together, attempt a strictly objective historical study of the Fathers apart from the views and positions of a later time. Possibly the Fathers said things which support no later view because they have no real bearing on it. Possibly they said things which in fact represent departures from the Bible, due perhaps to the intrusion of alien forms of thought and speech. Possibly there is much more variety and movement in patristic theology than is often conceded, as suggested by the divergent and not very closely defined presentations of the atonement. Possibly the Fathers will have some things to say which have been largely missed in later times but can add to our store of biblical understanding. The Fathers themselves must tell us these things.

The Fathers might also be pertinent in respect of what is perhaps an overdue evangelical self-appraisal. It is one thing to watch approvingly the Roman Catholic efforts at renewal, quite another to put into effect the principle that the church, every church, is always *ecclesia reformanda* and never finally in this world *ecclesia reformata*. Now, the supreme norm of doctrine and practice is Scripture. Yet, there are also subsidiary and relative norms, among which the Fathers hold an important place. The function of these secondary standards is to provide points of reference by which the biblical norm may be applied, or its application confirmed. Thus it is easy to compare one's own doctrine and practice with Scripture and again find only what one wants to find. The fact that other ages, making the same comparison, have found other things puts the question with new point and precision. Perhaps the other age is right, and an unsuspected nonconformity to Scripture is disclosed. Even if it is wrong, or partly wrong, there is something to learn from the way it is wrong and the reason or reasons it went wrong, for our own time might easily go wrong in similar ways or for similar reasons. Whether in the positive mode or the negative mode the aim of self-testing is thus in part fulfilled.

A third proposal, then, is that the doctrine and practice of the Fathers be intensively studied against the norm of Scripture and in comparison with other ages, especially our own. This may bring surprises. Possibly, as Aulen suggests in his *Christus Victor,* there is in the Fathers an aspect of soteriology which has often been overlooked. Again, as Cullmann stresses, the element of resurrection joy in the Lord's Supper is a biblical dimension we need to recapture. In evangelism and church life, for example, the field of discipline or Christian funding, the early church might focus no less searching a light on us than we on it. In relation to departures from the biblical norm, patristic study can illustrate the problem of stating biblical truth and living the biblical life in a pagan environment. This is a problem which affects every church and congregation, however zealously evangelical. It is easier to identify the problem (and the mistakes) in a past age. But until one can do this, the problem (and the mistakes) will often pass unnoticed in the present. An illusion of being biblical will thus in some measure replace the reality when the honest use of a point of reference might easily dispel the illusion.

Finally, a proper study of the Bible demands some knowledge of patristic exegesis. The patristic side of biblical study is not the most important. Even if the Fathers were the earliest exegetes and many of them spoke the same language as the New Testament and the Septuagint, they were not necessarily the best equipped or the most accurate. [89] The legitimate stress on fulfilled prophecy could produce some extravagant flights of fancy. [90] The growth of Alexandrian allegorizing was no great help. [91] Nevertheless, as the intertestamental writings, the Qumran texts and the Mandaean writings call for notice in relation to proper biblical understanding, the relevant body of patristic material is certainly not to be ignored.

A fourth and final proposal, then, is that greater attention be paid to the Fathers as at least a supplementary part of especially New Testament study. This will serve a direct purpose, for light can be shed on the meaning and application of Scripture at important points. It will also serve an indirect purpose. Only as patristic studies are incorporated in New Testament research can the first three proposals be carried out properly. Both the patristic age and all other ages have to be tested by Scripture if they are to be set in profitable interaction. The reassessment of the Fathers needs to be done along with the intensive investigation and under the critical scrutiny of the Bible. The

objective criterion is consolidated if and when early orthodoxy is seen to be in essentials identical with the message
and teaching of the apostles. Patristic study is in no sense an
alternative to biblical study. It is nevertheless an important
and salutary supplement both for the sake of biblical study
and also for its own sake.

FOOTNOTES

1. On the Reformation view, cf. Jacques de Senarclens, *Héritiers de la reformation* (Geneva: Labor et Fides, 1956), pp. 143 ff.

2. Cf. William Turner's work, *The Comparison Between the Olde Learnynge and the Newe* (London, 1537), a translation of Urbanus Rhegius, *Novae Doctrinae ad Veterem Collatio* (London, 1537, 1547, 1548), which appears in Leigh Richardson, *Fathers of the English Church*, 8 vols. (1807-12), vol. 4.

3. John Calvin, *Institutes of the Christian Religion*, ed. John T. McNeil, trans. Ford Lewis Battles; 2d ed. (Philadelphia: Westminster, 1960), 4, 4, 1 ff.

4. *The Works of John Jewel*, ed. John Ayre (Cambridge: U. Press, 1845-50).

5. *The Works of Thomas Cranmer*, ed. John Edmund Cox (Cambridge: U. Press, 1844-46), 2:1 ff.

6. Cf. B. B. Warfield, *Calvin and Augustine*, ed. Samuel G. Craig (Philadelphia: Presbyterian & Reformed, 1956).

7. Francis Procter, *A New History of the Book of Common Prayer*, 1st ed., 1855; revised and rewritten by Walter Howard Frere, 1901; reprinted with corrections (New York: Macmillan, 1902).

8. Cf. Henry Gwatkin, *Arian Controversy: Studies of Arianism* (Cambridge: Deighton Bell, 1882).

9. Irenaeus, *Haer.*, 5, 2, 1-2.

10. Cf. *Didache*, 14:1.

11. Justin, *I Apol.*, 61.

12. Clement, *I Clement*, 15:5.

13. Irenaeus, 3, 3, 4.

14. Tertullian, *De Praescr. haer.*, 21 f.

15. Cf. Cranmer, 1:35: "a sign or representation of the true sacrifice."

16. Ibid., p. 150.

17. Ibid., p. 352.
18. Cf. Henry S. Bettenson, *Documents of the Christian Church*, 2d ed. (New York: Oxford U., 1963), p. 307.
19. Irenaeus, *Demonstration of the Apostolic Preaching*, p. 33.
20. Ignatius, *Smyrn.*, 8:2.
21. Clement, 64:1.
22. This is especially true from the time of *The Shepherd of Hermas* onward.
23. For *libelli pacis*, cf. Cyprian, *Ep.*, 27, 1, 2.
24. Origen, *De Princ.* 1, 6, 3; 1, 8, 1; 2, 8, 3.
25 Ibid., 1, 2-8, 10.
26 Cyprian, *De unitate*, passim.
27 For a good account, cf. J. N. D. Kelly, *Early Christian Doctrines* (New York: Harper & Row, 1960).
28. Cf. Lessing's distinction between the religion of Christ and the Christian religion in his *The Religion of Christ* (1780), pp. 2 ff., reprinted in *Lessing's Theological Writings*, ed. H. Chadwick (Stanford: Stanford U., 1957), pp. 106 ff.
29. This is the main justification of the middle party at Nicea, but one should remember that it could not hold the pass against Arianism.
30. Cf. Ignatius, *Trall.*, 9:10.
31. Cf. Irenaeus, *Haer.*, 1:21.
32. For basic documents, cf. Henry Scowcroft Bettenson, *Documents of the Christian Church* (London: Oxford U., 1943), part 1, secs. 4, 5; part 2, sec. 1.
33. Ibid., pp. 32 F.
34. Athanasius, *De incarn. Verbi*, 8 ff.
35. Bettenson, pp. 49 f.
36. Irenaeus, *Haer.*, 5, 1, 1.
37. Origen, *In Matt.*, 16:8; Gregory of Nyssa, *Orat. Catech.*, vols. 21 ff.; Augustine, *Sermo*, 263:1.
38. Irenaeus, *Haer.*, 3:18.
39. Ibid., 5, preface.

40. Ibid., 3, 32, 2; 5, 1, 1.

41. Tertullian, *Adv. Marcion*, 4:21.

42. Cyril, *De recta fide*, 21.

43. Cyril, *Hom.*, 10:3.

44. Cf. John of Damascus, *Expos. Orthod.*, 4:4.

45. Clement, *Paed.*, 1, 3, 7.

46. Athanasius, *De incarn. Verbi*, vols. 14 ff.

47. Ignatius, *Rom.*, 2:2.

48. Clement, *I Clement*, 8:4.

49. Origen, *In Rom.*, 4:10.

50. Cf. Justin, *I Apol.*, 10:4; Tertullian, *Adv. Marcion*, 1:22; Clement, *Protr.*, 6:681; Origen, *De Princ.*, 3, 1, 2-4.

51. Cf. Augustine, *Ep.*, 157.

52. For the essential points, cf. Bettenson, pp. 52 ff.

53. Ibid., pp. 60-62.

54. Karl Barth, *Church Dogmatics*, ed. G. Bromiley, trans. G. T. Thomson et al. (Edinburgh: T. & T. Clark, 1936), 2:2.

55. Cranmer, 2:22.

56. Ibid., p. 24.

57. Ibid., p. 25.

58. Ibid., pp. 31 f.

59. Ibid., p. 33.

60. Cf. Ignatius, *Smyrn.*, 8, 1, 2; *Trall.*, 9:1.

61. Irenaeus, *Haer.*, 3, 3, 4.

62. The first extant use of "succession" is in Hegesippus (Eusebius, *HE*, 4, 22, 2.

63. Clement, *I Clement*, 44: 1-3 has often been pressed into service here.

64. Jewel, 2:103 ff.

65. Cf. Tertullian, *De Praescr. Haer.*, 20, 21.

66. Barth, 4, 1, par. 62, 2; cf. also 1, 2, 20.

67. *Didache*, 14:1-3.

68. Irenaeus, *Haer.*, 5, 2, 2-3.

69. Cf. Cyprian, *Ep.*, 63:14.

70. *Library of Christian Classics*, vol. 9: *A Scholastic Miscellany: Anselm to Ockham*, trans. and ed. Eugene Fairweather, 26 vols. (Philadelphia: Westminster, 1956), p. 126.

71. N. Ridley, *The Works of Nicolas Ridley*, ed. Henry Christmas (Cambridge: U. Press, 1843), p. 196; cf. Cranmer, 1:11, 91, 395.

72. Cf. *Library of Christian Classics*, vol. 24: *Zwingli and Bullinger*, trans. and ed. G. W. Bromiley, 26 vols. (Philadelphia: Westminster, 1953), pp. 231 ff. C. Gore agrees that though Augustine is obscure, it is at any rate certain that he did not believe in transubstantiation (Bettenson, p. 147).

73. Cf. Cranmer, 1:90 ff.; 221 ff.

74. Bettenson, pp. 307 ff.

75. Cranmer, 2:227, 457.

76. Cf. John of Damascus, *De fide orthodoxa*, for the Eastern view.

77. Vincent of Lerins, *Commonitorium*, 2:3.

78. Origen, *Contra Cels.*, 1, 28, 32.

79. Ibid., 4, 2, 3.

80. Ibid., 2:55.

81. Origen, *Hom. in Gen.*, 2:2.

82. Justin, *Dial.*, passim.

83. Cf. Hippolytus, *Ref.*, 7, 23, 2.

84. Origen, *De Princ.*, 1, 6, 3; 8, 1; 2, 8, 3, etc.

85. Ibid., 1, 6, 3.

86. Tertullian, *De Praescr. Haer.*, 7.

87. Ibid., 37.

88. Cf. the astonishing book by Hans Küng, *Justification: The Doctrine of Karl Barth and a Catholic Reflection*, trans. Thomas Collins et al. (London: Burns & Oates, 1964).

89. Cf. the odd exegesis of Mt. 6:16; 6:5; 6:9-13 in *Didache*, 8:1.

90. Cf. Barnabas, passim. Even the staid Irenaeus has some

strange things to say about the reason for four gospels in *Haer.*, 3, 11, 11.

91. Cf. Origen, *De princ.*, 4, 2, 4 for the principle and built-in examples.

THE FUTURE OF THE CHURCH

by
David F. Wells

Sociologists often predict that organized religion in the future will remain visibly organized even if it becomes inwardly godless. Radical theologians, who do not think that religious ideals need a cultus for their expression, hope that the Christianity of the future will remain inwardly vital while enjoying institutional emancipation.[1] In the one projection, Christianity will have no soul; in the other, it will have no body. The first prediction looks for religion without God while the second looks for God without religion. The church, then, will either become a mask which hides an inner emptiness or else it will become an absurd relic, the flotsam and jetsam of a past age.

These projections of godless religion and of religionless belief seem to refute the idea that the church's external shape is conditioned by its internal dynamic. In the one case there is a visible façade that exists unsupported by an inner dynamic; in the other, the dynamic flourishes without the aid of an outward form. Yet it must be remembered that religion which is godless is by definition not religious, and belief that is decorporated is by Christian standards not Christian. When the scope of our consideration is thus limited by the acceptance of a few broad theological principles it will be found that where tradition is weak there is, in fact, an intrinsic relationship between the nature of religious commitment and that form of corporate life which necessarily evolves to express it.[2] Pascal was almost correct when he said that "the history of the Church ought to be called the history of truth."[3]

This essay, then, endeavors to analyze the nature of the church's interior life in this century in an attempt to understand the many revolutionary changes which are taking place in the church's exterior structure. What forces explain the drift toward godlessness, and do these forces lead inevitably to restructured belief? Does historic Christianity have any contribution to make in the present agonized situation?

TOWARD GODLESS RELIGION

As the new decade begins, the dominant issue in theology, according to Marty and Peerman, is that of the transcendence of God.[4] But since divine transcendence always has to be thought of in relation to divine immanence, the dominant problem is more completely diagnosed and conceded as being God Himself. It is divine *reality,* according to Ogden, which "seems to have become the central problem of Protestant theology, if not of Christian theology in general."[5] Statistical evidence from sociologists Stark and Glock has provided an important underpinning for this conclusion. Among what they term Protestant "liberal" churches, only 43 percent of those members questioned believed that their religious commitment provided a meaningful perspective for their lives, as opposed to 84 percent of those from what they term "conservative" churches.[6] Only 43 percent of liberal Christians believed that they had had an experience of the supernatural order, as opposed to 89 percent among conservative Christians. And only 37 percent of Protestants in general had any "sense of being saved in Christ." [7] These figures may not be entirely accurate, for religious experience is difficult to interpret. Nevertheless, the sober fact remains that the absence of God seems to be the dominant element in the liberal Christian consciousness. [8] Moreover, as the modern church waits for Godot, and as it looks out over the wasted landscape of contemporary life, it is feeling the emptiness of its own experience. There can be little doubt that it is suffering a loss of nerve as a consequence.

E. L. Mascall is partly correct in affixing blame for this divine evacuation on Barth, though there is some irony in his accusation. [9] When Barth wrested theology from its liberal interloper in 1918 with his *Römerbrief*, he did so with the specific intention of *recovering* the reality of God. This had been lost through the liberals' anthropocentric concerns. Barth cursed them for the blight they had brought and he returned theology to its primary and proper concern of God in Christ. Barth undermined liberal anthropocentrism by his insistence on divine transcendence. However, Barth's followers, as Gilkey and Van A. Harvey have pointed out, have misunderstood his intentions. His doctrine of the transcendent God is nothing more, they say, than an alibi for man's sense of cosmic loneliness. They have discovered, as Augustine did centuries ago, that the Gnostic god is a deity of few words. Consequently they have turned away from Barth's transcendental realities to begin a fresh search for God, not in the airy realms "above," but in the concrete realms "below." The man who protested against the destruction of divine reality in the liberals' hands found himself similarly accused by even his own progeny, let alone his critics.

As a matter of fact, Barth himself appeared to be moving toward a reconsideration of this element in his theology. In

1956 he affirmed his willingness to counterbalance the old idea of transcendence with the newer concern for divine immanence. The old assertion of a qualitative difference between God and man had been understood as meaning that there is a total absence of relationship between them. Unless this development was checked, the world could be viewed quite legitimately as being an almost wholly self-enclosed and self-interpreting reality. Consequently, Barth affirmed that:

> Jesus Christ is in His own Person, as true *God*, *man's* loyal partner, and as true man, God's. He is the Lord humbled for communion with man and likewise the servant exalted to communion with God. He is the Word spoken from the loftiest, most luminous transcendence and likewise the Word heard in the deepest, darkest immanence. He is both without their being confused but also without their being divided; He is wholly the one and wholly the other. [10]

"In Him," Barth concluded, "the fact is once for all established that God does not exist without man," and consequently, that in Christ "genuine deity includes in itself genuine humanity." [11] Barth's double stress on immanence and transcendence is admirable but the dialectical relationship established between them has proved to be problematic. Barth's conclusion is amenable to rephrasing. If "genuine deity includes in itself genuine humanity" might it not also be said that genuine humanity includes in itself genuine deity? The rephrasing of the question does of course shift the locus of theology away from Christ to man but this is not considered undesirable. Barth's Christomonism, it is felt, stands in need of some correction. [12]

In different ways the rephrasing of Barth's conclusion

provided the substance of the theology of the 1960s. It is not easy to depict the mood of these years without incurring the charge of oversimplification. In speaking of a tendency in any period, one is simply finding the lowest common denominator shared by thinkers who may, at other points, be very different from one another. This task, though, is sufficiently consequential and fruitful to warrant the risk of perpetrating some injustice to those whose thought is considered.

In broad terms, then, it may be said that post-Barthian theology, especially in the 1960s, was attempting to relocate the traditional frontier that has divided the natural from the supernatural in the hope of recovering the lost reality of God. Indeed, it is the relationship of these orders in classical metaphysical theory which was blamed for God's absence from the world. [13] Instead of maintaining their alleged polar relationship, modern theology has attempted to work out a dialectical synthesis between them. The supernatural, it was argued, is no longer "above" the natural but "in" it. The sacred, then, is found in the secular, grace in nature, the objective in the subjective, and God in man. Between these orders there is a *coincidentia oppositorum*. Certain notions, irreconcilable in the structure of classical logic, have become united: the Absolute and the relative, the necessary and the contingent, Being and becoming.

In view of this, theology was given a new enterprise. As the two orders of reality were seen, not as adjoining one another, but as overlapping one another in substance, then theocentrism and anthropocentrism were no longer mutually exclusive concerns. They became coincidental. A theological anthropology not only became viable but, indeed, it held out the only hope of finding the elusive reality of God. Since the two orders of reality were seen to intersect one another in man, the theology of the 1960s celebrated this discovery by chanting a requiem over the death of classical metaphysics. Jürgen Moltmann depicted the new ideas well when he said:

> In modern times transcendence is more and more experienced in the inner dimension of human existence, in man's transcendental subjectivity. . . . Because the "boundary" between immanence and transcendence runs through himself, man comes to know this boundary in his own existence. Existentially man experiences finitude and infinitude simultaneously. He understands himself as God present on earth. Hence in place of the old correlation of "physics and metaphysics" the modern correlation of "existence and transcendence" advances to the foreground. . . . As a result of this change in metaphysics the whole traditional conceptualization of God has collapsed. 14

As the new theology looked at itself, though, it claimed that it was not attempting to delete the idea of divine transcendence; it was simply trying to redefine it. And, of course, within Moltmann's "existence and transcendence" model many variations on the theme are possible.

This point was made with some drama during the 1960s by the "new Cambridge theology" in England and the "death of God" theology in America. At the heart of both theologies was a repudiation of the supernatural in traditional terms together with the attempt, at least among the more temperate exponents, to find the Transcendent *in* the ebb and flow of human life. [15] Harvey Cox, for one, stated that theology should abandon the world "beyond" and concentrate on "this world" and "this time." Within temporal reality, in urban life and the secular processes, man would find the transcendent God. [16] Altizer, too, rejected the transcendent "otherness" of God and in doing so, he argued, he was opening himself to the immanence of God. [17] Yet, he evidently believed that the Absolute is to be found in the relative for he spoke of the uniqueness of the Word and of the events of Jesus' life. Christ is to be found behind the mask of profanity:

> The Jesus who is present in the midst of life is the Word made flesh, the Word which has finally and totally descended from the transcendent realm of Spirit. Once this descent has taken place, the life and movement of the Word are no longer present in a transcendent beyond. . . . 18

The drama and irreverence of the "death of God" debate left the impression that it was only these shadowy undertakers who were concerned with the death or transformation of the traditional Absolute. This is not the case. During the 1960s there was a broad stream of thinking, by and large rather more substantial and rather less irreverent than those who fleetingly stole the limelight, who were also concerned with precisely the same issue.

In existential circles, for instance, God was seen as a component in an ontological structure of which man is a part. God was related to man as Being is to being. Thus the external relationship of God to the world in terms of "otherness" was denied favor of an internal relationship in terms of "relatedness." God is a Being enclosed by temporal reality, not isolated "above" it. Finitude is clothed in infinitude, eternality is mingled with temporality. [19] In Tillich's utilization of this type of thought, strong emphasis was laid on God as internal Being rather than as an external Being. [20] Indeed, God is *the* Being within which other beings are rooted. God is their ground, the base line of their existence. Consequently, as Ogden has observed, the *via negationis et eminentiae* of classical metaphysics, in which "there is a denial that God is in any literal sense temporal or really related to the world," [21] is in process of dissolution.

Moltmann introduced an element of excitement into the

debate, but his proposal does not differ substantially from many of those offered during the 1960s. [22] He agreed that the Transcendent is not isolated "above" the historical. He looked, instead, beyond the temporal in the present. He defined transcendence as a future which is qualitatively different from the present, and one which will be ushered in through the revolutionary spirit. Moltmann's proposal, as a matter of fact, is present in germinal form in *Das Kapital*, though Moltmann has a sense of mystery which Marx did not.

From these different conceptions which, nevertheless, have certain elements in common, a new view of man is evolving. Many contemporary theologians are coming to see him as *Homo religiosus,* the point of integration between the orders. Because the consciousness of man is at this juncture, an aura of ultimacy is said to pervade his knowledge. Signals of transcendence intrude upon his thoughts. [23] They are the validation of a structural juncture between man's being and Being, or between man's humanity and the New Humanity divinized through the incarnation. [24] Troeltsch's notion of the religious a priori and Schleiermacher's idea of man's innate *sensus* of and *appetitus* for the Infinite are beginning to look attractive again. Barth's repudiation of liberal Protestantism is under reconsideration.

It is not generally realized, though, that Catholic theology has reached more or less similar conclusions and has done so in a rather less erratic and a rather more sophisticated manner. Moreover, in both Protestantism and Catholicism, the new quest for a theological anthropology is the reflex action to an exaggerated emphasis on divine transcendence. In Protestantism this dates from the 1940s when Barth's dominance over theology was effectively challenged, whereas in Catholicism it dates from the end of the last century when there was a powerful resurgence of scholasticism.

This resurgence was the consequence of Leo XIII's *Aeterni Patris,* issued in 1879 partly as an attempt to check the growing impulse toward anthropocentrism. As the orthodox erected their defenses, though, signs of heterodox dissent began to appear, especially in France. [25] To the dissenters, scholastic philosophy appeared to be aggravating the religious problem rather than resolving it. In opposition to the orthodox, the dissenters began to feel that a recovery of religious life depended on the recovery of the idea that God is active *within* human life. He is not isolated above it or separated from it. Christianity cannot survive if it is built over a rupture between the natural and supernatural. The new theologians returned to Romanticism for their answers rather than to Thomas. They repudiated intellectualism and established the religious consciousness as the datum for theology. Truth, as a consequence, began to be deduced inductively and intuitively rather than deductively and logically.

The shock waves of this departure can be traced through three discernible stages. First, between 1890 and 1910 some of the essential insights of the French philosophers Blondel, Laberthonnière and Ollé-Laprune were taken up and developed into the radical movement known as Catholic Modernism. [26] In due course the leaders, Tyrrell and Loisy, were excommunicated. Their theology was roundly condemned and their organization was eliminated by the orthodox storm troopers who constituted the movement known as *l'Intégrisme.* [27] Following the orthodox counterattack a stillness descended upon the church and the insights of the French theologians were laid to rest. However, in the 1940s the "Nouvelle Théologie" resurrected these ideas for the second time. [28] The contributors to this theology, principally de Lubac, Bouillard and von Balthasar, were rather more temperate than the Modernists and certainly more careful to remain within the structures of the church. Though the movement had to be checked in 1950 by *Humani Generis,* this encyclical was a paragon of moderation in comparison to its savage forerunner of 1907, *Pascendi dominici gregis.* In the third stage, some of the insights of the "Nouvelle Théologie," which in turn reflected earlier French philosophy, penetrated the chambers of the Second Vatican Council borne by such respected theologians as Karl Rahner and Yves Congar. These ideas, filled out from other sources and modified in certain respects, nevertheless introduced an entirely new element into official Catholic theology. In the documents issued by the council, traditional ideas are mingled with and correspondingly modified by notions which, at the turn of the century, were declared to be the quintessence of all heresy.

Central to the new Catholic anthropology is a rejection of the idea that man in his "natural" state is enclosed in a world structure which is, at least, unaffected by, if not dislocated from, the superstructure of grace by which it is crowned. Rightly or wrongly, the scholasticism of the nineteenth century is reputed to have taught that man's inward self-experience is purely "natural" and quite unalloyed with the Divine prior to sacramental union with God. The supernatural was thought to be secluded in a domain beyond the reach of natural experience. God's call of grace came as an unsought disturbance from "above." It emanated from distant and unknown quarters. Its reality was wholly foreign to man's inner experience. It was not woven into the fabric of his being. Man had no natural orientation to the grace to which his life was now suddenly conjoined. In traditional Catholicism, it is argued, this type of thinking remained in force as long as it was believed that all that the natural and supernatural have in common is the boundary which divides them from each other. [29]

The new theologians have repudiated this solution, affirming that grace is found *in* nature not *on* nature. Nature,

then, is never "pure" in the sense that it is severed on-
tologically and epistemologically from the Divine. The roots
of man's being reach down into the wellsprings of divine life.
   At the turn of the century, George Tyrrell endorsed this
view, saying that divine life

> is buried at the lowest depths of our spiritual being—deep down
> where its roots and fibres are seen to spread out under the soil and
> make one continuous network with those of all finite spirits, the
> whole clinging to the breasts of that common mother-earth from
> whom, and in whom, they move and have their being. [30]

   In a letter to a friend, he confessed that his conception of
God was

> reduced to a dialogue with that so evident and personal power
> within me which claims every moment my absolute worship and
> obedience; which is as real and self evident to me as the most
> constant impulses of my "nature" with which it is in perpetual and
> sensible conflict. My imagination is quite cured of the outside God;
> for I feel that the inward spirit pervades and transcends the whole
> universe. [31]

   In Tyrrellian theology, the religious sense or consciousness
is not the possession of an elite distinguished from the
others by their capacity for esoteric experience. Rather, this
sensus and *appetitus* is an intrinsic part of human nature and
is thus the possession of all men. Were man to be
dispossessed of this inner dimension he would be robbed of
an essential part of his humanity.
   The most brilliant exposition of these ideas in the
nineteenth century, however, was undertaken by Maurice
Blondel. Blondel's work has provided an important foun-

dation for much of the thought in recent decades. His influence is very pervasive, as can be seen, for instance, in Gregory Baum's new work, *Man Becoming: God in Secular Experience,* and Schillebeeckx's *God, the Future of Man.*

Blondel's most formidable and substantial work was his psychological analysis of human volition entitled *L'Action,* but for the purposes of the theme under consideration his *Histoire et dogme* and *Lettre sur l'apologétique* are equally illuminating. In these works, Blondel developed the idea that the Transcendent is to be found, not "above" the historical, but "in" it and permeating it. In his view the chief deficiency of nineteenth-century scholasticism was its failure to establish significance for the supernatural in the believer's life. There was, he thought, an unfortunate separation between the natural and the supernatural in traditional theology. The ideological sutures proposed by orthodoxy did little more than rip the sides of the wound.

Blondel, in fact, went on to attack those who were foolish enough to think that the natural could ever be emancipated from the supernatural. The former is immersed in and surrounded by the latter in much the same way as a fish is, in and by the water in which it swims. Miracles or signs, then, could no longer be conceived of as a breach in the uniformity of natural cause and effect. In *L'Action* Blondel provided the following definition of the miraculous, which he then utilized for his apologetic work:

> The idea of fixed laws in nature is only an idol; each phenomenon is a singular case and a unique solution. To go to the bottom of the matter, without doubt there is nothing more in the miracle than in the slightest of ordinary facts; but also there is nothing less in the most ordinary of facts than in the miracle. [32]

To Blondel, then, miracles are really the manifestation of the Divine from *within* the natural; they are neither a suspension of the natural sequence of cause and effect nor are they the consequence of a collision or intersection of the two orders of reality. In the Blondellian *schema,* science and religion could never be at odds with each other. Scientific work is an empirical activity and can therefore neither affirm nor deny that a miracle has taken place in the midst of "natural" events. Religion is nonempirical in its activities, concerned only with the "miraculous" content of natural events. It can neither affirm nor deny that an interruption in the *causal nexus* has taken place. Science and religion steam past each other like the proverbial ships in the night. Blondel's solution represents a remarkable anticipation of that adopted later by Protestant neoorthodoxy, at least on its left wing and probably on its right.

More recently, these ideas have been given a new lease of life by Hans Urs von Balthasar, especially in his *Theologie der Geschichte.* [33] Eternity, he has argued, is enclosed within time because the life of Christ is encased within the historical order. It is within the temporal plane that man encounters Christ. History does not derive its meaning from "above" but finds it in terms of its own interior reality. [34] In relating this notion to his view of man, Balthasar is not adverse to using the Schleiermacherian notion of absolute dependence, provided that the initiative for giving significance from "within" always rests with God and never with man. The repudiation of the scholastic superstructure of grace in Tyrrell, Blondel and Balthasar is accompanied, as one would expect, by a stridently antirational element.

With Karl Rahner, the question of the relationship between the natural and supernatural has been largely developed around his much celebrated notion of the "supernatural existential." [35] According to Rahner there is a certain supernatural element which has lodged in man's being. The resultant congeniality for grace, which he calls the Spirit's life, is a central and abiding element of man's inner life. It is the existential backdrop against which a more explicit Christian consciousness is formed.

There is discernible, then, in both Catholicism and Protestantism, an attempt at reshaping the classical metaphysical structure upon which the institutional church is said to have predicated itself and within which it is thought it has always understood itself. It is true, of course, that there are differences in the ways in which the old ideas are being rearranged and related to one another. At the heart of the new enterprise, though, is the conviction that the old metaphysical theory has not yielded the divine reality for which man is searching. Instead, as Schillebeeckx has argued, [36] man must now turn to his new secular culture in the hope that it will provide the source material for a fresh conception of and encounter with divine reality. If this quest fails, as it seems it must, the sociologists' prediction of a future religion devoid of inner godliness will prove accurate.

TOWARD RELIGIONLESS BELIEF

This new theorizing has important consequences for the future existence and shape of the church, though as Stark and Glock note, theologians have been rather tardy in carrying out this work of translating theory into practice:

> So far the new theology has not basically altered the structure, form or functioning of the institutional church. The churches continue to predicate their structure and activities upon a conception of a judging, personal, active God, *whether or not* the theological views predominant among clergy and laity still conceive of God in these terms. [37]

Despite this reluctance to work out the consequences, it would appear that the dissolution of institutional religion could take place at some point in the future, not for psychological reasons as Freud predicted, or for socio-logical reasons as Durkheim predicted, but for theological reasons.

It is true, of course, that there are those who dispute this judgment. Martin Marty, for example, has asserted that the work of the iconoclasts is "cheap" because "they shatter the forms that centuries have developed and that the good sense of Christian people has brought to maturity." [38] Traditionally, though, the institutional church has been predicated on the basis of theology rather than taste, and it is doubtful, now that the theology has changed, that that which was built upon it will remain in its historic form. Indeed, the iconoclasts are quite correct in wanting to change the outward form of the church. In theology, pumpkins should never be allowed to become carriages.

The new theological thinking has drastically undercut the vitality of the institutional church, as Stark and Glock have discovered:

> A general corrosion of commitment presently accompanies the acceptance of a modernized, liberal theology . . . if the erosion of traditional beliefs continues, as presumably it will, so long as the Church remains locked in its present institutional forms it stands in ever-increasing danger of both moral and literal bankruptcy . . . the liberal denominations are particularly vulnerable because the demise of traditional theology and a concomitant drop in other aspects of commitment is already widespread in these bodies. [39]

The erosion of commitment stems, they believe, from an erosion in an experiential belief in the supernatural. The consequent breakdown in Christian commitment is seen, for example, in the statistics relating to church attendance. Of those with attachments to what Stark and Glock call liberal churches, only 15 percent attend weekly as opposed to 59 percent of those committed to conservative views. A similar reluctance to support institutional religion is evident in their analysis of church finances. Only 18 percent of Protestant "liberals" contribute $7.50 or more per week while the comparable figure on the "conservative" side is 50 percent. [40]

This breakdown in the commitment to institutional religion obviously reflects the incompatibility of a church outwardly modeled along traditional lines but having inwardly rejected the rationale for its institutional existence. Paul Van Buren has discussed this ambiguity with reference to prayer. [41] The church, he observes, has always been in the habit of praying. In the old days, the godly were so confident that God superintended all natural events, that they would unhesitatingly pray that He would send rain on a stricken neighbor's fields. With the dissipation of this type of metaphysical theory, however, the church can no longer emulate this activity. For the modern man the object of the prayerful address, God, has disappeared. To pray for rain would be futile since there is no possibility of the interaction between the two orders of reality resulting in a rainstorm. Instead of praying, the modern man would best emulate the ancient attitude by building an irrigation ditch for the stricken neighbor.

One can agree with Ogden that "all talk of a Christianity *post mortem dei* is, in the last analysis, neither hyperbole nor evidence of originality but merely nonsense." [42] Yet it is doubtful if even the temperate expositions of the new metaphysic are really any less radical in their consequences for the institutional church in its form or in relation to such activities as prayer, preaching and missions.

Such consequences are already beginning to appear in the reshaping of the institutional church in Catholicism. These consequences are likely to be far more damaging there than in Protestantism. Traditional ecclesiology is of such a nature that its demise would result in the loss of the supernatural to its members. Yet it is precisely this conception which was partly undermined at Vatican II as a consequence of the new theological anthropology, and which has subsequently been openly assailed. As the church structure disintegrates, we can expect to see many more emancipated nuns, rebellious priests, independent theologians, and autonomous communities. In her book, *Divine Disobedience: Profiles in Catholic Radicalism*, Francine du Plessix Gray has shown that the new liberty in relation to the traditional church and its authority is being built on the idea of a transcendent authority said to be immanent in the new radicals.[43] This type of approach is the cause and harbinger of the breakdown in institutional Catholicism.

GOD AND THE CHURCH: A REASSESSMENT

Even if religion today is still visibly structured, it is clear that it has lost its inner dynamic. If the theologians' rather desperate search for God fails, the sociologist's prediction about godless religion in the future may be realized, at least in its godlessness. Whether an institutional mask will remain depends, of course, on the extent to which organized religion can be self-sustaining and on this there are differences of opinion. It is at least clear that if the present pattern of theological life continues it will drastically reshape and perhaps even eliminate organized religion. In view of this prognosis, the present spate of self-analysis in which theologians are engulfed achieves a new interest. Has contemporary theology understood why it has run into a cul-de-sac? Do contemporary theologians have any workable suggestions for recovering the lost knowledge of God?

The answers which we receive to these questions are disquieting. Theologians like Pittenger, Ogden and Kaufman, all of whom are deeply concerned with the recovery of a viable theism, say that the reason God's reality has been lost in recent decades is not due to man's

173

disobedience; rather, the church has been imprisoned within the Aristotelian metaphysic. Christianity, it is claimed, has been utilizing a theistic model which, it is now plain, is quite inadequate in its conceptualization of divine reality. The problem we are told, is intellectual, not moral.

The substance of this classical theism, Ogden states, uniquely combines "elements of classical Greek philosophy with religious insights drawn from the Hebrew-Christian Scriptures."[44] This amalgam, the *philosophia perennis,* has constituted that "common intellectual tradition that has served throughout Western history for the conception of his [God's] reality." [45] Ogden finds this metaphysic riddled with internal self-contradictions and quite incompatible with his experience in the secular world. There is, he says, "an irreconcilable opposition between the premise of this supernaturalistic theism and the whole direction of our experience and reflection as secular men." [46] In the face of these difficulties Ogden has abandoned classical theism. In doing so, it should be noted, he has also abandoned what he calls the "religious insights drawn from the Hebrew-Christian Scriptures" and he has done so on the odd assumption that biblical teaching is an inextricable part of the Aristotelian conception. The baby, it seems, is indistinguishable from the bath water.

This same confusion between biblical teaching and Aristotelianism is even more pronounced in Kaufman's case. He earnestly berates the biblical writers for holding the type of dualism that only came into vogue with the scholastic theologians of the late Middle Ages. It is a conception well described by Pittenger when he complains that classical theism

> has consistently stressed God's independence, absoluteness, and aseity, to the neglect of his relatedness to the world; one might say that a good deal of theism, in this mode, has been closer to a metaphysic of divine indifference than to one of love. [47]

But, of course, the biblical metaphysic is one of love, not of indifference, and to think otherwise represents serious misunderstanding. Moreover, it is equally wrong to attribute to historic Christianity what in fact it has never endorsed and what it has itself consistently opposed.

There is nothing novel or original in this rejection of Aristotelian metaphysics as these theologians seem to think; what is novel in the current polemic is the rather strange belief that biblical theism nestles comfortably in a niche within the Aristotelian structure. It is this confusion between Paul and Aristotle which has led recent theology to counter a false transcendence by an exclusive and equally false immanence with little regard for biblical teaching on either point.

It needs to be remembered that the Reformers rejected classical theism as vigorously as the new theology does. Their theology, though, succeeded in sailing between the Scylla of Aristotelianism and the Charybdis of relativism in a way that contemporary theology has not. For this reason it deserves more attention than it has received recently for it may well provide us with some insights that will be useful in the work of reconstruction which lies ahead.

That Luther rejected the scholastic metaphysic is plain. Aristotle was rejected in favor of Augustine; [48] the *theologia gloriae* (the knowledge of God by speculative logic and abstract reasoning) was replaced, in Luther's thought, by the *theologia crucis* (the knowledge of God through the incarnate and crucified Christ). The main impulse for this shift came from Luther's dissatisfaction with the dualistic metaphysic which he as a monk had inherited. [49] Medieval piety had been constructed on the notion that the Divine is largely isolated "above" and beyond the natural, that God's calling could only be perceived and followed out of all relation to the natural world. This type of piety was deliberately unnatural and unearthly and Luther found this to be inconsistent with the form of

175

identification which the Logos effected with man in the incarnation and with man's sin in the atonement. Building on this notion of identification through Christ, Luther affirmed that the calling of God can be pursued *within* the ordinary world and through the means of natural relationships. [50] God's undergirding of human life, and His structuring of human society provide the setting within which the divine purposes and presence are known.

In this regard, an important distinction which Luther reaffirmed and which Calvin developed is that which exists between the *Deus absconditus* and the *Deus revelatus*. To both Luther and Calvin, God, in His essential being, has placed Himself beyond the reach of natural experience and speculative logic. His revelation through the Word, both living and written, is prevenient and indispensable to a substantial knowledge of God. In view of God's voluntary hiddenness, man, if he is to touch divine reality, *must* approach God through the revelatory means which He Himself has established for this purpose. [51]

The Reformers' unique combination of the equivocal in the *Deus absconditus* and the univocal in the *Deus revelatus* makes the most cogent reply to the present period of questioning. By insisting against a notion of *Deus absconditus* that there are elements of contingency, finitude, relativity and mutability in the being of God, process theologians have been forced to deny the identity and self-subsistence of God no less than His sovereignty, and by further denying the notion of revelation from God, they have surrendered any univocal concept of truth. They must make their predications on the basis of a Tillichian view of the correlation between the infinite and the finite. Even if it may be said that such a correlation is productive of symbols which "contain" divine reality, there is no way of knowing whether the symbols correspond at all to the reality which they purport to represent and communicate. If the reality of God is in movement, as process theologians like Ogden and

Pittenger claim, then there is every reason to think that at best a symbol only represents God as He was in the recent past but which, in subsequent movement of time, has become obsolete through the change which has been effected in the reality of God. Skepticism is the inevitable result of such a position. The Reformers at least realized that the only alternative to speculative Aristotelian methodology is the one which acknowledges the hiddenness of God and therefore seeks to honor the revelation which He has given of Himself in Christ and Scripture.

This thrust from within the theology of the Reformation is epitomized in the thought of John Calvin. In relation to his medieval heritage, the essential novelty of Calvin's approach to the problems of theism emerges in the fact that the final edition of his *Institutio* entirely omits any systematic discussion on the nature, existence and attributes of God. This omission can hardly be explained by thinking that Calvin was disinterested in the subject or that, granting some interest, he had nothing to say about God. Rather, this omission represents on the one hand a serious attempt to utilize those means given to fix the substance and limits of a functional theism and, on the other, a determined attempt to jettison Aristotelian speculation. Consequently, Calvin deals with the doctrine of God, not as an isolated and abstract subject, but in conjunction with the essential concerns of revealed faith.

It is to the Word, both living and written, that man must turn if he is to know God and construct theistic models. "All knowledge without Christ," Calvin warns in one place, "is a vast abyss which immediately swallows up all our thoughts." [52] Again, he cautioned,

If we turn aside from the Word, as I have just now said, though we may strive with strenuous haste, yet since we have got off the track, we shall never reach the goal. For we should so reason that the splendour of the divine countenance, which even the apostle calls "unapproachable", is for us like an inexplicable labyrinth unless we are conducted into it by the thread of the Word; so that it is better to limp along this path than to dash with all speed outside it. [53]

This important methodological limitation which Calvin imposed upon himself obviously rests upon an acceptance of the distinction between the *Deus absconditus* and the *Deus revelatus*. Man is clearly limited both in *what* he can know about God and in *how* he should know God; revelation provides both the substance of the knowledge of God as well as the means of attaining it. This point was brought out well when Calvin said,

> We ought to observe that we are called to a knowledge of God: not that knowledge which, content with empty speculation merely flits in the brain, but that which will be solid and faithful if we duly perceive it, and if it takes root in the heart . . . we know the most perfect way of seeking God, and the most suitable order is not for us to attempt with bold curiosity to penetrate to the investigation of his essence, which we ought more to adore than to methodically search out, but for us to contemplate him in his works where he renders himself near and familiar to us and in some manner communicates himself to us. [54]

"When the Lord closes his holy mouth," Calvin concluded, "let us also stop the way, that we may not go farther." [55]

Aristotelian speculation Calvin rejected as leading to nothing but "doubts, ambiguities, and perplexities." [56] If we are to know God, it will not be "as He is in Himself, but as He is toward us, so that this recognition of Him consists more in living experience than in vain high-flown speculation" [57] What were normally classified as divine attributes, therefore, constituted for Calvin the sum and substance of his knowledge of God. It was this knowledge, objective in form and subjective in realization, that informed the whole body of his thought. Because of its pervasive and integrative role, Calvin dealt with the issues of theism, not synthetically and abstractly, but where their presence was most sharply felt in Christian life.

Calvin's approach to the doctrine of God is highly instructive in today's context. It counsels us, first, not to assume that the being of God is immersed in secular life; God is to some extent hidden and withdrawn. The immediate corollary of this is that divine revelation, rather than secular experience, is the indispensable prerequisite for a knowledge of God. Second, Calvin's approach warns against knowing more about God than He has chosen to reveal about Himself in Christ and Scripture. Theistic models not based on revelation are, in some shape or form, speculative in essence. It is a strange irony, therefore, that theologians like Ogden who so deride the empty speculation of classical theism should, in the final analysis, be forced to build their own theistic conceptions on nothing more substantial than another set of speculative propositions. Not surprisingly, the outcome of the new quest for a viable theism seems to be issuing in the same barren harvest of "doubts, ambiguities and perplexities" which Calvin said was the fruit of the medieval quest. The contemporary theologian, Van A. Harvey observes, has become as much a doubter as anyone else. [58]

The way ahead, therefore, lies in a fresh return to the biblical sources for man's knowledge of God, rather than to a further immersion in secular life. It is in the "enfleshed" Christ, Jesus of Nazareth, that God has spoken His final word to man. And it is on this foundation that God has built His church. Without the former, the latter does become ridiculous. This age-old truth was well expressed by Samuel Wesley when he wrote:

The Church's one Foundation is Jesus Christ her Lord;
She is His new creation, By water and the Word:
From heaven He came and sought her to be His holy bride;
With His own blood He bought her, And for her life He died.

Yet she on earth hath union With God the three in One,
And mystic sweet communion With those whose rest is won,
O happy ones and holy! Lord, give us grace that we,
Like them, the meek and lowly, On high may dwell with Thee.

FOOTNOTES

1. Public opinion seems to favor the view that institutional religion is declining. A Gallup poll taken in 1957 indicated that only 14 percent of those questioned believed that institutional religion was losing its effectiveness and influence. In 1967 the figure had risen to 57 percent and in 1970 it arrived at 70 percent. See Rodney Stark and Charles Y. Glock, *American Piety: The Nature of Religious Commitment* (Berkeley: U. California, 1968), p. 222. Cf. Paul M. Van Buren, *Theological Explorations* (New York: Macmillan, 1968), pp. 30-31; Richard L. Rubinstein, *After Auschwitz: Radical Theology and Contemporary Judaism* (Indianapolis: Bobbs-Merrill, 1966), pp. 191-208.

2. This conclusion does not concur with the opinions of many sociologists. In their view, religious form and substance tend to reflect the tension and difficulties of society. When society is in turmoil, religion will be automatically thrown into turmoil too. Its form derives more from its external relationships than its interior commitments. See J. Milton Yinger, *Religion, Society and the Individual: An Introduction to the Sociology of Religion* (New York: Macmillan, 1967), pp. 265-312; Peter L. Berger, *The Noise of Solemn Assemblies: Christian Commitment and the Religious Establishment in America* (New York: Doubleday, 1961), pp. 17-104. Cf. Helmut Richard Niebuhr, *The Social Sources of Denominationalism* (New York: H. Holt, 1927).

3. Blaise Pascal, *Pensées, the Provincial Letters*, trans. W. F. Trotter and Thomas M'Crie (New York: Random House, 1941), p. 304.

4. Martin E. Marty and Dean G. Peerman, eds., *New Theology No. 7: The Recovery of Transcendence* (New York: Macmillan, 1970), p. 9.

5. Schubert M. Ogden, *The Reality of God and Other Essays* (New York: Harper & Row, 1966), p. ix.

6. Stark and Glock, p. 222.

7. Ibid., p. 133.

8. Cf. Samuel Terrien, "Towards a New Theology of Presence?"

181

in *New Theology No. 7*, pp. 137-52.

9. E. L. Mascall, *The Secularization of Christianity: An Analysis and a Critique* (London: Darton, Longman & Todd, 1965), pp. 4-6, 25-26.

10. Karl Barth, *The Humanity of God*, trans. John M. Thomas and Thomas Wieser (Richmond: John Knox, 1960), pp. 46-47.

11. Ibid. Cf. Barth, *Church Dogmatics*, ed. G. W. Bromiley and T. F. Torrance; trans. J. W. Edwards, O. Bussey, and Harold Knight; 5 vols. (Edinburgh: T. & T. Clark, 1958—), 3:2; 55-324.

12. Roger L. Shinn, *Man: The New Humanism* (Philadelphia: Westminster, 1963), pp. 33-58.

13. Kaufman, for example, has blamed the eclipse or death of God on "the fundamental metaphysical-cosmological dualism found in the Bible" which he regards as "crude" and "unbelievable" (Gordon Kaufman, "On the Meaning of God: Transcendence Without Mythology," *Harvard Theological Review* 59, no. 2 (Apr., 1966): 106.

14. Jürgen Moltmann, *Religion, Revolution and the Future*, trans. M. Douglas Meeks (New York: Scribner, 1969), p. 182.

15. Cf. Gabriel Fackre, "The Issue of Transcendence in the New Theology, the New Morality and the New Forms" in *New Theology No. 4*, ed. Marty and Peerman (New York: Macmillan, 1967), pp. 178-94; Peter L. Berger, "A Sociological View of the Secularization of Theology," *Journal for the Scientific Study of Religion* 6 (Spring, 1967): 3-16.

16. Harvey Cox, *The Secular City: Secularization and Urbanization in Theological Perspective* (New York: Macmillan, 1965), pp. 2, 261. Cf. John Macquarrie, *God and Secularity* (Philadelphia: Westminster, 1966), pp. 62, 132-57.

17. Thomas J. Altizer, *The Gospel of Christian Atheism* (Philadelphia: Westminster, 1966), pp. 62, 132-57.

18. Ibid., p. 98.

19. Ogden, pp. 144-63.

20. Paul Tillich, *Systematic Theology*, 3 vols. (Chicago: U. Chicago, 1951-63), 1:163-284.

21. Ogden, p. 158. In this regard, note should also be made of the "process" theology stemming from the work of Whitehead and Hartshorne. See W. L. Reese and E. Freeman, eds., *Process and Divinity* (LaSalle, Ill.: Open Court, 1964); Norman Pittenger, *God in Process* (London: SCM, 1967).

22. Moltmann, *Theology of Hope*, trans. James W. Leitch (New York: Harper & Row, 1967).

23. This phenomena Berdyaev describes as "the disclosure of the divine element in man." Consequently, anthropology is for him the "Christology of man." Nicolas Berdyaev, *Truth and Revelation*, trans. R. M. French (New York: Harper, 1962), p. 122.

24. The idea that Christ, through the incarnation, has begun to divinize humanity was first effectively exploited by Irenaeus and then became the common currency of Eastern Orthodox theology. This notion, however, has begun to reappear in Western theology as can be seen in the following passages from Bonhoeffer and from the Second Vatican Council: "As they contemplated the miracle of the Incarnation, the early Fathers passionately contended that while it was true to say that God took human nature upon him, it was wrong to say that he chose a perfect individual man and united himself to him. God was made man, and while that means that he took upon him our entire human nature with all its infirmity, sinfulness and corruption, the whole of apostate humanity, it does not mean that he took upon him the man Jesus. Unless we draw this distinction we shall misunderstand the whole message of the gospel. The Body of Jesus Christ, in which we are taken up with the whole human race, has now become the ground of our salvation" (Dietrich Bonhoeffer, *The Cost of Discipleship*, trans. R. H. Fuller [New York: Macmillan, 1966] pp. 204-65). In the council's *Gaudium et Spes*, art. 22 says that "to the sons of Adam he restores the Divine likeness which had been disfigured from the first sin onward. Since human nature as he assumed it was not annulled by that very fact it has been raised up to a divine dignity in our respect too. For *by His incarnation* the Son of God has united Himself in some fashion with every man" (Walter Abbot, ed., *The Documents of Vatican II*, trans. Joseph Gallagher et al. [London: Geoffrey Chapman, 1967],

pp. 220-21). Cf. Philip Hefner, "The Churches and Evolution" in *Changing Man: The Threat and Promise*, ed. Kyle Haseldon and Philip Hefner (New York: Doubleday, 1968), pp. 117-23.

25. Edgar Hocedez, *Histoire de la Théologie au XIX siècle*, 3 vols. (Paris: Desclee de Brouwer, 1947), 3:13-319.

26. Blondel, it is true, dissociated himself from the Modernists and openly attacked Loisy's position. For his personal correspondence relating to this, see René Marlé, *Au Coeur de la crise moderniste: Le dossier d'une controverse inédite* (Paris: Montaigne, 1960), pp. 51, 62-64. Nevertheless, Tyrrell could still affirm himself to be a Blondellian in philosophy and he and von Hügel became avid disseminators of Blondel's works in England.

27. Jean Madiran, *L'Intégrisme: Histoire d'une histoire* (Paris: Nouvelles Édition Latines, 1964).

28. The resurrection was accompanied by murmurs against the new Modernism in some quarters. See R. Garrigou-Lagrange, "La Nouvelle Theologie ou va-t-elle?" *Angelicum* 23 (1946): 126-45; cf. Léonce de Grandmaison, "Une Nouvelle Crise Moderniste est-elle Possible?" *Etudes* 176 (1923): 641-43: B. M. G. Reardon, "The Prelude to the Contemporary Crisis in Roman Catholicism," *The Expository Times* 79, no. 7 (Apr., 1968): 202.

29. This is Rahner's analysis and it is based on the type of dogmatics manual used at the turn of the century. See, for example, A. Tanquerey, *Manual of Dogmatic Theology*, trans. John J. Byrnes (New York: Desclee, 1959), pp. 11-48, 394-430. The Latin edition, *Brevior Synopsis Theologiae Dogmaticae*, was in wide usage at the beginning of this century. See also J. M. Bellamy, *La Théologie Catholique au XIXe Siècle* (Paris: Gabriel Beauchesne, 1904), pp. 243-66.

30. George Tyrrell, "Vita Nuova," *Month* 102 (Oct., 1903): 30.

31. M. D. Petre, *Autobiography and Life of George Tyrrell*, 2 vols. (London: Edward Arnold, 1912), 2: 414.

32. Maurice Blondel, *L'Action: Essai d'une critique de la vie et d'une science de la pratique* (Paris: Ancienne Libraire Gemer Baillière, 1893), p. 398.

184

33. See also Hans Urs von Balthasar's *Verbum Caro* (Einsiedeln: Johannes, 1960), pp. 28-99, 245-75; *A Theological Anthropology* (New York: Sheed & Ward, 1967); *The God Question and Modern Man*, trans. Hilda Graef (New York: Seabury, 1959).

34. Cf. Leslie Dewart, *The Future of Belief* (New York: Herder & Herder, 1966), pp. 171-216. Dewart has attempted, like the other thinkers under consideration, to reinterpret transcendence in terms of temporal experience.

35. See Karl Rahner, *Theological Investigations*, trans. Cornelius Ernst; 5 vols. (London: Darton, Longmann & Todd, 1961—), 1:297-347; Rahner, *Nature and Grace*, trans. Dinah Wharton (London: Sheed & Ward, 1963). Cf. Paul Claudel, *Présence et Prophétie* (Fribourg: Libraire do l'Université, 1942), pp. 4-130; and Henri de Lubac, *Le Mystère du Supernatural* (Paris: Aubier, 1965).

36. E. Schillebeeckx, *God the Future of Man*, trans. N. D. Smith (New York: Sheed & Ward, 1968). It is this tendency in modern theology which probably explains the cultic enthusiasm which has developed for the work of Teilhard de Chardin.

37. Stark and Glock, pp. 210-11.

38. Marty, *The New Shape of American Religion* (New York: Harper, 1958), p. 122.

39. Stark and Glock, pp. 215-16.

40. Ibid., p. 222.

41. Paul M. Van Buren, *The Secular Meaning of the Gospel* (New York: Macmillan, 1963), p. 191.

42. Ogden, p. 15.

43. Cf. Schillebeeckx, "Un Nouveau Type de Laïc" in *La Nouvelle Image de l'Eglise*, ed. Bernard Lambert (Paris: Maine, 1967), pp. 177 ff.

44. Ogden, p. 17.

45. Ibid., p. 16.

46. Ibid., p. 17.

47. Norman Pittenger, "Process Theology Revisited," *Theology Today* 27, no. 2 (July, 1970): 212.

48. Cf. Henri de Lubac, *Augustinianism and Modern Theology,* trans. Lancelot Sheppard (New York: Herder & Herder, 1969), pp. 118-63.

49. The type of medieval piety that grew out of this metaphysical understanding is well described by J. A. Symonds in his account of Bernard of Clairvaux. During one of his many travels, Bernard found himself riding along the shores of a particularly beautiful lake. He rode, we are told, without noticing "the azure of the waters, the radiance of the mountains with their robe of sun and snow, but instead bent his thought-burdened forehead over the neck of his mule, and at the end of the journey, when his companions referred to the lake, inquired, 'What lake?' Even so were men of that day pilgrims intent on sin, death, and judgment" (Symonds as quoted by Roland Bainton, "Man, God, and the Church in the Age of the Renaissance" in *The Renaissance* [New York: Harper & Row, 1962], p. 77). This concern with sin, death and judgment was, however, an unusual one. Sin and death were thought to be wholly localized and contained within the natural and material order; salvation was conceived of as liberation from this. Thus we note an overwhelming concern with the soul and the spiritual and a matching disregard for the body and the material. It is this fact which explains the church's total indifference to the stench of rotting humanity that clung to the structures of every large medieval city. In the few instances where social concern was manifest, as in the case of the Franciscans, the church felt threatened by some strange new heresy.

50. See John Oliver Nelson, ed., *Work and Vocation: A Christian Discussion* (New York: Harper, 1954).

51. See T. H. L. Parker, "Calvin's Concept of Revelation," *Scottish Journal of Theology* 2 (Mar., 1949): 29-47; B. B. Warfield, "Calvin's Doctrine of the Knowledge of God," *Calvin and Calvinism* (New York: Oxford U., 1931), pp. 29-132; Kenneth Kantzer, "Calvin and the Holy Scriptures" in *Inspiration and Interpretation,* ed. John Walvoord (Grand Rapids: Eerdmans, 1957), pp. 115-55.

52. John Calvin, *Commentary on the Epistle of Paul the Apostle to the Romans,* trans. John Owen (Grand Rapids: Eerdmans,

1948), pp. 353-54.

53. Calvin, *Institutes of the Christian Religion*, trans. Ford Battles, vols. 20, 21. *The Library of Christian Classics*, ed. John Baillie, John McNeil, and Henry van Dusen (Philadelphia: Westminster, 1960),1 , 6, 3.

54. Ibid., 1, 9, 2.

55. Calvin, *Commentary* . . . p. 354.

56. Henry Cole, ed., *Calvin's Calvinism* (Grand Rapids: Eerdmans, 1956), pp. 111-12. On the matter of speculation, see Calvin's interesting letter to Lelio Socinus in Jules Bonnet, ed., *Letters of John Calvin*, trans. Marcus Gilchrist, 4 vols. (Philadelphia: Presbyterian Board of Pubn., 1858), 2:230-31.

57. Calvin, *Institutes*, 1, 10, 2.

58. "One of the most striking characteristics of Protestant theology in the last two centuries," Van A. Harvey says, "has been the emergence of what I shall call the alienated theologian, the professional who is concerned with the articulation of the faith of the Christian community but who is himself as much a doubter as a believer. This is a new phenomenon in the history of Christendom, because it has always been assumed that the Christian theologian is a believer who differs from other believers only by virtue of his office, to clarify and defend the Christian faith. But beginning with the Christian Deists in the eighteenth century and culminating in the radical theologians of the last decade, we see the Christian theologian gradually accepting the premises of the unbelief it has always been his office to overcome" (Van A. Harvey, "The Alienated Theologian," *McCormick Quarterly* 23, no. 4 [May, 1970]: 234).

ETHICS IN THE THEOLOGIES OF HOPE

by

Bernard Ramm

HISTORICAL INTRODUCTION

When the great leaders in theology from 1920 to 1960 retired or died, the theological world wondered what would come next.[1] The answer soon came in the publication of Jürgen Moltmann's *The Theology of Hope*.[2] Not that it was the only answer, for a revival of process theology was also in the making.[3] However, the interesting subtitle to Moltmann's book was: *On the Ground and Implications of a Christian Eschatology*. It stirred up such a controversy that another "debate book" was published (in Germany).[4]

When the reader gets past Moltmann's criticisms of Barth and Brunner he discovers that the main inspiration for Moltmann was Ernst Bloch. In order to understand the theology of hope in some depth and with this its ethics, some attention must be given to understanding Bloch.[5]

Bloch is a Marxist revisionist.[6] Although he taught in the University of Leipzig in Eastern Germany, his relationship with the government was always uneasy. A definitive set of his works is in the process of being printed, the greatest part of which is the three volumes entitled *Das Prinzip Hoff-*

nung. They are not typical books written in academic fashion. Instead there is a mixture of learning, insights, and unusual interpretations, written more in a poetic or lyrical style than that of prose. Many of his interpreters think that his main source of inspiration was not really Marx but Hegel.

Although Bloch's influence upon American thought has come very late and with not too much of his work translated, he has already had a great impact upon Continental scholars. This is apparent in the number of German scholars participating in the volume edited by Wolf-Dieter Marsch, *Diskussion uber die 'Theologie der hoffnung' von Jürgen Moltmann,* and Siegfrieg Unseld's *Ernst Bloch zu ehren,* which included not only philosophers but also a number of theologians. The best source book for English-speaking students to study both Bloch, Moltmann, and the theology of hope is *The Future of Hope,* edited by Walter Capps.

In differing degrees Bloch has influenced such theologians as Moltmann, Betz, Braaten, Cox, Cauthen,[7] Pannenberg, Alves, Tillich and Rahner. Bloch's ideas of hope received their first major theological treatment in Moltmann's *Theology of Hope.* In it are the beginnings of a Christian ethic based on a theology of hope.[8]

THE FUNDAMENTAL ASSUMPTIONS BEHIND THE ETHICS OF THE THEOLOGIES OF HOPE

Although there are other sources pouring into the theologies of hope, the main core of ideas comes from Bloch. Some of the leading ideas derived from him in support of the new ethics are:

1. The universe is not fixed or settled or determined. In Bloch's words, "The world is not yet determined completely; it is still open to a degree, similar to tomorrow's weather conditions."[9] The world is not determined by strict

physical or scientific law. The story is told that Bloch was once asked to summarize his philosophy in one sentence. After much apology he said his philosophy could be summarized by the sentence, "S is not yet P." [10] If one says, "S is S," then he falsifies the universe, as the universe is always on the move.

Schilling discusses Bloch's concepts of the "front" and of "matter." [11] By the category of the "front," Bloch means that the cosmos is a reality that is continuously moving forward. The parallel here with process theology is very close. The edge of the "front" is the "not" and the anticipation is the "not-yet." Man lives in this world of becoming from the *not* to the *not-yet* to the *novum*.

"Matter" is another category of Bloch's but it is not the hard stuff of traditional materialism. It is the dynamic stuff of dialectical materialism. Hence, matter, too, has its openness; and if matter has this, the universe can be further characterized as dynamic, rich in qualities, endless in possibilities, and continuously in process.

2. History is an open-ended as the universe. Bloch's notion of history has greatly impressed Rühle, for he comments on it as follows:

> This concept of the openness and undecidedness of history is possibly the most exciting feature of Bloch's thought: it throws the rattling machinery of dialectical materialism entirely overboard and gives new scope to the freedom of the will and the power of decision. [12]

Or as Bloch puts it, "The world [has an] unfinished character." [13]

3. If the cosmos is in process and if history is pliable, then it follows that man has no fixed nature. Human nature, like the world and history, has an open-ended character. The openness of history is the presupposition for possibilities, and man is open to history and its possibilities, which in-

clude the *novum*. Or to put it another way, according to Bloch, man exists in freedom which is "the unconditional indeterminate." [14]

4. If the world, history and man are open-ended, then the true *novum* can appear. The category of the *novum* is fundamental to Bloch and many theologians of the theology of hope.

The real *novum* cannot be anticipated in any manner. Commenting on the *novum,* Bloch says that "in [dialectical reality] new things truly happen. Things happen which have never occurred to any man. Things happen which likewise have never happened before." [15]

In the same essay he gives another definition of the *novum:*

> Openness toward the future is a large category with a sort of step-mother character. One must plunge beyond the horizon into that very difficult sphere of reality, the sphere of the *novum.* And this is not the reality which is being present . . . nor the reality of the not yet. . . . This is the sphere of the *novum,* the place where deeds are measured, the realm of fear as well as hope. [16]

5. Because there is the possibility of the *novum,* there is also the possibility of utopia. Bloch does not picture utopia, for we do not know its contours until it arrives, but we can characterize it. In fact, the impression is given that there is a series of utopias spiraling up in a way that almost duplicates the Hegelian movement of history. Homeland *(Heimat)* is used as a synonym for utopia; it means the end of all alienations. Man is then "at home" with his neighbor and his world. Yet another word associated with utopia is *mediation.* The opposite of alienation is division or splitting. The overcoming of these splits is the process of *mediation.* Utopia arrives when all alienations have been healed through mediation. Another facet of this idea is the *humanization* of man which will be realized in the future.

This is one of the points where Bloch rubbed traditional Marxism the wrong way. Bloch felt that present-day Marxism was inhuman in the way it treated man, but that true Marxism means the humanization of man—that is, he is to be free from all pressures, forces, dictates, enforced systems, etc., so that he can truly be himself. [17]

6. All of these add up to a philosophy of hope (the real counterpart in Christian theology being the theology of promise, for biblical hope rests on the prior promise of God, and therefore the promise is more fundamental than the hope). *Man can hope for the novum.* In a world that is open-ended, in a history that is not determined, and with man as a bundle of possibilities and potentials, the *novum* can appear; and if the *novum* can appear, man can hope for it.

Lombardi approaches the idea of hope from a different angle. [18] In that man's basic drive is mediation (a Hegelian concept), it appears in man as a hunger. If a man hungers, he also *hopes* for that which will satisfy his hunger. Because of the openness of the cosmos, history and man there are endless possibilities, and man may hope for a better world by the emergence of the best of the potential possibilities. The main drive-spring in man, therefore, is hope.

Our concern is with the ethics of the theologies of hope; in particular we wish to show that Bloch's ideas provide the foundation for this new ethical system. Theologians have not absorbed Bloch *in toto,* but some important insights have been assimilated from him. Chief among these are:

1. Moltmann sees in Bloch's philosophy of hope a new possibility of eschatology becoming the motif which harmonizes the Scriptures. God tells man what He will do in the future; man hopes in God's promise that the new situation will arise. Hence, eschatology, built on the promise-hope schema, can harmonize the entire scope of biblical history.

2. The great events of history in Scripture are "promise-events." The exodus is a promise for a new freedom for the Israelites. The coming of the kingdom in Christ is the

promise of the future coming of the kingdom. [19] The resurrection of Christ is the supreme event of promise for it is not only a promise of future liberation but it also yields the final meaning of history in an anticipatory (proleptic) way.

3. The philosophy of hope lays the foundations for a new version of Christian ethics which makes Christian ethics relevant for our times. The member of this school who makes the most of this notion, and with great force at that, is Ruben Alves. [20]

4. Bloch's philosophy of hope is of hope *for all men*. This is part of the notion of *humanizing* Marxism. The Christians respond to this affirmatively: *Christian promises are for all men. The Christian hope is a hope for the world.* This leads them to be very critical of and even vindictive toward those who advocate "personal ethics" or "personal religion."

5. Harvey Cox thinks that the only philosopher of any stature to arise in our times and offer to the theologians a philosophy as great and viable as that of Heidegger is Ernst Bloch. [21]

6. Bloch helps us get eschatology in perspective. Just as some have said that C. H. Dodd's eschatology was "self-realizing" eschatology, one may say the theology of hope is "self-realizing" hope.

7. Justification by faith is not an event in a preaching situation, for faith forces us not only to love but also to hope. The old adage that "faith leads the intellect" may be replaced by "hope leads the intellect." Hope is a power directed toward the future. But it is a special kind of power. It is the kind of power that wishes to produce good works and to correct the political, social and economic evils of our entire globe.

8. In view of Bloch's writings, Christians have taken a new look at revolution. [22] The liberals' (political and religious) belief in gradual progress and the belief of those who see in pacifism a kind of transforming force are judged

inadequate. Present evils are too great to be handled in any other way than by that of revolution.

ETHICS OF THE THEOLOGIES OF HOPE

When Moltmann's *Theology of Hope* was first published it was received with enthusiasm by many on both sides of the Atlantic. The reasons were: (1) it seemed to give biblical eschatology a new, creative interpretation; (2) it sternly attacked Bultmann for reducing hope to faith when he described hope as only an attitude about the future; (3) he seemed to defend the historicity of the bodily resurrection of Christ; and (4) he attempted to interact with secular history more positively than had Barth or Bultmann.

When Moltmann later published *Religion, Revolution and the Future*, he made us catch our breath. There seemed to be a new Moltmann. Had we read *Theology of Hope* too optimistically? Or had Moltmann made a radical shift in his stance? Upon rereading the first book in the light of the second we could see the revolutionary elements carefully hidden in the first. For example, the notion that ethics is only and inevitably social ethics is already in *Theology of Hope*. [23] However, in that his ethical theory comes out most clearly in *Religion, Revolution and the Future*, our concern will be much more with the latter work than with the former.

What are the shifts from *Theology of Hope* to *Religion, Revolution and the Future*? We can spot at least four:

1. The amount of biblical material in the first work is considerably reduced in the second. Although there are some references to Scripture and to theological topics in the second book, the names of Bloch, Marx, Hegel and Marcuse occur frequently.

2. Whereas in *Theology of Hope* Moltmann seems to maintain the bodily resurrection of Christ, it is much more difficult to determine what he means by the resurrection in

the second book. In the latter work he seems to move toward a Bultmannian view of the resurrection as suggested in the following texts: "We are therefore able to say that Jesus' resurrection is only *indirectly,* but the meaning of his cross is *directly* the foundation of the Christian hope for justice and life. . . . Here [in the interpretation of the resurrection] we find the justification for existential interpretation and its necessity."[24] In *Theology of Hope* at least two passages seem to question the *bodily* resurrection of Christ. [25]

The problem is complicated by his distinction of a society of *being* and a society of *having,* upon which our version of the resurrection depends. Perhaps it is in *this* context that the bodily resurrection is to be understood, but at any rate his opinions on the resurrection as an event are somewhat ambiguous. What is equally as serious is that the resurrection is transferred away from its usual location in the doctrines of justification and salvation. Instead, it is relocated and made to serve as the major fulcrum in the social ethics of the theology of hope.

3. With a qualifying phrase here and there, Moltmann retains the place of personal ethics in Christian theology, but the preponderance of his thought in *Religion, Revolution and the Future* is with social ethics (later dubbed "Political Theology") [26] Actually, the whole literature of the ethics of the theology of hope has left untouched the concepts of sainthood, profound personal piety, or Christian character. In fact, both Betz and Moltmann, the two leading theoreticians of the ethics of a theology of hope, made a number of caustic remarks about personal religion and personal ethics. [27]

It is true that Moltmann recognizes with Sartre that the Marxist man may be an empty man. But he leaves the implications of this untouched. A really vital, personal spirituality and devotion to the person of Christ and personal leadership of the Holy Spirit go uncultivated. [28]

4. He advocates a Christian theology of revolution. The concept of revolution differs among the theologians of hope, so we return to an exposition of it later.

Macquarrie is right in saying that there are now a number of theologies of hope rather than one single theology of hope. [29] They include men like Moltmann, Alves and Betz and others who have been mentioned previously. These men all agree that the real sins of men are not so much the personal ones of man against man but of one part of society oppressing another part. The victims of the oppressors are the poor, the sick, the hungry, and the defranchized (i.e., those systematically excluded from various privileges or rights). Moltmann names what he considers the three great alienations of modern man: (1) economic alienation; (2) political alienation; and (3) racial alienation. [30] When listing typical modern ills, he mentions poverty, hunger, illness and suffering. [31]

Unexpectedly, one of the strongest advocates of the theology of hope is a Roman Catholic theologian, Johannes Betz. He speaks of political theology, and Moltmann accepts the validity of this expression. By this, Betz and Moltmann mean that social ethics is not a secondary study in theology or a paragraph in the doctrine of sanctification. Social ethics is to be considered a major discipline in theology. To emphasize this conviction instead of speaking of social ethics, Betz speaks of political theology. [32]

In agreement with Betz, Moltmann writes:

> Together with Joh. B. Betz, I call it *political theology* in order to make it clear that ethics is not an appendix to dogmatics and also not only a consequence of faith, but that faith itself has a messianic context in which it becomes meaningful and that theology itself stands in a political dimension in which it becomes relevant. [33]

He goes on to say that ethics is concerned with bringing the power of the future world into the trouble spots of the present world, personally, socially and politically. [34]

Betz believes that the first step in creating a political theology is "the deprivatizing of theology." [35] What is meant by this odd expression is that faith or Christian experience can never be confined to one's inner being or one's own personal concerns. Political theology demands that Christian ethics—for both the individual and the church—be unashamedly and wholly social rather than personal in its concerns.

As we noticed, one of Bloch's main ideas was that of the humanization of Marxism. This concept of humanization is picked up by the ethics of the theology of hope. It presupposes that all forms of social evil depersonalize man. To be oppressed, deprived and discriminated against is to be depersonalized. Political theology seeks the alleviation of all such evils and, in doing so, humanizes society and its structures.

Robert Jenson develops his ethics of the theology of hope in a different direction. [36] He thinks that a theology of the future is the only workable theology for our decade. To be viable, future ethics must be programmatic, inspired by love; and in the nature of the case, programmatic love is eschatological and futuristic. It is a kind of action that is oriented to the future and anticipates benevolent deeds. So love provides the dynamic of the new ethic; the theology of hope of which it is a part offers the only meaningful option for our time.

Carl Braaten has an entire book on the theology of hope, or "Futurology" as he calls it, though we can only mention a suggestion or two of his. [37] Essentially, he treats the righteousness of God in the same manner in which Jenson treats love. God's righteousness is the sum of God's actions. It is the way God has, does, and will act. There is, therefore, a futuristic or eschatological dimension to the righteousness of God. Righteousness as so programmatically understood is, then, part of the ethics of hope.

The basic concept with which Ruben Alves works is "messianic humanism." [38] We have already discussed what is meant by the humanization of society. The addition of "messianic" gives it its futuristic or "hope" dimension. Although Alves tries to make his "messianic humanism" a biblical and Christian humanism, the amount of genuinely biblical and theological material is slim.

In his essay, "Some Thoughts on a Program for Ethics," [39] Alves gives us his definition of ethics:

> Ethical thought is a critique of the present from the perspective of the future. The urgent task which Christian ethics has to fulfill today is the liberation of the imagination. The world will be liberated only if man liberates it. The task of Christian ethics, thus, is to take the often hidden and unconscious groaning of the oppressed, their aspirations and values, to transform them in conscious language and to give them back to those to whom they belong—but now no longer as simple groanings but as a tool for the understanding of the world. Ethics has to do with the creation of a new world. [40]

Perhaps the boldest concept of all is the incorporation of revolutionary elements into the ethics of the theology of hope, though the concept of revolution is not entirely new to the theology of hope nor to Christian theology, historically speaking. It is, however, becoming increasingly fashionable in our general culture. [41]

Moltmann gives us the most cautious definition of revolution: "I understand revolution to mean a transformation in the foundations of a system—whether of economics, or politics, or morality, or religion." [42]

He advocates revolution on the basis that the people who have the customary forces of policemen and armies are the oppressors. Ordinary means of seeking justice are of no avail in such a context. Only by revolution can society be broken up and reformed so that justice and equity may prevail. For the same reason Alves advocates violence which is similar to revolution. [43]

Of all the writers on revolution, the one who has most painfully struggled with it is Braaten. [44] In the presence of massive social evil, what is a Christian to do? Part of his answer is that "the Christian is free to be a hippie, a fool for Christ's sake. Or he may be a revolutionary, who seeks to replace the present social, political, and economic order with one more humanizing." [45]

It is the more militant response which is favored in some of the articles in *New Theology No. 6,* where it is claimed that the Christian must move into the violent phase of revolution. Vernon Grounds cites a Lutheran pastor who says that the Christian may have to involve himself in "an armed overthrow of the existing order" if it is necessary. [46]

CRITIQUE OF THE ETHICS OF THE THEOLOGIES OF HOPE

GENERAL CRITIQUE OF PRINCIPLES

1. The shadow of Stalinism falls over the entire system of ethics spawned by the theologies of hope. Moltmann and Bloch are very much aware of it and go out of their way to mention it. The question is this: *Can we have revolution without its degenerating into Stalinism?* What assurance do we have that the revolutionaries who march under the banner of Christ are going to uphold Christian virtues and not sink to the usual brutality of revolutionaries?

The reflective Christian thinks of East Berlin in the early fifties when every moving creature—man, woman, child or animal—was leveled by machine-gun fire. He thinks of the Communists in Budapest who countered opposition by bombing out the lower floors of suspected buildings, thus leaving the building to crush its inhabitants. He remembers the gaping wounds left by the Communists' illegal usage of dumdum bullets. The Czechoslovakian massacre occurred after Moltmann wrote his book.

This does not mean there is never a place for a revolution.

But for Christians to toss the idea around as an easy alternative, like changing one's political affiliation and not reckoning with the potential Stalinism or Hitlerism in any revolution, is certainly naïve and unrealistic.

2. There is a self-righteousness that usually goes with the revolutionary. The revolutionary is so *completely* right and the oppressor is so *completely* wrong that discussion is meaningless. Moltmann is aware of this glaring conceit on the part of the revolutionary. [47] But does he really let it modulate his thinking? For example, he writes that "as long as Christians refrain from acting in a revolutionary way, *they have no right to make theological declarations about revolution.*" [48] But what makes a revolutionary so holy and right that he is beyond criticism? Why am I denied the right to act before I meditate upon the act? I would say that no one has the right to revolution who has not done some premeditation. [49]

Again, does not an unabashed self-righteousness appear in Moltmann's remark that if churches do not follow the pattern of *his* revolution and *his* theology of politics, then these churches are class-conscious, racialistic and heretical churches? [50] If churches are heretical because of unhealthy structures, what church is healthy enough in *any* dimension or *any* criterion not to be heretical?

3. Can there really be a *novum*—a totally new thing? Bloch apparently thinks so. But Christian theologians are caught in a bind at this point. *There is biblical history.* There is the Scripture itself, *a book of the past!* And there is the person of Christ, His cross and resurrection, upon which so many of the theologies of hope rest their theological claims. The idea of a *novum* cut off from this rootage is impossible. Israel knew the God of the *now* or the *present.* One of the names of God in Scripture is "who is and who was and who is to come" (Rev. 1:4, RSV). A theologian cannot be true to Scripture and cut off the God who is to come from the God who was and the God who is. The problem with the

theologians of hope is that the God of the past and the God of the now are never firmly woven into the fabric of their theology, even though they recognize that God is both of the past and of the now.

4. Although the inspiration for the theologies of hope may appear to be biblical eschatology, the actual meat or substance of the exposition is provided by the philosophies of Hegel, Marx and Bloch. Moltmann expressed his admiration for Bloch when he wrote, "It is only today that we find in Ernst Bloch, a magnificent philosophy of hope, in which the *novum* is made the central theme." [51] Moltmann, it is true, does toss theological concepts around in *Religion, Revolution and the Future,* but the real substance is from Bloch and it is surprising how many times Marx is cited.

Barth objected to Nazism on the basis that it was willfully trying to corrupt the message of Scripture. It therefore had to be resisted, and this resistance came to expression in the famous *Theological Declaration of Barmen* (1934). When he was asked why he was not equally adverse to Communism, he replied that Communism made no attempt to fuse Christianity and Communism, so the purity of the biblical message was not in danger. But has not the dependence of the theologies of hope on Bloch and Marx's ideology recreated the Nazi problem? Are not the theologies of hope being so penetrated by Marxian concepts that the message of Scripture is again in danger? Do we need a new Barmen declaration to say afresh that the one Word of God to man is Jesus Christ rather than Karl Marx and his wayward disciple, Ernst Bloch?

5. It is Hordern's opinion that the theology of hope is in danger of reviving the theory of inevitability of progress. [52] This notion that historical motion inevitably spirals upward has been severely criticized in recent years. In the idea of hope there is a breath of optimism. But here is where theologians of hope must be faced with some hard questions: Is not evil as much an option as the *novum*? Why

think that there can be no more Hitlers or Stalins in the future? Have psychiatrists informed us that all our terrible political psychopaths are in the past and that we may now breathe easier? Can we be sure that there will never be another Dachau?

6. In a sharp review of Braaten's *The Future of God,* Grover Foley asks whether there is going to be a future. [53] If there is going to be an atomic war, there will not be any people left to enjoy the *novum.*

In 1967 Rene Dubos asked the question: Does man have a future? [54] Among the items he mentions is the danger of extermination through pollution. What terrible cycle might we be starting? Dubos mentions that lichens readily sponge up strontium 90. Reindeer eat the lichens, and man eats the reindeer. Where does the cycle stop?

7. Moltmann proposes that the universities be the centers to help create the revolutions, the new social order, and the new world. This is the function of the *total* university, for "every science is questioned about its socio-political function." [55]

In America this program, it has been felt, will result in the *destruction* of the universities. Departments of black studies, created in good faith and with the best of intentions and in keeping with Moltmann's idea, have had to be terminated in many universities. Rather than being centers of cultural studies of black people, they became centers for planning violence and revolution. That which blights Communist universities, namely, that *all* subjects are "political," is the very thing Moltmann is advocating. A number of American professors resigned their posts when their universities were forced into social and political functions, because that meant the end of academic freedom.

8. Most of the critics of the theology of hope agree that if all the really big and important things of God are with the future generations, then the past and present generations

are but "the garbage dumps of history." If the real thing is the future *novum* with the future world order and the future utopia of social righteousness, then previous generations are nothing but temporary stepping-stones or rungs on a ladder whose meaning is gone once the kingdom of God has moved beyond them.

9. The word *revolution* is very common today in theological as well as secular literature. In the history of ethics and in the philosophy of politics the issue of a "just revolution" has been discussed, as well as the concept of a "just war." It is my impression in reading the literature of the theologies of hope and their call for revolution that *they have not seriously weighed the risk in any revolution.* That a political and economic system can reach such a point of deterioration that revolution is the only remedy is conceded. Our American nation was created by a revolution, and certainly revolution has ended some terrible national administrations.

But those who have written on the subject of revolution with patience, reflection, and historical perspective are very cautious about indicating the possible losses as well as anticipated gains in a revolution. *Our generation of more radical theologians has not taken the trouble to count up the risks of revolution.* For example, if the revolution fails, the oppression may be measurably increased. Or, if the revolutionary force is not strong enough, instead of revolution there will be a terrible slaughter and rivers of blood. If the revolution succeeds, the new regime may be more wicked or oppressive than the older regime. The revolution may solve one set of problems only to create another.

10. Bloch's metaphysical statements, to the effect that the cosmos, history and man are open-ended, should not be taken as gospel truth without intense philosophical scrutiny. Bloch may be right. But the easy way in which theologians of hope gulp down these metaphysical assertions of Bloch is very disturbing.

THEOLOGICAL CRITIQUE OF ETHICS OF
THEOLOGIES OF HOPE

1. Our principal concern is that Christian ethics be derived fundamentally from Scripture. The development of ethical principles is more complex than simply exegeting a moral principle from Scripture and then seeking to apply it today. But Christian ethics must have *genuine* Christian roots, and that means having genuinely biblical roots. My impression in reading the theologies of hope and futurology is that the basic framework is not biblical but stems from some sort of amalgamation of Hegel, Marx and Bloch. The appeal to Scripture occurs *after* the acceptance of the assumptions, despite the fact that these men want a Christian and not a humanistic or Marxist ethics. It is the methodology of the theology of hope which is at issue; those who appeal to Scripture after determining their premises about economics—be they capitalist or Communist—have, at best, only placed a Christian veneer on their thinking. Even if capitalism is the system which best harmonizes with Holy Scripture, Adam Smith is no more to be found there than is Marx or Bloch.

In his *Theology of Hope,* Moltmann made the resurrection the promise of all promises in that it contained the clue to the meaning of history and the anticipation of the hope of all hopes. This was reinforced by the repeated attacks upon Bultmann for reducing the cross, resurrection and kerygma to a *now* existential (and in Bultmann's peculiar definition of eschatology) eschatological encounter. But *Religion, Revolution and the Future* seemed to cast doubts on Moltmann's interpretation of the resurrection as a bodily resurrection. The difference between Bultmann and Moltmann would now appear that whereas Bultmann retains the resurrection as the "new life" aspect and "openness to the future" aspect of the kerygma, Moltmann would say the resurrection (whatever it was) promises specific things in the future like a *novum* or a *utopia*.

However, Carl Braaten in his book, *The Future of God,* has himself given one instance of a theologian of the theology of hope who has developed a theology that does not require a *bodily* resurrection. Braaten believes that something happened which could be called a resurrection, and this resurrection is necessary for a theology of hope. But what kind of event took place is *completely* negotiable. Braaten lists a series of possible interpretations of the resurrection and says, in so many words, "Take your pick as the theology of hope is not dependent upon any particular version of the *eventness* of the resurrection." [56]

Two things may be said of this generous offer to take our pick among the options about the *eventness* of the resurrection:

1. The options are contradictory. The very fact that it can be said that the options are contradictory materially undetermines any one option. If the *eventness* of an event is capable of contradictory interpretations, then the *eventness* itself evaporates. To be specific, if the subjective-vision theory of Otto is just as much an option as the physical theory of the fundamentalists, then how can there be any common theology of hope built on contradictory interpretations of the most fundamental event for the theology of hope?

2. If a *bodily* resurrection is only an option and not the definitive doctrine of the resurrection, then the Evangelical feels that we are back to the old liberal game of theological counterfeiting. The Evangelical suspects that theologies of hope are counterfeiting the concept of the resurrection of Christ when they will accept a number of alternatives other than a bodily resurrection, and further state that these alternatives have as much status with them as the version of a bodily resurrection.

3. There is no second coming in the theologies of hope.

206

In *Theology of Hope* Moltmann did speak of the *parousia* of Christ, which is a specific New Testament word meaning the second coming of Christ. But that concept vanishes in *Religion, Revolution and the Future;* the perpetual ongoing of God, Christ and the kingdom of the future eliminate it. It would seem that Betz, a Roman Catholic, would be committed to the resurrection and the second coming. But in the materials that we have available of Betz there is no place in his political theology for the return of Christ. The same is true with Braaten. There is a future—Christianity is eschatological through and through—but no return of Christ appears in the exposition about the future of Christ.

4. Theologies of hope throw the doctrine of creation into confusion. Certainly there is no doctrine of creation in Bloch and we don't expect one from a Marxist. The situation is similar to the problem of Jesus Christ and the Old Testament. A theologian may be so anxious to preserve the unity of Scripture that he makes the Old Testament almost completely into a Christological book. In so doing he undermines the inherent worth of the Old Testament as a revelation of God in its own right. When the theologians of hope throw the whole weight of Christian theology into the future they unwittingly undermine the integrity of the doctrine of creation. It may be true that we understand history from the end (eschatology) and not from the beginning (creation), but eschatology must not be so stressed that creation is made virtually irrelevant to Christian theology and Christian ethics.

Moltmann's lack of interest in the doctrine of creation is expressed in the following: "(The New Testament with its eschatologically oriented faith) is not interested in an event that took place at the beginning of time in explaining why the world exists and why it is as it is." [57]

First, Moltmann has simply not done his homework on the number of times creation is referred to in the New Testament and the theological use made of it.

Second, it is difficult to understand a theologian of Moltmann's learning ignoring the Christological passages *which refer to Christ as Creator* (e.g., Jn. 1:1; Col. 1:16; Heb. 1:10) in order to enhance the dignity of the person and work of Jesus Christ.

5. In Holy Scripture, God is the God of *eternity.* This means He is very God of very God in the past, that He is very God of very God in the present—in the now, and that He is very God of very God in the future. Macquarrie is very unhappy with the completely futuristic reality of God..58

Two doctrines of special abhorrence to theologians of hope are, first of all, the doctrine of eternal recurrence, no matter how it is expressed. That little prefix *re* is specially anathema to them, for it collides with the idea of lineal progress implied in the concept of the *novum.* The other doctrine which is abhorrent is that of an *epiphany,* namely, a vision or manifestation of God. To them it is like a frozen picture. Pictures are not movies; history, though, is a movie and not a picture. Our theology must be like a movie and not like a picture.

The theologians of hope are wrong, however, in glossing over the epiphanies and not giving them the status they have in Scripture. Moreover—and here is where Macquarrie bears down hard—how will Christians of the future recognize God if they have not become familiar with Him from the epiphanies of the past?

6. In general, Harvey Cox is appreciative of Bloch. 59 He thinks that he is the only other philosopher besides Heidegger that can give the modern theologian a working model. But he has doubts about the all-encompassing concern with the future. First, he observes what has been said many times before (starting with Pr. 13:12, RSV, "Hope deferred makes the heart sick"): that a hope beyond the horizon yields more to despair than to inspiration.

Then he adds another and more profound criticism: *the importance of the individual has been lost in an ethics that is purely social.* Vernon Venable has explored the Marxists' view of man. [60] He notes that in their literature the preoccupation is with man or mankind or the masses. In fact, he observes, there seems to be a distaste of the individual.

Man wants some sort of meaning to his life *now,* and he wants some sort of recognition of his own *personal* worth. If the real action is in the future, with mankind as the hero of it, contemporary man feels cheated out of life. The theologies of hope tend to ape the Marxists in putting the emphasis upon the future, thereby robbing the *now* of intrinsic significance or value, and in speaking of mankind or the world, and thereby depriving the individual of that *uniqueness* which at least for him makes life worth the pain.

Moltmann and Betz will occasionally admit that alleviating all the social, political, economic and racial ills of man can still leave man empty and frustrated. But this is never taken so seriously as to be built into their political theology. The reason is quite obvious. If too much attention is given to the individual and his sense of worth, meaning or spirituality, then Christian ethics is in danger of losing its equation with political theology. What theologians of hope have not shown is that "deprivatization" of Christian ethics is not to be equated with "depersonalizing."

7. Moltmann wrote: "It seems to me that Christian theology of today should turn away from a dogmatic theology to a critical one, from beginning with answers about God to the unsolved asking for God." [61] But what does all of this mean? Criticism presupposes a stance from which that criticism is made. If a theologian surrenders dogmatic theology, he has surrendered the grounds from which to operate critically. And if answers are ruled out, revelation is inevitably ruled out too. Then man's problems have overcome God's revelation. Can one really believe in the incarnation and affirm that we have no answers about

God? Is there not here capitulation to the ill-conceived irreligion of our times?

8. Finally, there is a denial of the significance of the church in most of the theologies of hope and their ethical stance. The entities of "church" and "world," we are told, are relative, not absolute. But, again, what do we do with passage after passage of Scripture? Is the world the body of Christ? Is the world the temple of the living God? Does the world have any sacraments? The absolute difference of world and church does not mean the absolute isolation of the church from the world. The church is always open to the world. And the church can and must have this openness to the world without surrendering its absolute character as the unique body of Christ.

If the above has seemed excessively critical we can say a word of appreciation for the theologies of hope and their ethics:

1. They have showed the church afresh that the resurrection cannot be negotiated away but stands at the center of the Christian message.

2. They have showed the theologians that they can yet have a healthy, historical eschatology without critically denying it, or giving it a peculair twist like Dodd's realized eschatology or Bultmann's existential-perpendicular eschatology.

3. They have reminded us that compassion for men in their need of salvation must also include compassion that they be fed, clothed and protected. It is a healthy reminder of the truth in the old Salvation Army slogan of "Soup, soap, and salvation."

4. When forces of nihilism and pessimism and emptiness are pressing upon Western man's consciousness, they have raised a sound of joy and hope that the future may be better and not worse than the past. To live by hope—as thin as its support may be—is always more redemptive and healthy than to live by pessimism and nihilism and skepticism.

1. James Smart thinks that for all the variations in theology after Barth and Bultmann, theologians will return to their options as the only great ones of our century. See James Smart, *The Divided Mind of Modern Theology* (Philadelphia: Westminster, 1967).

2. Jürgen Moltmann, *The Theology of Hope* (New York: Harper & Row, 1967).

3. This was initiated by John Cobb's *A Christian Natural Theology* (Philadelphia: Westminster, 1965). A general introduction with bibliography on process theology is found in Norman Pittenger, *Process Thought and Christian Faith* (New York: Macmillan, 1968).

4. Wolf-Dieter Marsch, ed., *Diskussion über die 'Theologie der Hoffnung'* (Munich: C. Kaiser, 1967).

5. Ernst Bloch's work is being slowly translated into English. See his books entitled *On Karl Marx* (New York: Herder & Herder, 1970); *Spirit of Utopia* (New York: Herder & Herder, 1970); *A Philosophy of the Future* (New York: Herder & Herder, 1970); and *Man on His Own* (New York: Herder & Herder, 1970).

His most famous work, *Das Prinzip Hoffnung* (Frankfurt: Suhrkamp, 1959) of three volumes has not yet been translated. It would also be a real help in the English-speaking world if Siegfried Unseld, ed., *Ernst Bloch in zu ehren (sic.)* (Frankfurt: Suhrkamp, 1965) were translated.

For a bibliography of materials on Bloch in English, cf. Walter Capps, ed., *The Future of Hope* (Philadelphia: Fortress, 1970), p. 45, n. 22. Cf. also Jürgen Rühle, "The Philosophy of Hope" in *Revisionism: Essays on the History of Marxist Ideas*, ed. Leopold Labedz (New York: Praeger, 1962), pp. 166-78; Franco Lombardi, "Ernst Bloch" in *The Encyclopedia of Philosophy*, 1:321-23; Gerald G. O'Collins, "Spes Quaerens Intelltum, *Interpretation* 22 (Jan., 1966): 36-52; Harvey Cox, "Ernst Bloch, and 'The Pull of the Future,' " *Theology No. 5*, eds. M. Marty and D. Peerman (New York: Macmillan, 1968), pp. 191-202; Francis Golffing, "Bloch's 'Summa,' " *Books*

Abroad 34 (Fall, 1960): 358-59; and S. Paul Schilling, "Ernst Bloch, Philosopher of the Not Yet," *The Christian Century* 84 (Nov. 15, 1967): 455-58. *Philosophy Today* 14 (Winter, 1970) is an entire issue devoted to articles on Bloch and contains many details and much information not contained in the above references.

6. For the details of Bloch's life, his involvement with the East German government, and his settlement in retirement at Tübingen, cf. Rühle's "The Philosophy of Hope"; also see Jürgen Moltmann, "Introduction" in Bloch's *Man on His Own*, pp. 19-29.

7. Kenneth Cauthen, *Science, Secularization and God: Toward a Theology of the Future* (New York: Abingdon, 1969). The relationship of the theology of hope and process theology (which Cauthen belongs to) is discussed by Capps, *The Future of Hope*, pp. 9 ff. The last sentence of Cauthen's book reads: "This book, then, is written as a suggestion toward the development of a theology of the future and for the future—a theology of hope" (p. 229).

8. So new is the ethics emerging from the theology-of-hope movement that discussion on this is omitted from such recent works as Gene H. Outka and Paul Ramsey, eds., *Norm and Content in Christian Ethics* (New York: Scribner, 1968); Ian T. Ramsey, ed., *Christian Ethics and Contemporary Philosophy* (London: SCM, 1966); and Edward LeRoy Long, Jr., *A Survey of Christian Ethics* (New York: Oxford U., 1967).

9. Ernst Bloch, "Man as Possibility" in *The Future of Hope*, ed. Capps, p. 63.

10. Reported by Harvey Cox in the foreword to Bloch, *Man on His Own*, p. 9. Cox makes the observation that this does not violate the law of identity (S is S) as a new logic of change is called for.

11. Schilling, p. 1456.

12. Rühle, p. 172.

13. Bloch, "Man as Possibility," p. 63.

14. Ibid., p. 38.

15. Ibid., p. 61.

16. Ibid., p. 63. German terms omitted.

17. The dehumanization of man in present-day Russia glares at the reader on every page of Alecksandr I. Solzhenitsyn's *The First Circle* (New York: Bantam Books, 1968).

18. Lombardi, p. 322. Tillich points out that Bloch is unique in his interpretation of hope for he makes hope an inward driving force like faith and love. It is part of man's *daily* experience and not a passive attitude of expectancy. Cf. Paul Tillich, "Das Recht auf Hoffnung" in *Ernst Bloch zu ehren*, ed. Unseld, pp. 265 f.

19. This is a point especially made by Wolfhart Pannenberg in "Appearance as the Arrival of the Future" in *Theology No. 5*, pp. 112-29.

20. Ruben Alves, "Some Thoughts on a Program for Ethics," *Union Seminary Quarterly Review* 26 (Winter, 1970): 153-70. Cf. also his important book, *A Theology of Human Hope* (Washington: Corpus Books, 1969).

21. Cox, "Ernst Bloch . . .," p. 203.

22. Cf. Marty and Peerman, eds., *New Theology No. 6: On Revolution and Non-Revolution, Violence and Non-Violence, Peace and Power* (New York: Macmillan, 1969); and Vernon Grounds, "Bombs or Bible? Get Ready for Revolution," *Christianity Today* 25 (Jan. 15, 1971): 4-6.

23. Moltmann, pp. 304, 328.

24. Moltmann, *Religion, Revolution and the Future*, pp. 53-54. H. M. Kuitert suggests that Moltmann has not really left the existential camp but that he develops its theology on a different axis. See Kuitert's "Erläuterungen zu Jürgen Moltmanns Theologie der Hoffnung" in *Diskussion über die "Theologie der Hoffnung,"* ed. Wolf-Dieter Marsch, pp. 184-88.

25. Moltmann, *The Theology of Hope*, pp. 181, 194. But now his second book makes us suspect his meaning in the first book. Cf. the denials in *Religion, . . .*, pp. 33, 48.

26. Moltmann, *Religion, . . .*, p. 59.

27. Ibid., p. 114. The parallels between the ethics of the theology of hope and the ethics defended in the new evangelical journal, *Vanguard* (the publication of a very articulate and highly

socially motivated group of Evangelicals) are many and very close. Both deplore the traditional emphasis on "personal ethics." Both wish to "deprivatize" (a concept we develop later) Christian ethics. Both want to enlarge greatly what is meant by evangelism. However, the editors of *Vanguard* are careful to preserve what is good in the personal spirituality of historic Christianity—something which cannot be said for most theologians of hope.

28. Moltmann, *Religion*, . . ., p. 105, n. 26; and p. 127.

29. John Macquarrie, "Theologies of Hope," *The Expository Times* 82 (Jan., 1971): 100-5.

30. Moltmann, *Religion*, . . ., pp. 38-40.

31. Ibid., p. 123.

32. Johannes Betz, "A Political Theology" in *The Future of Hope*, ed. Capps, pp. 136-54.

33. Moltmann, *Religion*, . . ., p. 218.

34. Ibid., p. 202.

35. Betz, p. 140.

36. Robert W. Jenson, "The Futurist Option of Speaking of God" in *New Theology No. 7*, eds. M. Marty and D. Peerman (New York: Macmillan, 1970), pp. 207-9.

37. Carl E. Braaten, *The Future of God*, pp. 92 ff. We say more of Braaten when we discuss the concept of revolution.

38. Alves, *A Theology of Human Hope.*

39. Alves, "Some Thoughts . . .," pp. 153-70.

40. Ibid., pp. 165-67, 169. "A new social order" (p. 160) is apparently a synonym for the "creation of a new world." Although the specific ethical norms are not stated, they are obviously political, sociological and economic. Alves, too, rejects the idea that one may claim to have personal ethics and ignore social ethics—an a priori in the theologies of hope that needs careful sifting before uncritical acceptance. Personal ethics, to Alves, is mockery if it does not lead to political theology.

41. Cf. Abbie Hoffman, *Revolution for the Hell of It* (New York: Dial, 1968), and Jerry Rubin, *Do It* (New York: Simon & Schuster, 1970).

42. Moltmann, *Religion,* . . ., p. 131.
43. Ibid.
44. Braaten, chap. 5: "The Politics of Hope—Society."
45. Ibid., p. 163.
46. Grounds, p. 5.
47. Moltmann, *Religion,* . . ., p. 145.
48. Ibid., p. 133. Italics ours.
49. Judge Samuel W. Gardiner has written a very mature and judicious commentary on revolution and violence in their relationship to justice and democracy which anybody who wants to throw a brick, burn a building, or club a pig ought to read before he "does his thing." See *The Center Magazine* 4 (Mar. / Apr., 1971):80.
50. Moltmann, *Religion,* . . ., p. 141.
51. Ibid., p. 15. Moltmann says he defends a "humanistic Marxism" and not a "Stalinistic Marxism" (p. 70). It would be interesting to have Alexander Dubcek's commentary on the realism of this distinction. S. Paul Schilling's criticisms will be found in his previously cited essay from *The Christian Century* (Nov. 15, 1967). Further criticisms of Bloch will be found in Ferdinand Kirstien's "Hope" in *Sacramentum Mundi,* ed. Karl Rahner et al. (New York: Herder & Herder, 1969), 3:61-65.
52. William Hordern, "The Theology of Hope in America," *Lutheran Quarterly* 21 (Nov., 1969): 342-51.
53. Grover Foley, " 'The Future of God' by Carl E. Braaten," *Interpretation* 24 (Oct., 1970): 515-17.
54. See reprint in Rene Dubos, "Does Man Have a Future?" *The Center Magazine* 4 (Mar. / Apr., 1971): 56-62.
55. Moltmann, *Religion,* . . ., pp. 131-32.
56. Braaten, pp. 74-75.
57. Moltmann, *Religion,* . . ., p. 5.
58. Macquarrie, pp. 100-5.
59. Cox, "Afterword" in *The Secular City Debate,* ed. Daniel Callaghan (New York: Macmillan, 1966), pp. 179-204.

60. Vernon Venable, *Human Nature: The Marxian View* (New York: Knopf, 1945), p. 3.

61. Moltmann, *Religion, . . .,* p. 65.

PROCLAMATION FOR A NEW AGE

by
Harold J. Ockenga

"Ours is an age of preaching and of able preachers,"
wrote Edgar DeWitt Jones in 1933.[1] Quite the reverse is true
today.[2] There is a void of great preaching and a scarcity of
great preachers. The pulpit masters of the last generation are gone—Joseph Fort Newton, Clarence Edward
Macartney, Charles Clayton Morrison, George W. Truett,
Joseph Anderson Vance, G. Campbell Morgan, Frederick
B. Fisher, W. E. Sangster, George A. Buttrick, Mark A.
Matthews, etc. Where are their successors? A survey of the
cities of America leaves us with no outstanding array of
dominant voices.

In the 1930s the cry was often heard: "Let's have a
moratorium on preaching." That moratorium has come, but
not as expected—through a dearth of eminent preachers.
The church buildings are occupied, the sermons are being
preached, the people are still attending church. Yet the
greatness of preaching is absent. The golden age of
preaching is past. Even S. Parkes Cadman, one of the
"greats," sensed this when he advocated

that no more books of sermons be printed for twenty-five years, so that ministers might be driven to read and study the great old classics,. . .and so be inspired to dig out their own sermons instead of utilizing material so easily pilfered from sermonic literature.[3]

The reason for the present famine is the practice of substituting social ethics, political activism, psychological counseling, group therapy, and new liturgies for preaching. Primacy is being given to secular relevance. Emphasis in theological seminaries and ministerial conferences is upon social activism which will change environment, rather than on renewal of individuals who, in turn, will transform environment.[4] The minister is made to feel guilty if he is not building bridges between the races, fighting for legislation in behalf of the underprivileged, establishing communes to protest materialism, and participating in black studies. The quiet hours of study so essential to great preaching are like stolen fruit to the average minister charged with administration, interviewing, protesting and serving.[5] Reinhold Niebuhr, George Webber, Harvey Cox and a host of writers have browbeaten the preacher into believing that preaching per se is irrelevant. The question most asked in ministerial groups to which I have spoken is, "How can we be relevant to the problems of our day?" Relevance is a fetish before which the present generation of preachers bows in idolatry.

In a treatise called *Eutychus: or the Future of the Pulpit,* the novelist, Winifred Holtby, adds an addendum to Fénelon's "Dialogues on Eloquence":

On the opening page Anthony, a young intellectual, has just returned from a play. He complains that he finds religious drama, such as he had been witnessing, tedious in the extreme. "How those allusions to Deity date, don't they?" he observes in his sceptically superior way. "We've done with the ages of faith, thank heaven!" At this point Fénelon, mysteriously recalled to the twentieth century, enquires whether such gratitude is not somewhat misplaced.

218

"Is it indeed to heaven that we owe thanks for an end of faith?" he asks. "I should have looked elsewhere." Anthony's interest is aroused by this strange intruder. He wants to know who he is and what he is doing. Fénelon gravely explains that he is visiting England to collect material for his little work on *The Future of the Pulpit*. Anthony is vastly amused at the idea of such a subject. "Alas, my poor Archbishop," he exclaims, "you came too late! The pulpit has a past now, but no future."[6]

The disparagement of preaching is quite general among young men entering the theological seminaries. Disillusioned by what they have seen and heard in the churches, yet internally called of God to minister in the kingdom, they are casting about for a proper sphere of service. Preaching seems to them to be antiquated and out-of-date in a world of astronauts and atomic power. The great task of the seminary is to reinculcate in ministerial students a new confidence in the authority of the Word of God, and an awareness that preaching is the ordained means of dissemination of the Word.[7]

No matter how complete the eclipse of preaching by modern activism, the darkness will pass with the emergence of the unbound Word and the emanation of that Word through preaching. The eternal Word is perennially relevant to the needs of the human family. Only as its principles, precepts, promises and provisions are proclaimed will Christianity prosper and men be motivated to establish righteousness. Not by extolling virtue and exhorting social reform will the world be changed, but by the proclamation of the grand center point of revelation in the redemptive acts of God by incarnation, atonement and resurrection are the forces released which bring regeneration and reform.

The challenge to preaching is to make this changeless and durable Word applicable in our modern milieu. Concepts held in high value in the late twentieth century are justice, love, brotherhood, togetherness and sharing. The consciousness of social responsibility is universal among the new generation of Christians. The expression of this mood is found in the ecclesiastical plan of union called "Cocu," which has won the support of the socially minded clergy. The cost of "togetherness for others" as so expressed, has been the disparagement of biblical doctrines and theological statements of faith. The Reformation has been circumvented; evangelism as confrontation for decision with the claims of Christ has been replaced by social action; and both truth and morals have been declared relative. Preaching as proclamation of truth is discredited and is replaced by dialogue of modern dialectic discourse. Pulpits are occupied by men using the conversational method instead of rhetorical, didactic and forensic delivery. As Jones complained, "When it comes to the content of contemporary preaching, it is not nearly so doctrinal, expository and dialectic as the sermonic content of other generations."[8] The great question is, Should and can great preaching be revived?

One plan advanced in modern theological circles is the collegium principle.[9] In certain large churches of today or in the projected parishes of the "Cocu Plan," a group of ministers may be attached to one parish. By this means expertise can be attained in various areas of service—preaching, counseling, legal assistance, welfare advice or assistance, student leadership, and direction for the aged. The interaction of the spiritual with the material and physical ministries will enable the church to treat the whole person of the individual. The preacher may thus devote himself to the explication of the revealed Word in both personal and social areas with lucidity and freedom because he is part of a team implementing the application of these spiritual insights. Revelance of the spiritual and prophetic message can thus be guaranteed. The current problems of society in poverty, racism, violence, pollution and isolation demand that the gospel be preached with relevance. We do not live in and we cannot preach in a vacuum.

PREACHING IN HISTORY

The history of the church has been adorned by many great preachers. Of these John Chrysostom (345-407) was eminent. Called Χρυσόστομος, or "golden-mouthed," he charmed the multitudes, first at Antioch of Syria, and then at Constantinople. At thirty-five his sermons catapulted him into popularity so that he swayed the people of Antioch toward moral restraint, righteousness, and probity. They preferred hearing his sermons to the entertainments of the theater and the circus. Elevated to the bishopric and then the archbishopric of Constantinople, he demanded among his clergy the discipline he exercised in his own life. He separated the ecclesiastics from the lay sisters they used as concubines, and he removed thirteen bishops for simony and licentiousness. Against the vices, pride, pomp and profane honors of the court, especially of Empress Eudoxia, he thundered from St. Sophia's pulpit. His pure and copious vocabulary, his inexhaustible fund of metaphors and similitudes, his dramatic exposure of the folly and turpitude of vice, and his deep moral earnestness won the unfailing fidelity of the masses of people. His preaching was based upon an intimate acquaintance with Scripture, grammatical study, knowledge of the original circumstances of composition, and forceful application to the needs of his day. Twice exiled by envious and resentful enemies, he maintained great power through his pulpit eloquence, and exerted wide influence over the church of East and West until his death. [10]

Another "great" of God's preachers was Girolamo Savonarola (1452-98), the Italian Dominican monk who died a martyr to the truth he so eloquently proclaimed in Florence. Precocious as a child, brilliant as a student, industrious as a priest, inspired as a preacher, and incisive as a political leader, he ruled Florence as undisputed sovereign for nearly a decade. The sources of his power were his

221

ascetic personal discipline, his firm stand on the Bible, his courageous rebuke of personal and ecclesiastical vice, his eloquent and moving sermons on righteousness, his concern for the poor and exploited, and his belief in personal spiritual guidance.

The preaching of Savonarola reproved the vanities of professing Christians, denounced hyprocrisy and vice in church leaders, called for sacrifice and generosity to the poor, outlined social reform for amelioration of human suffering, summoned the courts to legislate righteousness, all based upon the justice and mercy of God as revealed in the Bible. His call was to repentance and change, or to face the judgment and wrath of God. A child of his time in use of visions and prophecies, nevertheless, he moved a city, kings and popes by his preaching. The power of the preached Word controlled Florence under his ministry. [11]

Best known of all the Reformers as preachers was Martin Luther (1488-1553). Converted from legal studies at Erfurt to theological vocation by confrontation with God in a thunderstorm while returning from Mansfeld, he entered the Dominican priesthood studies, first at the University of Erfurt, and then at the University of Wittenberg. In the Augustinian monastery of Wittenberg he passed through the soul struggles which eventuated in his famous transformation by grasping the truth of justification by faith. From the Psalms, then Romans, and finally Galatians as lecturer, he entered the firm conviction of *sola fidei,* or the primacy of faith in Christ's finished redemption as the means of salvation. This set him in opposition to the dominant teaching and practice of Rome. Through his Ninety-Five Theses, his debates with John Eck, his conversations with Cardinal Cajetan, his trial at Worms, and his incarceration as Knight George, he emerged the champion of reform. The steps were taken in conjunction with his preaching to the townspeople of Wittenberg. In St. Andrew's Church he instructed parishioners in their freedoms;

in the castle chapel he admonished Frederick the Wise on virtue and political action; in the university he expounded the biblical and philosophical grounds of reformed Christianity; in his home he expatiated on problems and questions raised by students and friends. His sermons were disseminated in printed form over Germany and throughout Europe until the reasoning, pleas and instruction swept half of Europe out of the Roman Church. [12]

Though George Whitefield (1714-70) was by far the more eloquent and moving preacher of the evangelical revival in England, John Wesley (1703-91) was the more influential. Whitefield was possessed of a powerful voice which could be heard by over 20,000 people at once, his manner of speaking was dramatic, his use of events and figures of speech was so emotionally moving that the common people in great crowds heard him gladly. He burned himself out preaching a score or more times a week in his evangelistic ministry in England, Wales, Scotland and America.

Wesley was calmer, more methodical, more of an author (he wrote some three hundred books), a better organizer and administrator so that his influence became more permanent. Yet Wesley preached as often and as effectively as did Whitefield. Whitefield influenced him to take to the open air at Moorfields, after which he preached outdoors for forty years.

Originally a stiff Anglican high churchman, insisting on all the rubrics, Wesley gradually moved into innovations which became the grist of his organization of Methodism. Fervent from the experience of being "strangely warmed in heart," he communicated his zeal for personal religious experience and scriptural holiness to his people. He held forth on the possibility of victory over sin, of perfection in love, and appealed to consciences in the clearest language supported by cogent argument and personal conviction. Hearers, who felt that every word was aimed at themselves, were brought under conviction and, through repentance of sin and faith in Christ's atonement, were renewed and transformed. No preacher of the eighteenth century had greater mastery over his audiences. This spiritual power, combined with social concern expressed in providing work for the poor, clothes and food for the distressed, and aid to the debtors, made such an impact upon England as to transform society. [13]

Modern preachers have all been eclipsed by Billy Graham. His radio ministry has extended farther than that of preachers representing councils of churches, denominations or independent constituencies. His use of television has surpassed that of heads of nations. His personal appearance as preacher has reached more persons than any man in history—all this for the sake of preaching the gospel of Jesus Christ. This gifted preacher speaks simply, with short, understandable words and sentences, dynamically with great conviction, pictorially with vivid illustrations, and scripturally with biblical content. The result is a positive response from the masses, a personal fascination to political leaders, a popular acceptability to famous people, and a purifying influence upon the churches. His spoken word moves the minds and hearts of men as does that of no other man. Chosen of God and gifted in ability, under the unction of the Spirit, Billy Graham demonstrates the power of the preached Word of God. [14] This influence and effect of preaching is not confined to any one age.

THE PERMANENT BASIS OF PREACHING

After hundreds of years of prophetic silence, John the Baptist came preaching. [15] His physical appearance was startling: bronzed in the sun, clothed with camel's hair and leather, eating the simplest food. His manner was shocking: rebuking ecclesiastical leaders, kings and military. His message was shattering: repent or be doomed by ax and fire. Here was a preacher, sent of God, speaking to church and nation, and ministering to the masses. His voice was heard and men and society were changed.

Then "Jesus began to preach," [16] and went about for three years teaching and preaching. [17] In synagogues, in homes, in open fields, on mountains, from boats on the sea, and in the temple He preached. The crowds gathered whenever He appeared and followed Him, hanging upon His words and saying, "Whence hath this man such wisdom?" or "Never man spake like this man." Some of the sermons of Jesus have been gathered for us by the synoptists and by John: the Sermon on the Mount, [18] the seven parables by the sea, [19] the Olivet discourse on prophecy, [20] and the message to the Pharisees on hypocrisy. [21] Moreover, He sent the seventy disciples out to preach [22] and commissioned the church through His apostles to preach the gospel to every creature [23] and in all the world. [24]

And preach they did. The apostles and early Christians preached in Jerusalem, [25] in Samaria, [26] and everywhere. [27] The foundation of the New Testament church was laid by preaching the good news of the gospel. Emphasis is laid upon preaching the life, sufferings, death and resurrection of Jesus, especially in Peter's sermons. [28] The attestation of the Spirit's presence and blessing accompanied the apostolic preaching. [29]

Paul testified to his call to preach and the encumbency which rested upon him to fulfill this ministry of proclamation. [30] The content of the gospel Paul preached was given by revelation, [31] and was the exclusive message given for salvation. [32] By hearing and believing this gospel of the death of Christ for their sins and His resurrection from the dead, Paul declared that the Corinthians were saved. [33] To fulfill this commission, Paul undertook his strenuous missionary journeys and suffered innumerable hardships. His concluding testimony was that he had preached the gospel where Christ was not named, lest he should build upon another man's foundation, and was still intending to journey into Spain to preach the gospel. [34]

To the church Paul gave instruction that the work of the ministry would depend upon the exercise of the gifts of the Spirit from the resurrected and ascended Christ. Thus, some would be apostles, some prophets, some evangelists and some pastors and teachers "for the perfecting of the saints, for the work of the ministry, for the edifying of the body of Christ." [35] He left a body of instructions for the ministers of the church in the epistles to Timothy and to Titus, urging Timothy to "preach the word; be instant in season, out of season; reprove, rebuke, exhort with all longsuffering and doctrine." [36] Paul left no doubt that preaching is basic to the ongoing work of extending and upbuilding the church of Christ. Other ministries may supplement that of preaching, but nothing can ever substitute for it. "It pleased God by the foolishness of preaching [the thing preached] to save them that believe." [37]

THE KINDS OF PREACHING

In extracting the heart out of the Yale Lectures, called the Lyman Beecher Lectureship on Preaching, Batsell Baxter [38] emphasized the conviction by Phillips Brooks and Paul Scherer that all types of sermons should be merged in preaching.

> I am inclined to think that the idea of a sermon is so properly a unit, that a sermon involves of necessity such elements in combination, the absence of any one of which weakens the sermon-nature, that the ordinary classifications of sermons are of little consequence. [39]

> You are familiar with different types of sermons: doctrinal, expository, ethical, pastoral, evangelistic. Let me only say again that I have never preached or heard or read a sermon worthy of the name which was not to a greater or less degree all five of these

together . . . . A sermon without exposition, with noting which leads to a clearer understanding of God's Word, is without its highest sanction. A sermon of the cardinal tenets of the Christian faith, is without foundation. A sermon without the ethical is pointless . . . . A sermon without the pastoral is spiritless. And a sermon without the evangelistic is Christless and useless altogether! 40

While recognizing the wisdom of the above, I found in my experience of forty years as pastor and forty-five years of constant preaching, that there are predominant types of sermons which are especially valuable for different purposes. I would underscore the truth that biblical exegesis, doctrine, ethics and application must be present in every sermon. Some messages, however, are predominantly expository, or doctrinal, or biographical, or prophetic, or experiential, or textual, or topical. A pastor should be skilled in the use of all kinds of sermons.

He who would enjoy a long pastorate in one congregation should master the expository method of preaching. Thereby he will always have a fresh and inexhaustible supply of material. In my first church I read of Ulrich Zwingli's practice at Einsideln and Zürich of beginning to preach at Matthew 1:1 and preaching through the New Testament. Incidentally, he preached himself into the Reformation. I said, "If he could do it, so can I." I began expository preaching and followed the method on Sunday mornings and at most midweek services for forty years. No other method of preaching is so calculated to instruct the people in biblical truth and life. I used doctrinal, biographical, prophetic, and topical preaching on Sunday evenings, but my primary method was expository.

To prepare an expository sermon, one must accept the message of the scriptural passage. This means reading the book in the original and then rereading it many times in English. Dr. G. Campbell Morgan claimed to read a book of the Bible fifty times before expounding it. Along with this, one must outline the book so that each division and subhead is in context. The section used will have a developmental connection with the remainder and derive its meaning from it. It is a sin to wrest the meaning of Scripture to support some theory. The section chosen for the sermon may be a book, a chapter, a paragraph, a text, a phrase, or a word. Each division must stand alone as an independent unit. Some transients will hear only that one sermon and it must stand alone in completeness of thought and treatment. The topic of the sermon must express the meaning of the text. By this method the minister will always know what his next subject will be. He is never at a loss for texts. Moreover, all reading and study become cumulative, contributing to future sermons.

The aim of the sermon must be clear. What truth or experience are you trying to convey? If this is not clear to the preacher, it cannot be communicated to the people. That is derived from the text. The text must be analyzed. Most time ought to be spent on the outline. This comes from the meaning, the divisions and the development of the text. That outline should express the truth in logical form. Syllogism, alliteration and antithesis should be used. Each point must land one directly before the next point to be developed. The analogy of Scripture should be used. If the sermon is a true exposition of Scripture, a wealth of texts will be available to express or to illustrate the truth. The best illustrations are those taken from the Bible itself. This treatment must be amplified with theology. Powerful preaching is impossible without a positive theology. The preacher must know what he believes and why he believes it. With this goes the courage to enter the theological arena with those who deny the biblical truth.

Thus, an expository sermon may be polemic. It must be applied to the people and to the times. We do not preach in a vacuum. People lack carry-over power to apply truths to themselves and situations. Blind spots exist in everyone's moral conscience. A gospel which is both personal and social must be applied. [41] Hereby, the "thus saith the Lord" becomes authoritative over against relative truth or the opinions of men, or the authentic moment of the existentialist.

Doctrinal preaching is intended to establish faith in the great guidelines of truth. [42] By it mileposts of thinking are established by which one's spiritual journey may be measured. Limited in extent, it may be used in series or in occasional sermons to relieve the expository method. Evening doctrinal series on the person and work of Christ, the Holy Spirit, the steps of salvation, the second coming, the Apostle's Creed or the confessions, the deeper life, prayer, etc., will attract wide interest of students and serious-minded people. I spent one entire year of midweek addresses on the great doctrines of Scripture and used doctrinal series regularly.

Biographical preaching should be ranked with expository preaching. The Bible is an inexhaustible source of characters. In addition, general biography may be used as illustrative material. By this vivid means, all truths and valid Christian experiences can be portrayed. Life itself throws constant light on these characters. Experts in this field were Alexander White and Clarence E. Macartney. Macartney's biographical preaching packed the old First Church of Pittsburgh through winter Sunday evenings. The writer's own excursions into this field were many, such as "Pentecost in Personality," dealing with the Spirit-filled experience of New Testament characters, or "Men of Power," dealing with the thirty leading characters of the Old Testament. People enjoy biographical preaching, especially on little-known persons of Scripture. Every character is worthy of at least one message. Attempt to bring him up to date with trials and triumphs corresponding to those of modern persons.

Topical sermons may be timely or even sensational, but must be current. Though this was Jesus' primary method, it is one which taxes the ingenuity and creativity of the preacher. Albert Edward Day urged this type of preaching in *Jesus and Human Personality.*

> He did not take a passage from the law and the prophets, unravel its general principles, and then look about to discover if there were some place where those principles might be having an immediate application. Rather did he address himself to the human situation before him, guided by familiarity with the moral vision of yesterday but also by his own fresh and unique insight. He was, if anything, a topical preacher. 43

The parallel between events in the history of Israel and our own history affords a remarkable opportunity to prepare a full series of topical sermons addressed to the nation, such as "The Origin of a Nation" (Abraham), "The Constitution of a Nation" (Moses), "The Prodigality of a Nation" (Elijah), "The Revivalist of a Nation" (Hezekiah), "The Doom of a Nation" (Jeremiah). Others can treat Communism and the Christian faith, ideas of God, man, the state, law, freedom, etc., or Christian education, or the new morality, or missions, or sociological tension points. These may border on politics, but the minister at times must speak as a prophet.

Polemic sermons have their place. Times arise when it is necessary to define and defend the Christian faith over against new and old errors. In some areas so many people are committed to an antibiblical view of Christianity or to some of the cults that no converts would ever be made without apologetic preaching. The nature of these sermons changes with the issue confronted, but the philosophy underlying them is ever the same. Although there is a new rapprochement between Romanism and Protestantism today, sermons sharpening our perspective on the different points of teaching are very necessary. Heresy trials may be out of favor, but error must be refuted when it rears its head in any movement.

Every sermon ought to have something of the evangelistic thrust in it. This means that the content of the gospel should be present, man's need for the gospel analyzed, and the way of application stated. This Paul did to the Corinthians:

> I declare [certify] unto you the gospel which I preached unto you, which also ye have received, and wherein ye stand; by which also ye are saved, . . . how that Christ died for our sins . . . that he was buried, and that he rose again the third day . . . . [44]

Men must see that they cannot save themselves, that Christ through His death and resurrection can save them, and that this becomes applied by a choice of the will to receive Him. Enlightenment in the methodology of evangelistic preaching can come from reading the sermons of John Wesley, Charles G. Finney, Dwight L. Moody and Billy Graham.

A type of preaching rarely used is the experiential sermon. This begins not with a text or truth or proposition, but with a snatch of human experience. It may be a full story received in counseling, or an experience related in correspondence, or a conversation overheard on a streetcar or on the street, but it vividly states some biblical truth which can be developed from the experience. The title is taken from the experience and attracts because of its startling nature. The introduction narrates the experience and the sermon develops the ramifications of the subject.

During World War II, the author was walking on the Boston Common where thousands of soldiers and sailors gathered to meet girls or to while away the time, a fact which impelled me to initiate outdoors services for them. On one occasion I overheard two servicemen talking, one married and one unmarried, but both about to go abroad to fight. Said one, "But I wanted a baby before I die." This afforded me a title in a series of "Sermons from Human

Experience," which I used with great effect in speaking of death, immortality, sacrifice, family relationships, etc. Dr. C. E. Macartney used this method often and called these messages "Sermons from Life." [45] By these, the full gamut of life can be covered from the biblical perspective.

PREPARATION TO PREACH

The preacher's weekly routine is a very important part of preaching. Happy is the man who charts the periods of each day so as to discipline his activity through the week. Since no boss sits in judgment on the preacher's use of time, he must learn to discipline himself. Let each half hour of the waking day be outlined. Time for devotions should be strictly observed, either in the morning or at a set time of day. If a preacher does not saturate his life with prayer, he may go through the motions of spiritual ministry, but he shall be ineffectual. [46] Many sermon topics or whole messages will be born in prayer. Let a prayer list in book form be kept with specific entries by date and subject and a scrupulous record of answers. He who thus prays will keep himself alert in all areas of his responsibility. While praying, keep a blank sheet of paper at hand on which a record of the items God speaks about may be made. When devotions are over, attempt to accomplish these items first. Luther said, "To have prayed well is to have studied well."

The weekly schedule begins with a rest day on Monday. The preacher's week builds up to Sunday and necessitates a letdown on Monday. The biblical law of one day of rest in seven is as obligatory on the preacher as on a working man. It may not be possible to keep oneself free from occasional funerals or sick calls or other obligations on Monday, but the attempt should be made. Some retreat a few miles away from home is a great aid to this. Even with a complete break in activity, the preacher's mind will be homing toward texts, ideas or sermons.

On Tuesday morning, topics and announcements for the church bulletin must be in. Then work begins on the Sunday evening sermon. Here the use of a series helps, for there is no casting about for a topic. If the work is slow, keep at it until the sparks begin to fly. A goodly portion of Tuesday's work time must be given to this sermon. In the afternoon, break off in order to visit the parishioners or to do organizational work, or to keep up with correspondence.

Wednesday morning get back to the Sunday evening sermon and keep at it until it is finished. The afternoon may be given to interviewing, counseling or calling.

Thursday should find the preacher at his study for the Sunday morning sermon, or if the midweek meeting comes on Thursday night, then get to that task. Since my midweek lecture came on Friday, I gave Thursday morning to sermon preparation. The evening was devoted to organizational meetings.

Friday morning I attacked the lecture to be given that night and continued until it was completed. Group gatherings were always associated with the Friday night lecture.

Saturday morning I returned to my Sunday morning sermon and shut myself in until it was done, regardless of time. The afternoons I kept for a walk, or some calls, or family affairs. Saturday night was kept inviolable for prayer and study of the Sunday sermons. I memorized my outlines and quotations so as to be able to preach without notes. By this method, I unloaded first that which was prepared last; first, the Friday lecture prepared that day; second, the Sunday morning sermon prepared on Thursday morning and on Saturday, and then the Sunday night sermon prepared on Tuesday and Wednesday. This system enabled me always to preach without notes.

Preaching is as permanent as the need of men for the Word of God. Though the practice may become suspect, or the ability be vitiated, or the influence be eclipsed, preaching is the means ordained of God for the building of His church. In times of famine of the Word, unsung and unhonored in small fields and out-of-the-way places, faithful men of God are proclaiming the gospel and the revealed truth. Honored of God, if not of men, they are being used to build the church of Christ. Sooner or later, eras of great preaching return. They will continue until Jesus comes. Their presence, however, depends upon the institutions which train the men.

Preachers are educated in theological seminaries. These schools are the reservoirs of the church's preachers. Since great confusion exists among the seminaries on curriculum, philosophy and goals of theological education, this will be reflected in the future preachers. Many believe that the seminary courses should be relevant to all the practical demands of modern life, such as labor relations, welfare, political action, family problems, and urban redevelopment. If the curriculum seeks to prepare men in these practical fields, the time traditionally given to the great theological disciplines must be reduced or surrendered. No man can have training in all the areas of need which he will face upon entering the ministry. Far better is it to be trained in the great facts of linguistics, philosophy, history, theology, psychology and rhetoric, so that he has the principles to apply in the practical field. Many men are entering seminary with scientific or secular education because of a call during the university period. To give them practical courses without the core theological disciplines is to equip them for very limited service. There is a timelessness about true theological education which prepares a preacher to find the area of his power and influence.

Let those who come to seminary and who will ultimately preach be sure that God has called them to preach. [47] Jesus said, "The Spirit of the Lord is upon me, because he hath anointed me to preach . . . ." [48] Let the theological student have such a call. Let him seek piety through spiritual discipline which will make his future career, giving the heartthrob of intimacy with God. Let him master the theological disciplines prerequisite to sermon preparation by intellectual effort. Let him sense his Christian responsibility to social causes due to an awareness of evil and corruption. Let him humbly begin in a field to which the Holy Spirit leads by open doors, preaching wherever he can. Let the passion move him which moved the Baptist, Jesus, Paul and the preachers of the ages, and we will not need to be anxious concerning the availability nor ministry of great preaching in the days to come.

FOOTNOTES

1. "To be sure, there are no Henry Ward Beechers, Theodore Parkers, Phillips Brookses, Matthew Simpsons or George A. Gordons, towering above their preaching brethren, as heaven-kissing hills overshadow the lesser ranges. But a little lower than these Angels of Light there is today a shining company" (Edgar DeWitt Jones, *American Preachers of Today* (Indianapolis: Bobbs-Merrill, 1933], p. 11).

2. "Moreover in these thirty years the number of scholarly American preachers with a nationwide, interdenominational reputation has dropped from twenty or more to an indifferent number. And, what is much more tragic, in the average parish the will to preach—the joy, enthusiasm, and urgency of preaching—diminished in our generation until preaching becomes a monotonous and dreaded routine for some ministers and a dreaded ordeal for others" (Kyle Haselden, *The Urgency of Preaching* [New York: Harper & Row, 1963], p. 9).

3. Jones, p. 13.

4. Will Oursler, "The New Evangelism—Blessing or Blight," *The Christian Herald* (June, 1964).

5. Elton Trueblood, *The New Man for Our Time* (New York: Harper & Row, 1969), pp. 15-35.

6. A. Skevington Wood, *The Art of Preaching* (Grand Rapids: Zondervan, 1963), p. 7.

7. George A. Buttrick, *Jesus Came Preaching* (New York: Scribner, 1931), Preface, p. x. Cf. Wood, p. 36.

8. Jones, p. 13.

9. Charles Shelby Rooks, *Enoch Pond Lectures* (Bangor, Maine: Bangor Theological Seminary, 1971).

10. T. Harwood Pattison, *The History of Christian Preaching* (Philadelphia: American Baptist Pubn. Soc., 1903), pp. 63-72.

11. Ibid., pp. 125-30.

12. Roland Bainton, *Here I Stand* (New York: Abingdon-Cokesbury, 1950).

13. Edwin N. Hardy, *George Whitefield* (New York: American

Tract Soc., 1938). Cf. Arnold Lunn, *John Wesley* (New York: Dial, 1929).

14. John Pollock, *Billy Graham* (New York: McGraw-Hill, 1966).
15. Mt. 3:1.
16. Mt. 4:17.
17. Mt. 4:23.
18. Mt. 5, 6 and 7.
19. Mt. 13.
20. Mt. 25 and 26.
21. Mt. 23.
22. Mt. 10.
23. Mk. 16:15.
24. Mt. 28:18-20.
25. Ac. 2:15-36; 3:12-26.
26. Ac. 8:5.
27. Ac. 8:4; 11:19.
28. Ac. 4:8-12; 10:34-43.
29. 1 Pe. 1:12.
30. Ac. 26:16-18.
31. Gal. 1:11.
32. Gal. 1:8.
33. 1 Co. 15:1-3.
34. Ro. 15:20-24.
35. Eph. 4:11-13.
36. 2 Ti. 4:2.
37. 1 Co. 1:21. See vv. 18-25.
38. Batsell Barrett Baxter, *The Heart of the Yale Lectures* (New York: Macmillan, 1950), pp. 210-16.
39. Phillips Brooks, *Lectures on Preaching* (New York: Dutton, 1898), pp. 129-30.
40. Paul Scherer, *For We Have the Treasure* (New York: Harper, 1944), p. 165.
41. Trueblood, p. 81.

42. Ibid. p. 113.

43. Baxter, p. 211.

44. 1 Co. 15:1-4.

45. Charles Edward Macartney, *Sermons from Life* (Nashville: Abingdon-Cokesbury, 1933).

46. E. M. Bounds, *The Preacher and Prayer* (Chicago: Christian Witness, 1907).

47. 1 Co. 9:16; Wood, p. 19.

48. Lk. 4:18.

THEOLOGY AND CULTURE

H. D. MC DONALD

The term *culture* is an ambiguous one. It has been made to yield a variety of meanings, some of which appear to be contradictory. Sociologists and theologians give their own significance to the word according to their own presuppositions; among each of these groups there are differences concerning what is to be understood by the concept which make for a virtual reversal of connotations. [1] Yet no man can successfully escape from the reality which the term so vaguely seems to express.

The word itself comes from the Latin *cultura,* meaning the act of tilling the soil to prepare it for growing crops. More particularly, it denotes that studied attention to cultivation by which improvements and new forms of bacilli are produced. From this primary agricultural and horticultural usage the term comes to designate the man of good taste who cultivates the desirable values of truth, goodness and beauty. Such a man is indeed the cultured man.

This "essentially aristocratic Greek understanding of the

term," as Henry B. Clark states, was introduced into Western thought by Kant, following the earlier suggestion of Herder.[2] Then it was imported into North America by Lister B. Ward and contrasted with the concept *civilization*. In this context, culture was regarded as the control of the natural order by men of artistic and scientific ability in distinction from civilization which connotes the effort to subject man's natural instincts in general by political and moral laws. This restricted significance of the term *culture* continues, finding popular and philosophical expression. To most people, the cultured man still is regarded as the person who is refined, enlightened and civilized, and especially appreciative of the artistic and the aesthetic.

Sociologists, however, have on the whole tended to give a wider and more passive meaning to the concept, some continuing to distinguish between culture and civilization, and others almost equating the two. Thus Robert MacIver and Jacob Burckhardt, to name but two, conceive of a people's culture as their nonmaterial purposes, values and goals in contrast with their state of civilization which marks the standard of their scientific and material achievements. On the other hand, Carl Brinkmann and Bronislaw Malinowski, for example, are unable to find any special features which could be said to differentiate the one word from the other. This view of culture is in general elaborated by T. S. Eliot who remarks that "culture is doubled by the word *civilization.*"[3] Yet Eliot would admit some sort of distinction between the two.[4]

The theologian H. Richard Niebuhr prefers the term *culture* to be identified with civilization. It signifies, he declares, "that total process of human activity and that total result of that activity to which now the name *culture,* now the name *civilization* is applied in common speech."[5] Maintaining that culture is a "reality *sui generis,*" Niebuhr conceives it to be what the New Testament writers sometimes had in mind when they spoke of "the world."

Some of the characteristic features of culture which he suggests seem to be unnecessarily tautologous. Granted that it is correct to refer to culture as that "artificial, secondary environment which man superimposes upon the world," it is quite evidently a social activity and a human achievement. The culture of a people certainly arises out of their concern for values, and for those values which are held to be "good," worthwhile realizing and conserving.[6] However, Niebuhr is right in giving attention to that aspect of a people's culture as "the temporal and material realization of values." But this must not be taken to mean that cultural achievement is merely concerned with that which gives material and temporal satisfaction. There are always those within any society who are aware that man is not just a somatic creature, for certain intangible and immaterial realities can only become part of a cultural heritage by being embodied. Thus "culture in all its aspects—ideological, sociological, and technological—serves man's inner, spiritual needs as well as his outer, material needs."[7] A people's culture will, then, include its literature, philosophy, art, music, laws and whatever derives from and enters into social life. Consequently, culture is a social phenomenon. This fact reveals its pluralistic nature.[8] For, in any society, dominant sectional interests arise from different views of what is essential, valuable and worthy. Thus the perpetual task confronting every civilization is to attempt to conserve those various goods and to mediate between the often conflicting efforts of the manifold groups within it so that the best that all have to give may find a place in the cultural complex.

To summarize, then, by a people's culture we mean that wider significance of the term which refers to the climate of opinion, and network of ideas and values which form the social environment within which each individual lives his life. It includes, as Eliot says, "all the characteristic activities and interests of a people."[9] Man creates his own environment because he is human and has the ability to feel, think and act. In the physical and organic areas of existence, as M. K. Opler observes, culture is irrelevant. It is only when we cross the line of human experience that it becomes significant. For "man is unique: he is the only living being that has a culture."[10]

In the light, then, of what has been contended regarding culture, the question which immediately forces itself upon the Christian is this: What should be my relation, as one who seeks to live under the lordship of Christ, to the culture in which I find myself? Historical answers given to this question depend largely on whether faith is conceived of as opposed to, equal with, or related to culture.

Our procedure here is first to seek, with an eye on Niebuhr's treatment, some of these attitudes and to give a constructive statement. Then we discuss the secular outlook of modern culture and the humanist contention that a man's life can find complete fulfillment therein. A brief concluding note is added on how Christian theology and faith fare in such a context.

Niebuhr declares that "in his single-minded direction towards God, Christ leads men away from the temporality and pluralism of culture. In its concern for the conservation of the many values of the past, culture rejects the Christ who bids men to rely on grace."[11] While Niebuhr seems to be taking his stance among those who advocate the repudiation of culture, this is not finally true in his case. Throughout history, however, there have been those, such as Tertullian in the early age of the church, and Tolstoy in more recent times, as well as numerous Christian groups, who have taken up the Christ-against-culture position. The viewpoint has attractions, especially if culture is fully equated with "the world," from which the people of God are regarded as delivered to become citizens of another kingdom not of this realm. However, the very fact of this withdrawal and separation from the life of society has had unexpected and far-reaching consequences for culture. In this way the necessary distinction has been kept alive between the things that belong to Caesar and the things that belong to God. And, by a strange irony, men and movements which have been foremost in repudiating culture have had the strongest influence upon its formation and shaping.

True, this influence may have been unintentional, but it has been nonetheless decisive. Perhaps the second-century Christians rarely dreamed of social reform, but they did prepare the way for the social triumph of the church and the conversion of the pagan world into a Christian civilization. Perhaps monasticism was inspired merely by the spirit of withdrawal from the worldly, but it became the greatest conserver and transmitter of culture. Perhaps, also, the many Protestant sectarians were driven by an understandable desire to get away from a system which, however much it labeled itself "Christian," was too much of this world, yet from them sprang the demand for liberty of thought and the many social reforms which have become part of the cultural context of modern life.

A specific instance of the religious rejection of culture can be seen in the Puritan repudiation of art. This revolt is certainly understandable even if it was extreme, for in "Cultural Catholicism" all human endeavor was blessed and its churches overstocked with the works of men's hands in rituals, images and pictures. However, even if, as Dorner suggests, the more spiritual a religion the less will it be encumbered by forms of art, it still was an excessive rejection of the artistic as an expression of Christian faith. In repudiating the aesthetic, Puritanism virtually canonized the ugly; it almost hallowed the hideous and sanctified the secular. The fact is, however, the time came when the Puritan attitude was taken in all seriousness by the nonreligious person, and when art, following the lead of science and morality, asserted its autonomy, the cry went forth which is still ringing in our ears: "Art for art's sake!" [12]

Such facts serve to bring to the fore the seemingly inevitable tension between faith and culture whenever an individual or group seeks to live out life under the absolute lordship of Christ. As Niebuhr indeed contends, the relationship of the authority of Jesus Christ to the authority of culture is of such a nature that every Christian must often feel himself claimed by the Lord to reject the world: the pluralism and temporality of its culture, the makeshift compromises of its many interests, and the hypnotic obsession with the love of life and the fear of death.

Yet, however necessary the movement of withdrawal and renunciation, the Christ-against-culture answer does not really work. There is always the difficulty of separating ourselves from the world of culture around us and from the very needs within us which give rise to it. The position can easily lead to that of a sharp dualism which abandons the world to the devil, leaving no room for any point of contact between the two realms. A consequence of the view would even be to compromise that very lordship of Christ of which so much is made. For this is the very world of which Christ is the creative voice and the sustaining power, and over its history He presides and is Himself its goal. The earth is the Lord's and the fullness thereof, the whole world and they that dwell therein. This is surely God's world; it does not do justice to the full sweep of Christian theology to begin at the second clause of the so-called Apostles' Creed and to neglect the first. What is needed for a fully assured Christian faith is a clear understanding of the biblical doctrine of creation; for, as Emil Brunner rightly contends, to understand what the Bible means by creation is to understand the whole Bible and the Christian religion. [13] Thus the repudiation of culture easily involves a suspicion of nature and of the God of nature.

On the other extreme stand those who virtually merge Christianity with culture. The tension between social laws and the faith of the gospel, between human effort and divine grace, between world and church, is no longer felt. In this context Christ is conceived of as little more than the inspirer of social action and the educator of human life. The so-called "Cultural Protestantism," of which Kant was the philosophical spokesman and Schleiermacher the theological precursor, was marked by the way it accomodated Christ to culture. In America the "social gospel" of Rauschenbush, and in Great Britain the "Christian socialism" of F. D. Maurice were but phases of the same general outlook.[14] It would take us too far afield to give any account of their views. Suffice it to say that for Maurice the church and state were regarded virtually as two sides of the one coin. Both, he contended in his "Lectures on National Education" and elsewhere, promote the same end and both alike are religious societies. God, he asserted, has "ordained an eternal connection between the law, which is embodied in the state, and the religious life-giving principle, which is embodied in the church."[15] To this view the "earlier William Temple" confessed to be committed. Until the outbreak of the Second World War he had regarded the church as the channel and vehicle of the kingdom of God which was destined to father all national groups within itself, thus "making Christianity coextensive with the world."[16] He considered the principles of secular progress and the divine revelation of Christ to be identical.[17] However, writing just ten months before his death, Temple recalled, almost with astonishment if not quite with shame, his early optimistic illusion about the worldwide progress of Christian principles and ideals. He had been trained under and been influenced by those theologians who supposed it to be their task to show that Christianity makes sense of the world. "I was still talking like that," he confessed, "when Hitler became Chancellor of the German Reich."[18] The outbreak of the Second World War shattered for Temple, and the others who still dared to call themselves believers,[19] this rosy view of inevitable progress and of Christianity as "the clue to a universal synthesis." But what brought the "later Temple" to a new understanding of the relation between church and civilization, between the gospel and culture, was his discovery of the biblical doctrine of sin, touched off by his growing realistic awareness of the havoc which man's evil had let loose upon the earth, and by his fuller appreciation of the New Testament insistence upon redemption as the only sure source of world transformation. [20]

There need be no grudging to the liberal Christianity of the Christ-of-culture advocates of whatever values they found in the gospel. It was certainly a merit to lift Christianity out of all narrow exclusivism and to make it applicable to the whole world and the whole man. The danger was in its tendency to make the whole world, the only world; and the physical and / or intellectual man, the whole man. But it did score in that it gave Christianity a contemporary social relevance, imparting to it an impetus toward needed social reform. But its harmartological concept, its philosophical presupposition, and its Christological doctrine were too weak to bear the superstructure. [21] Sin was conceived generally as the survival of animal instincts destined to die out as man became fully human; progress was proclaimed as inevitable as the law of nature; and Christ was set forth as little more than an ideal figure, the goal of the evolutionary process who, as the supreme teacher of the good life, presented mankind with the blueprint of the highest possible social culture. It is easy, of course, in the hindsight of history to see how naïve and nebulous were such ideas.

But the tragedy of the situation was that such notions were proclaimed as new "insights" into the meaning of the Christian gospel which elevated their advocates to the high platform of intellectual superiority from which they looked upon the orthodox Christian as a mere traditionalist and obscurantist. Here, however, is a fact that should speak to the present-day *illumaniti* who proclaim their own latest "insights" under the vogue of the most recent scientific discoveries as the one "relevant" understanding of the Christian message. Too often, as history has shown, that which is fashionable today becomes outmoded tomorrow, so quickly does the up-to-date become the out-of-date.

The resolution of the Christ-culture tension by the either-or method has not commended itself as finally satisfactory. Culture cannot be rightly regarded as a frivolous obstruction of the spiritual life, nor can religion be understood as a natural pursuit for human well-being touched by emotion. As a consequence, other positions have been taken which refuse either to repudiate culture in the interests of Christ or to identify Christ with the interests of culture in any absolute sense. Such views seek neither to reject the *fact* of human culture nor to minimize the blackness of human sinfulness. There is a certain dualism between grace and works, between gospel and world, between Christ and culture, which remains to a greater or lesser extent, depending on whether culture is conceived of as the evidence of human depravity or as the product of human ability.

The difficulty in seeking to separate the possibilities here is that the various theses are not clean-cut. Teachers who set forth apparently conflicting views often stand within the same Christian tradition, while ideas which they develop constantly overlap and intertwine. Nevertheless, three broad distinctions can be made which we will designate as the totalist, the oppositionalist, and the leavenist.

The first is referred to as totalist because its characteristic note is the assertion that culture and Christianity, while retaining their separate spheres of reference, are yet one under God and church. Christ, in this view, is proclaimed as both Logos and Lord and is intimately related to the Father who is both Creator and Redeemer. Human culture, however, is not regarded as sinful in itself, while at the same time it is not denied that man is a sinner. But there is a law of social life and a way of social living (a general ethic, in fact) which come in the form of imperatives basic to the structure of any adequate culture and which can be traced back to an ultimate divine authority. The disjunction in the form of an either-or—either Christian faith or human culture—no longer holds. It is a case of both-and, yet neither can exist apart from God.

Niebuhr considers Clement of Alexandria, at a time when the church was outlawed, as the precursor of this view. Clement certainly would not have thought of even the prevailing culture of his day as being a form of man's rebellion against God. He could not have conceived of there being any ultimate disharmony between Athens and Jerusalem. In the knowledge of Greek philosophy, which was at the time the surest mark of a cultured man, Clement took special delight. He saw Plato as an ally of Paul, despite the fact that "the Christian ethics and etiquette" of his book, *The Instructor,* "correspond to the content of Stoic handbooks of morality current at the time."[22]

But Thomas Aquinas must be accorded the prize as the most thorough spokesman of the totalist view. Limited space prevents any meaningful account of the way he "combined without confusing philosophy and theology, state and church, civic and Christian virtues, natural and divine laws, Christ and culture."[23] It was a magnificent attempt to draw together all these realities into one cathedrallike structure under the God of the temple. Aquinas, however, did not seek for culture a position of equality with faith. To him, culture referred to life now present, whereas faith has reference to the future. Yet, within its own sphere, culture is not to be despised, for it is the discovery of man's God-given reason of the eternal and divine principles of human existence and morality. Over and above these, there is the law of Christ which the natural man does not fully know and cannot fully obey without super-natural grace. This grace does not destroy but perfects nature. For Aquinas, "grace" is not opposed to "nature." It comes as a *donum super-additum* to the native power of man. With him the medieval maxim "Naturam non tollit gratia sed perficit" finds its supreme advocate.[24]

The merits of Aquinas' position can be seen at once. The clearest emphasis is given to the lordship of God as at once Creator and Redeemer. The case is well made for a general ethic, for the necessity for every man to do that which is right and just. This is the very law of the universe. Never-theless, there are problems. The view that sees Christianity as almost a higher law could easily lead to a deistic un-derstanding which regards it as the mere republication of the one eternal law of right conduct. To place natural law in brackets with the supernatural, culture with grace, however lower in the scale the former may be thought to be, is to leave the way open for the idea that there is merit in the fulfillment of law and thus to compromise the biblical conception of grace. "Grace is not," we have declared elsewhere, "the mere addition to man's best endeavours. The Cross is not God's method of toning and tuning up the music of man's natural life. Christ, the very grace of God incarnate, did not come to supplement man at his best, but to redeem man at his worst. In the end it is not cheer that we need but salvation, not help but rescue, not a stimulus but a change, not tonics but life."[25]

The oppositionalist thesis deepens the divide between culture and Christ by placing the emphasis upon God's relation to man rather than on His relation to the world. In this context, culture takes on a different aspect. Here the question about the worth and value of culture is no longer put by man but by God. It is consequently viewed as the outworking of man's depravity rather than the evidence of his superiority; to fulfill its demands as one must, is no cause for boasting. Culture and Christ stand therefore in a position of contrast and conflict. Cultured man is no less sinful, and be he ever so cultured he is not self-sufficient. Man "come of age" is still of "this age"; of himself he can never make for himself the "age of the kingdom of God." Indeed, at this point his very culture breaks into idolatry. Thwarted in his efforts to make himself godlike and divine by means of his culture, he turns to things which he can control and create, to live as a god without God. "The creative power of the human spirit craved after pure creation—jealous, as it were, of God, who was tactless enough to create before us."[26] Thus does man seek in science, in art, in morality—and even in religion, Barth and Bonhoeffer would add—to find satisfaction for his own cultural creations. [27] "If man is made for God, the absence of God in his life leaves a tremendous vacuum. This is apt to be fulfilled by disproportitate developments of other interest and in a predominantly secular age, disorders of this kind also may wreck havoc in the affairs of men and society."[28] The higher pursuits which should be higher immediacies take the place of the highest realities, and in this way the most worthy aspects of human culture become idolatrous.

Luther, perhaps, is the best spokesman of this opposition between Christ and culture, as is expounded in his idea of the "two kingdoms." He saw the created kingdom as sold to sin and under the bondage of corruption. Such a kingdom can only be held in check by the restraints of law and justice. Consequently, Luther believed the state to be God's instrument for keeping man's evil within bounds. "Every statement made by Luther on civic and social life," says Heinrich Bornkamm, "stems from the firm conviction that a corrupt world can be saved only by reason and force."[29] The state, the law, and community life he regarded as having their own sovereignty and sanction, and no longer subject to ecclesiastical laws.

Yet, although the two realms are so divided, they are still

related in Luther's thinking. Four volumes titled *The Christian in Society* are allotted to Luther's discussions on this subject in a recent American edition of the Reformer's works.[30] Here Luther makes clear that there is a duty to the society in which one lives. He has, therefore, what has been called "an Evangelical theology of society" in the sense that while "the two kingdoms must always be properly distinguished," they must "never be separated in secularism or equated in clericalism."[31] The Christian will not despise culture, however; he will approach it as a man redeemed and seek it even for its own sake, but under God. Luther can, therefore, confess to a liking for music as being, next to theology, God's greatest gift to men. He will seek, too, as a Christian, to do something by way of curing the ills of society, for believers alone are best qualified to do so. It is only those who are possessed by the love of God which has appeared in the world in Christ who have the divine dynamic to accomplish something of lasting worth for society.

Luther's position on culture, with an existential flavor, is expounded with their own peculiar emphasis by Kierkegaard in *Attack on Christendom,* by Niebuhr in *The Nature and Destiny of Man,* and by Brunner in *Christianity and Civilization.* Brunner sees the social order as secular, sinful and satanic. He conceives of the whole of human culture as being in marked opposition to the creative purpose of God, and contends, quite bluntly, that the state represents man's sinfulness on a large scale. The state can only exist by compulsion, and compulsion is contradictory to the divine law of love.[32] Brunner, therefore, regards the gospel of God as standing in judgment of civilization and culture. Indeed, as J. C. Bennett contends, Brunner takes a static view of the world order. He sees the whole human situation as so controlled by sin that a radical reconstruction of society is out of the question. But there is yet a glimmer of hope in his most gloomy pictures since, as Bennett contends, there are always two Brunners in every book.

251

Niebuhr gives more prominence to that aspect which appears to be absent in Brunner, and consequently he has a more balanced view of the relation between Christ and culture. He is no less insistent than Brunner upon the radical sinfulness of all human institutions, yet he allows a place for the operation of love with justice. He states, for example, that all the structures of justice do in fact presuppose the sinfulness of man, and that all are partly systems of restraint which prevent the conflict of wills and interests from resulting in a consistent anarchy. But he goes on to insist that there are mechanisms by which men fulfill their obligations to their fellowmen, beyond the possibilities offered in direct and personal relationships. The kingdom of God and the demands of love are consequently relevant to every political system and impinge upon every situation in which the self seeks to come to terms with the claims of other life. [33]

There is a good deal to be said in favor of this approach. Niebuhr, while allowing for the reality of human sinfulness, does not release us from our human responsibilities and from the need to preserve human culture. For, as Berdyaev remarks, to return to the One is not to turn away from the many.

The leavenist view takes the duality of Christ and culture, of church and state, as still real, but would contend for the ennobeling influence of the former on the latter. This is, perhaps, the historic view of the relationship which began in the early days of the postapostolic church and came to focus in Augustine. C. N. Cochrane has shown how pagan culture underwent a radical transformation under the impact of Christian trinitarian thinking throughout the period from Augustus to Augustine. [34] The driving concept of this regeneration of human culture reached a climax in the classical statement of the view in Augustine's *City of God.* Augustine had a strong conception of human sinfulness, one of the results of which he saw to be the disruption of human society.[35] But he knew from his own experience, and proclaimed with infinite passion, that for the one whose perverted and corrupt nature was healed and redeemed, human culture and convention can be used both for the advantage of the renewed life and for the glory of God. The man in Christ could rejoice in God's creation and serve all His creatures in the spirit of divine love.

In like manner, Calvin, as an authentic Augustinian, viewed the relationship between Christ and culture. He, too, was deeply aware of the profound consequences of man's sin. But he did not write off the world as altogether outside the leavening influences of the Christian message. His experiment in Geneva suggests, rather, that he considered it possible to Christianize a community by permeating it with Christian principles and ideals. In this regard it is legitimate to speak, as Troeltsch does, of Calvinism as "Christian socialism." And it is so in the sense that it sought to mold in a corporate way the whole life in the state and society, in the family and in the economic sphere, in public and in private, to accord with the principles of the Christian gospel. [36]

The "later Temple," having abandoned his earlier idealistic dream of incorporating all cultures into one Christian society, came to regard the church as the leaven within society. But he continued to contend strongly for the right of the church to influence society and he argued for love as the regulating principle of human relationships. [37] Here, perhaps, was a relic of his earlier idealism. It is doubtful, however, whether the leavening of social life can be attained so easily and be made to work so smoothly as Temple seemed to think, in a society where sin remains unmasked, unfaced and unforgiven.

This view of the relationship between the Christian gospel and culture, in which the former is regarded as the leavening influence in the latter, appears as a one-way relationship. But there are those who prefer to see a two-way commerce between them. Accordingly, as William Horosz contends, "The culture is free to recast its religion; and the religion is free to transform the culture in which it operates." [38] There can be no doubt, as the history of Christian thought shows clearly, that not only are essential Christian doctrines cast in the mold of the prevailing culture, but that they often have to be interpreted in the light of it. Does not Anselm's doctrine of sin, as a robbing of God of the honor due to Him, for example, reflect a period when chivalry manifested itself in the romance of knight-errantry and the high adventures of the Crusades?[39] It was a time, when as H. T. Buckle says, "Chivalry was to manners what feudalism was to politics,"[40] and when to seek satisfaction when one's honor was questioned or despoiled was itself a matter of honor.

How far the gospel can be reinterpreted in the terms of the cultural vogue, without losing its distinctive Christian message and meaning, is always an urgent issue. It is perilously easy for the Christian preacher, and more particularly for the Christian theologian, to be found uttering the shibboleths of the hour under the delusion that they are making the eternal gospel cogent for contemporary man. It seems that Paul Tillich comes near to this folly—so close, in fact, that it might be argued that he should be put among the Christ-of-culture advocates. Yet, to do him justice, Tillich does distinguish between religion and the cultural forms in which it actualized itself. He does regard the church as standing over against culture and as being, in the exercise of its prophetic role, "the guardian who reveals dynamic structures in society and undercuts their demonic power by revealing them."[41] At the same time Tillich can draw both religion and culture into closer relationship. He affirms, therefore, that "religion as ultimate concern is the meaning-giving substance of culture, and culture is the totality of forms in which the basic concern of religion expresses itself. In abbreviation: religion is the substance of culture, culture is the form of religion. Such a consideration definitely prevents the establishment of a dualism of religion and culture." [42]

In whatever way the relation between the faith of the gospel and the culture of the day is understood, one fact stands secure: the community of the redeemed people of God is within human society as its preserving flavor and its illuminating factor. For whatever the foibles and futilities of the church of the living Christ, it remains the salt of the earth and the light of the world. Without it culture would corrupt and society would stagnate. But salt attacks and light attacts. There must be some participation between the redeemed life and the social structure, between the church and the wider realm of mankind. But the method and the measure of this involvement remain the ever present and ever pressing question for Christian personal and social ethics.

At this point let us look at the second part of our study: the secular outlook of modern culture, and the humanist contention that man can find in it complete fulfillment of all his needs.

First, let us begin by contrasting the cultural context of the world outside the environs of Judaism, which had provided the first preachers of the Christian gospel with the immediate point of contact, with our contemporary world in which the same saving message must be proclaimed. It is always necessary to remember that "cultures change with time and therefore always have histories." [43]

In broadest terms it may be said that the general cultural outlook of the earliest centuries of the Christian era was spiritualistic, universalistic and rationalistic. Today it is almost the opposite of these, for the *Weltanschauung* in which modern life is cast is characteristically naturalistic, individualistic and empirical. This is not, of course, an exact description of the contrast between the cultural context of the first era of the Christian church and the present. At the same time, when brought within the narrower setting of a doctrine of man, the contrast between the basic anthropological approach of the two periods is certainly revealing. In an age when the spiritual world was thought of as more "real" than the material, it was easy to regard man as a sort of celestial being temporarily resident in flesh. For the modern, to whom the idea of another world is at best problematic and at worst superstitious, the notion of man as more than a product of natural forces has become virtually impossible to conceive and very difficult to accept. The cultural context of contemporary Western civilization can, then, be broadly designated "humanistic." And it is so, precisely because it is man-in-the-world that is conceived to be the sanction and the summit of the total natural process. It is, therefore, from this anthropological perspective that the cultural context of the early period of the church's existence and that of the present stands out the most strikingly.

This fact can best be illustrated by reference to ancient gnosticism and contemporary humanism. In the early days of the church, gnosticism presented itself as a serious rival to the faith of the gospel. Today humanism is proclaimed as the only live option for modern man. Gnosticism flourished in a period when the present world was less actual than was the supermundane realm of spiritual realities. It was therefore spiritualistic in its approach and expressed itself as a sort of theosophy. It sought to find a place for the Christian faith within its system by divorcing it from its historic foundations. It cast out that which it could not assimilate and presented itself as an adequate gospel for spiritual beings.

But whereas gnosticism approached from the spiritualistic side and found the floating ideas of its day congenial for its constructions, today humanism, the opposite view, claims to provide man with the sole and sufficient philosophy for living. Contemporary culture is shot through with this humanistic spirit. In a period when the spiritual world has receded far from the thinking of men and when empiricism dominates with its basic philosophy that the real is what is observable, and its epistemological dictum that the true is what is verifiable by the senses, it seems difficult for modern man to acknowledge the reality of anything other than the present scene. Thus it is easy for humanism to present itself as the cultural context of an age in which man is regarded as the measure of all things. And has not science made him a veritable god with the powers to create new things to meet his developing needs?[44] The humanist account expresses in its own grandiose form the contemporary outlook. To be sure, some of its more devout advocates have incorporated what they could of the Christian ethic into its system and its statements, but only after divorcing it from its basic doctrinal setting. If, then, the cultural activity of man of the early centuries was conceived of as that of man in necessary dependence upon God, that of modern man is conceived of as man in final dependence upon himself.

It may be worthwhile to interject at this point a remark that should make humanists think again. Gnosticism had conceived of man so spiritualistically that it had no earthly answers to the questions of his presence and need in his terrestrial existence. By its airy view of human nature it failed to take seriously man's total being and consequently only managed to register a passing success. But humanism comes with a view equally one-sided and half-baked. It conceives of man so naturalistically that it has no satisfactory answer to the recurring questions arising from his feeling and need for a more-than-earthly context. If, then, gnosticism failed because it sought to detach man's feet from the solid earth, will not humanism be proved inadequate by its effort to pluck man's heart from the eternities? Gnosticism saw man as all spirit but could give no convincing account of his earthliness. Humanism

257

conceives of man as all earthliness but can give no adequate explanation of his awareness of his otherness. The fact of the matter is, of course, that man is neither a chip of divinity nor a complex of animality. He is both of the ground and of God, a combination of dust and deity. Man is neither an angel or an ape. He cannot be treated as the former and we dare not treat him as the latter.

Our concern here is to underscore the fact of the humanistic outlook of contemporary culture. David L. Edwards describes the twentieth century as the age of secularization. The term *secular,* he recalls, was coined by George Jacob Holyoake, who died in 1906 as an ardent and arrogant unbeliever who had once spent six months in jail for blasphemy. The *Oxford English Dictionary* says that it was his "doctrine that morality should be based on regard to the well-being of mankind in the present life, to the exclusion of all considerations drawn from belief in God or a future life." That such a doctrine is atheistic is obvious, but the same ideas "become established and respectable" under the term *humanism.* Although Edwards gives the term *secularization* a connotation which holds a less hardened attitude toward religion than that which he apparently believes belongs to humanism, he can still declare that "the achievement of our time—most dramatic in Russian and Chinese Communism's liberation of the peasants, but most powerful in the growth of American capitalism—has been the extension of humanism to include humanity." He can therefore state quite emphatically, "This is, therefore, a time of *humanism."* [45]

When, however, we search for a definition of *humanism* we find ourselves at a loss, for the term has been stretched to cover a large variety of sometimes conflicting views. *Humanism* is what Ralph Barton Perry calls a very versatile word. At the same time it is impossible to dispense with it, as there is no other term which so readily characterizes that which we have contended is the broad outlook of recent and contemporary thought. Of course, there have always been humanists, but it is only in modern times that humanist ideas have permeated the social milieu so decisively as to become its distinguishing feature.

The nineteenth century, according to Henri de Lubac, witnessed the rise of three types of humanism: the Nietzschean, the Comtean, and the Marxist. Michele Federico Sciacca refers to Nietzsche as the mystic of both humanism and atheism, even though his humanistic doctrine is self-refuting by reason of the fact that he admitted that it could only be attained beyond the human.[46] Comte, in his positivism, regarded the present world as the only reality. By translating worship of God into service of man, he succeeded, as Beatrice Webb says, in turning around his head to worship his own tail. Marxian Communism posits a humanism so total as to leave no room for God. Believing religion to be a human invention, Marx declared that "the more that man posits in God, the less he retains for himself."[47] Here, then, is the fundamental principle of the humanist doctrine, which, whatever the differences between these three systems, can be singled out as the rejection of God in the interests of man.[48] And while these systems are avowedly atheistic in theory and practice, general European and American humanism is atheistic in practice in that the interests of man have led to a neglect of God. The modern "permissive" society can be regarded as one of the most significant and sinister expressions of this demand for the uninhibited "rights" of man without God. S. E. Morison, surveying the American scene, says, "After three centuries in which Christian morals had been maintained by law, religion, and custom, 'permissiveness' has conquered St. Augustine and John Milton, becoming a dominant principle in education and sexual relations."[49]

Specific definitions of humanism tend to fall on the philosophical or the moral side. Schiller, for example, says that humanism is really in itself the simplest of philosophical

259

standpoints. It is merely the perception that the philosophical problem concerns human beings striving to comprehend the world of human experience by the resources of the human mind. The intention of this, and like statements, is to cut the reality of faith out of reckoning. On the other side are those who place the emphasis on man as the object of the humanist concern. In this sense humanism may be regarded as an outright reinterpretation of the concept *God* in terms of humanity. Man, it is held, is the highest type of known existent; therefore, if there is any proper object of religious devotion and real "god," it can only be mankind considered in its noblest aspirations and capacities, together with nature, so far as it is expressed in and serviceable to humanity. Thus, whereas the philosophical emphasis intends to deny the existence of a spiritual realm, the moral emphasis seeks to secularize religious worship.

Evidently, then, humanism can be best understood by its denials and its affirmations. It denies the existence of anything other than the natural. There is no spiritual realm, no other-world reality, no personal God and, obviously, no life beyond the grave. It affirms that man is explicable in purely earthly terms; that "conscience in human beings, the sense of right and wrong, and the insistent call of one's better, more idealistic, more social-minded self, is a social product."[50] Humanism places man in the center, and puts the human existent on the temple throne.[51] Humanism is truly, as Berdyaev contends, an anthropology masquerading as a religion.

Professor Corliss Lamont, the "archdruid"—because "archbishop" might be considered too much of a religious term—of the American Humanist Association, regards humanism as a philosophy of joyous service for the greatest good of humanity in this natural world according to the methods of reason and democracy. And he sets out ten particulars which he considers essential declarations of a humanist creed. They may be called the "ten points" of humanism and reduced as follows:

1. Humanism is a naturalistic metaphysic which excludes all forms of the supernatural as a myth.

2. Humanism regards man as an evolutionary product who exists in an inseparable union of body and brain; this means that after the dissolution of death there can be no conscious survival.

3. Humanists conceive of man as possessing the power and potentiality of solving his own problems by reliance upon reason and his use of science.

4. Humanists reject all theories of determinism and fatalism in the conviction that man is master of his own fate and is thus free to choose and act.

5. Humanists believe in a morality that bases all values on experiences and relationships in the present world.

6. Humanism teaches as an ethical ideal the self-adjustment of the individual to the development of society, to the welfare of which he should seek to contribute.

7. Humanists contend that the aesthetic experiences are open to all who may be taught to appreciate nature's loveliness and splendor.

8. Humanists hold out the promise of an eternity of peace and plenty in a "this-world" condition.

9. Humanism preaches that in its universe of bliss, man will be free to express himself through all areas of economic, political and cultural life.

10. Humanism claims to be a developing philosophy ready to discard any dogmas no longer open to scientific verification.[52]

All this, of course, is very impressive. But it is not, according to Kingsley Martin, utopian. For has not humanism, too, had its reformation? The old unreformed humanists may still persist in their optimistic dream of man as essentially reasonable and good, and of the brave new world

261

as being just around the corner. But the modern reformed humanist is less cocksure. The pressure of circumstances has led him to acknowledge that the world is hell-bent on its own destruction. Martin admits, "Men are more nationalistic, violent, and stupid than they thought they were. We control the earth and the air, but not the tiger, the ape and the donkey inside ourselves." It might be well to underscore that word *inside,* for He who knew what was in man, long since declared that from *within,* from man's inner being, come those things which defile a man and destroy human life.[53] But humanism has poorly learned that truth, even after its reformation.[54]

And does not the pleasant hope of a heaven on earth, when the tiger, the ape and the donkey shall have emerged from their inner sanctuary and bother man no more, still linger? The grim reality of events has not quenched, even among the enlightened humanists, the hope of making it in the end. In the end—but, how long? Martin, at least, has no immediate date for his earthly paradise. He surely believes that the humanist gospel can "still point the way to a better society and better human beings," but the fulfillment of the promise belongs to the far future. Humanism must "not make the mistake of promising unlimited improvement and uninterrupted progress."[55] For, after all, tigers are not easily tamed, apes are quite unpredictable, and donkeys are stubborn creatures.

With all this, then, is humanism a religion? Humanists themselves are not too sure. H. J. Blackham would prefer that it should not be so described. "To become a religion, as to become a philosophy, would be the death of humanism."[56] Above all, it must not become sectarian, he demands; but, alas, his counsel has come too late. For there are as many sects—and with less reason except for the perversity of human nature—of humanists as there are of Christians: existential, liberal, scientific, positivist, religious, secular, popular, to name a few. Indeed, humanists are as divided on dogma as are Christians, and, for all their profession, are highly intolerant of others bearing the same general label who do not sing to the same tune and hoist the same flag.

Renford Bambrough says that after he had joined a humanist group in Cambridge, he was compelled to subscribe to a student magazine published by the Rationalist Press Association. Finding himself in disagreement with the committee, he resigned, only to learn later that had he not done so, he would have been "expelled from the Heretics for heresy."[57] Humanism, Blackham contends, is "a way of life." But Julian Huxley does not relish this plainer diet of humanism; a blend with a savoring of religion is more to his taste,[58] yet, of course, not religion of the traditional Christian brand with its doctrine of a transcendent God and a redeeming Christ. "What the world needs," says Huxley, taking to himself the divine prerogative of omniscience, "is not merely a rational denial of the old but a religious affirmation of something new."[59] Of something new—as if there were anything!

It is not, however, our special purpose to develop a critique of humanism. Rather, it is to call attention to the fact that in theory and practice the humanist viewpoint is the pervading and persuasive element in our contemporary culture. We live, as Erich Fromm says, in a "humanoid" culture. And Christians have responded to it in a variety of ways. Space will only permit a passing reference. Broadly, there have been those who have taken the way of acceptance or the way of rejection, and among each group there are extremists and moderates.

The extreme "acceptationists" are those who seem to regard the humanist denials and affirmations as finally true and who seek to squeeze Christian theology into a secular framework.[60] The attempts made in this regard by Altizer, by Van Buren, and by Harvey Cox, are well known. For Altizer, God is dead. That, he insists, is the good news.[61]

Van Buren is quite sure that the Christian gospel can be proclaimed without allusion to the word *God*. Being a Christian in the modern world, he assures, is learning to live without the need of the God-hypothesis. "A Christian who is himself a secular man may understand the Gospel in a secular way by seeing it as an expression of a historical perspective."[62] The upshot of Harvey Cox's thesis in *The Secular City* is to reduce Christianity to a secular vocabulary and to rid it of its supernatural elements. The Christian is one who lives openly toward his neighbor, for such a man, whatever his creed and need, is really being an authentic person and living after the fashion of the "religionless" Jesus of Nazareth. One must accept modern society for what it is and make no attempt to "religionize" it. For, as Cox sees it, secularization is liberation.[63]

These attempts are made to transfer the whole gospel of Christ into the concepts of the secular humanism of contemporary culture. In the transfer, however, it has ceased to be Christian; for, as Langdon B. Gilkey has pointed out in a review of Van Buren's book, the "logic" of the theological language which Van Buren uses is no longer the logic of the historic faith, but "of his own contemporary secular understanding of the gospel."[64] Besides, and more cogent, a secularized gospel is not the sufficient word for a secular world. The Christian is indeed called upon to serve the world, but precisely because it is the world that God loves and has acted in Christ to redeem. To serve man "in the whole range of our humanity" is right and good, but it is false to assume that to serve man in that extent—which in fact only One has done—is the same as the gospel of God.

The professed concern of the moderate acceptationists is with the problem of communicating the gospel to a secular world. Only in secular terms, it is contended, can the message of Christianity be made meaningful to modern man. This was, according to Bultmann, his purpose in demythologizing the New Testament.[65] Only by ridding it of what he supposed were its mythological setting and drapery could it find response in a scientifically orientated age. But the tragedy was, as the subsequent story demonstrates, that the gospel was lost in the process and robbed of all objective "factuality," language about God was turned into language about man, and talk about God's act in Christ was resolved into talk about one's subjective quest for authentic existence. Here, indeed, as T. R. Torrance says, is the supreme sin of man—of always identifying God with the depths of his own self-consciousness.[66] Yet there is this to be learned, at least, from the effort: that to speak about God to our day we must speak meaningfully. For the gospel needs always a contemporary voice, since Christ is ever a reality in the living present:

> For last year's words belong to last year's language
> And next year's words await another voice. [67]

The extreme repudiationists, either from a neo-Calvinist or a neo-Puritan perspective, would repudiate all humanism as sinful folly. The best endeavors of man are but evidences of his depravity; and all the works of his hands are marked and marred by his native sinfulness. [68] Without God, man is nothing. Without God, in words borrowed from W. B. Yeats,

> Things fall apart; the center
> Cannot hold.... [69]

This certainly is a necessary reminder for a humanistic culture in a day when evil is called good, when the iron in society has been replaced by brittle metal, and when the saving salt within culture has given place to sickly syrup.

If the extreme repudiationists see all culture as false, the moderates would regard it as inadequate. Here points of contact are sought with humanism, and an apologetic is worked out in an effort to show that humanism may be true in some of its affirmations, but is false in most of its denials. The main thrust of the moderate repudiationists is the contention that the chief error in humanism is just its fatal contentment with the human. And if humanism were indeed consistent with itself and true to the logic of its own presuppositions it would be driven beyond the human.

It is necessary, therefore, according to W. S. Urquhart, to seek a higher humanism which allows to man that which is beyond the human. For the inadequacy of all humanists lies in the break they make by their isolation of man "as belonging to time" from "his participation in eternity." Humanism encourages man to depend upon his own resources as adequate, but human power, which is believed to be unrestricted, soon assumes the position of a tyrant and thus destroys that very faith which it claims as its own supreme glory. By its failure to place the ladder by which it would have men ascend to the bar of heaven, humanism has given itself no secure hold. It is the verdict of psychology and history alike that ladders without some support in a meaningful cosmic reality sooner or later must come tumbling down. [70]

Charles Hartshorne contends that by refusing man the worship of God, humanism falls back into egoism and state worship. And he charges that humanists must be either too cautious or too busy to consider the possibility of a more-than-human; "too cautious to look beyond the obvious relations of man to his fellows for the essential values of life," or maybe, "too busy defending their position" not "to have regard to what is beyond the human scene." [71] Maritain believes that Christianity alone holds the true humanism. And he quotes a remark of Aristotle, that to offer man only what is human is to betray him. There is that element in man which calls for "something better than a purely human life." [72] Martin Buber contends that the Old Testament teachers proclaimed a right regard for man by dealing with every aspect of his being. "Biblical humanism," he declares, "is concerned with a concrete transformation of our total—and not alone our inner—lives." [73]

The Christian, then, in contemporary humanistic culture has something vital to communicate. He can point to the manger of Bethlehem as the standing reminder that there is nothing mean in the state of humanness. To take flesh was not a condition too lowly for the Son of God. Of our human ways, the incarnation makes clear, there is "nothing to be ashamed of but—sin."[74] And the cross on Golgotha provides for man a permanent resort to which, as sinner, he may come for healing and help, so that man may live in God's world as a being of eternity. Thus will the reality of Christ ever be for culture its norm and its touchstone; in the twin facts of the incarnation and the cross, humanism can find at once the best evidence of man's dignity and the only answer to man's depravity. A humanistic culture may produce good humans—good enough, that is, for human society. There is no need to deny that. But a divine Christ can make humans good—good enough, that is, for the kingdom of God. There is every reason to affirm that.

FOOTNOTES

1. "There are real problems of translation. . .take a word like 'culture'—an abstract, difficult word. The English don't like it at all and use it only with embarrassment. Other nations use it with different confidence" (Richard Hoggart, Assistant Director General of Culture for UNESCO, talking about the difficulties of administering a program involving 125 different states, in interview by Stacy Waddy, "The Uses of Culture," London *Guardian* [Aug. 31, 1970], p. 6).

2. Henry B. Clark, "Culture, Society and Community" in *A Dictionary of Christian Ethics*, ed. John MacQuarrie (Philadelphia: Westminster, 1967), p. 79.

3. T.S. Eliot, *Notes Towards the Definition of Culture* (London: Faber & Faber, 1947), p. 15.

4. "*Civilization* is often synonymous with *culture;* in reality, however, each has its own peculiar meaning. *Civilization* indicates a process and a state. As a *process*, it refers to the progress of a people towards a higher form of social life. As a *state*, it indicates an advanced condition of social life characterized by relative progress in the arts, sciences, customs, and government. *Culture* is a particular aspect of civilization, with particular reference to the intellectual achievements of a certain people or a particular period of its history" (Carlo Rizzo, "Civilization" in *Dictionary of Moral Theology*, ed. H. E. Cardinal Roberti and Pietro Palazzini [London: Burns & Oats, 1962], p. 236).

5. H. Richard Niebuhr, *Christ and Culture* (New York: Harper & Row, 1951), p. 32.

6. "A culture comes into being when the manifold interests and activities of a people can be made to derive their deepest significance from a common understanding of the meaning and value of human life" (E. D. Martin, *Liberty* as quoted in W. S. Urquhart, *Humanism and Christianity* [Edinburgh: T. & T. Clark, 1945], p. 49).

7. Leslie A. White, "The Evolution of Culture" in *Cultural and Social Anthropology*, ed. Peter B. Hammond (New York: Macmillan, 1964), p. 411.

8. Cf. Ralph L. Beal and Harry Hoijer, *An Introduction to Anthropology* (3d ed.; Los Angeles: U. California, 1965), chap. 9.

9. Ibid., p. 31.

10. White, p. 406.

11. Niebuhr, p. 39.

12. "This strange but predictable product of antinatural voluntarism found a ready ally in Greek philosophical naturalism, revived by the Renaissance. The theological critique of sanctifying grace, in association with the humanist rebellion against the so-called Augustinian denigrations of nature, produced a variety of humanistic theologies which stressed nature, human capacities, and human will, over against supernatural destiny, divine initiative, and divine grace" (Eugene R. Fairweather, "Christianity and the Supernatural" in *The New Theology No. 1*, ed. Martin E. Marty and Dean G. Peerman [New York: Macmillan, 1964], p. 251). See H. R. Rookmaaker, *Modern Art and the Death of a Culture* (London: Tyndale, 1970). According to Rookmaaker, modern art reflects the dying nature of contemporary culture.

13. Emil Brunner, *Our Faith* (London: Scribner, 1936), pp. 16 ff.

14. Cf. Robert T. Handy, ed., *The Social Gospel in America* (New York: Oxford, 1966), pp. 251-389.

15. F. D. Maurice, *The Kingdom of Christ* (London: Macmillan, 1883), p. 106; cf. *The Life and Letters of Frederick Denison Maurice Chiefly Told in His Letters*, ed. Frederick Maurice, 2 vols. (London: Macmillan, 1884), vol. 2, chaps. 1-3; F. Higham, *Frederick Denison Maurice* (London: SCM, 1947), chap. 5; W. Merlin Davies, *An Introduction to F. D. Maurice's Theology* (London: SCM, 1964), pp. 109 ff.; Alec R. Vidler, *F. D. Maurice and Company: Nineteenth Century Studies* (London: SCM, 1966), chap. 7.

16. *Mens Creatrix* (1917; reprint ed.; London: Macmillan, 1923), p. 346.

17. William Temple, *Church and Nation* (London: Macmillan, 1915), p. 14.

18. Temple, "What Christians Stand for in the Secular World," *The Christian News-Letter*, no. 198 (Dec. 29, 1943), p. 5.

19. Cf. C. E. M. Joad, *The Recovery of Belief* (London: Faber &

Faber, 1951), pp. 59 ff.

20. Temple, "Theology To-day," *Theology* 39, no. 233 (Nov., 1939): 329 ff.

21. Cf. Brunner, *The Mediator* (London: Lutterworth, 1934), chaps. 1-14.

22. Niebuhr, p. 125.

23. Ibid., p. 130.

24. The extreme totalist view is given effect in the "papalist" theory of the church as above state and culture, being, it is claimed, gifted by God with this sovereignty. This doctrine was first defined by Boniface VIII in 1302 in the bull "Unam Sanctum" and reaffirmed in 1925 by Pius IX in the encyclical "Quas Primas." "This is the ultimate goal of the Church in its centuries of drive to make divine the human world. . .such reflects the totalitarian spirit of the Church, which is an anti-democratic institution" (Vittorio Gorresio, "On the Balance Between Church and State," *Manchester Guardian* [Sept. 16, 1970]).

25. H. D. McDonald, *I and He* (London: Epworth, 1966), p. 83. Cf. P. T. Forsyth, *Positive Preaching and the Modern Mind* (London: Hodder & Stoughton, 1907), p. 56.

26. Jacques Maritain, *Challenges and Renewals*, ed. Joseph W. Evans and Leo R. Ward (Notre Dame, Ind.: U. Notre Dame, 1966), p. 37.

27. "Religion and morality are the greatest dangers to the understanding of divine grace" (Dietrich Bonhoeffer in his first sermon to his Barcelona congregation, cited by Eberhard Bethge, *Dietrich Bonhoeffer; Man of Vision, Man of Courage*, trans. Eric Mosbacher; ed. Edwin Robertson [London: Collins, 1970], p. 80).

28. H. D. Lewis, "Worship and Idolatry" in *Contemporary British Philosophy*, ed. H. D. Lewis (London: Geo. Allen & Unwin, 1956), p. 274.

29. Heinrich Bornkamm, *Luther's World of Thought*, trans. M. H. Bertram (St. Louis: Concordia, 1965), p. 268.

30. *Luther's Works*, ed. Helmut T. Lehman (Philadelphia: Fortress, 1962—), vols. 44-47.

31. Ibid., 44: xiii.

32. Cf. Brunner, *The Divine Imperative* (London: Lutterworth, 1949), pp. 444 ff.

33. Cf. Niebuhr, *The Nature and Destiny of Man*, 2 vols. (London: Nisbet, 1941), vol. 1, chaps. 7-10; vol. 2, chaps. 5-9.

34. C. N. Cochrane, *Christianity and Classical Culture: A Study in Thought and Action from Augustus to Augustine* (New York: Oxford U., 1957).

35. Cf. Augustine, *The City of God* 14: 15 ff.; Cochrane, chaps. 10-12; Peter Brown, *Augustine of Hippo: A Biography* (London: Faber & Faber, 1969), chaps. 25-28.

36. Cf. E. Troeltsch, *The Social Teaching of the Christian Churches*, trans. Olive Wyon, 2 vols. (London: Geo. Allen & Unwin, 1931), 2:622 ff.

37. Cf. Temple, *Citizen and Churchman* (London: Eyre & Spottiswoode, 1941), pp. 76 ff.; F. A. Iremonger, *William Temple: Archbishop of Canterbury: His Life and Letters* (London: Oxford U., 1948), chaps. 15 ff.; Robert Craig, *The Social Concern of William Temple* (London: Gollancz, 1963); and W. E. Baker, *William Temple and His Message* (London: Penguin Books, 1946).

38. William Horosz, "Religion and Culture in Modern Perspective" in *Religion in Philosophical and Cultural Perspective*, ed. J. Clayton Feaver and William Horosz (New York: D. Van Nostrand, 1967), p. 306.

39. Cf. Anselm, *Cur Deus Homo?* pp. xiii-xv.

40. Cf. H. T. Buckle, *History of Civilization*, 2 vols. (London: John Parker, 1857-61), vol. 2, chap. 2.

41. Paul Tillich, *Theology of Culture*, ed. Robert Kimball (New York: Oxford U., 1964), p. 50.

42. Ibid., p. 42.

43. George P. Murdock, "Changing Emphasis in Social Structure" in *Cultural and Social Anthropology*, p. 445.

44. "The central factor contributing towards man's newly creative stance towards the world. . .is the rise and triumph of modern science" (R. O. Johann, "Modern Atheism" in *New Themes in*

Christian Philosophy, ed. Ralph M. McInerny (Notre Dame, Ind.: [U. Notre Dame, 1968], p. 351).

45. Cf. David L. Edwards, *Religion and Culture* (London: Hodder & Stoughton, 1969), chap. 1. "The modern world more and more is coming to define itself as secular" (Marty and Peerman, "Introducing New Theology" in *The New Theology No. 1,* p. 12). "We have to face the growing secularization of life..." (Sergius Bulgakoff, "The Orthodox Church" in *Revelation,* ed. John Baillie and H. Martin [London: Faber, 1937], p. 175); cf. Harvey Cox, *The Secular City* (London: SCM, 1966), chap. 1.

46. Cf. Michele F. Sciacca, *Philosophical Trends in the Contemporary World,* trans. Attilio M. Salerino (Notre Dame, Ind.: U. Notre Dame, 1964), pp. 14 f.

47. "Marx's terrible mistake was in having thought that to escape from fate it is necessary also to escape from God" (Maritain, *True Humanism,* trans. M. R. Anderson [London: Geoff. Bles, 1938], p. 125).

48. "Since the beginning of the 18th century God has been moved from the power field of man's activity. He has been put alongside the world without permission to interfere with it because every interference would disturb man's technical calculations. The result is that God has become superfluous and the universe left to man as its master" (Tillich, pp. 43-44). "Modern atheism is really a new humanism bent on exploiting the potentialities of this life and stressing man's inalienable responsibility in the task" (Johann, p. 249).

49. S. E. Morison, *The Oxford History of the American People* (New York: Oxford U., 1965), p. 917. "Recent American faith in progress has been grounded, not on history, but on confidence on our human and natural resources" (Herbert W. Schneider, *A History of American Philosophy* [2d ed.; New York: Columbia U., 1963], p. 487). "Much of American Humanism is infected with scandalous ambiguity" (C. Hartshorne, *Beyond Humanism* [Lincoln, Nebr.: U. Nebraska, 1968], p. 65).

50. Corliss Lamont, *The Philosophy of Humanism* (New York: Philosophical Library, 1961), p. 192.

51. "In the best sense 'humanism' is simply the expression of an instinct in man; in the worst sense it is this instinct become a

monomania. . ." (Hartshorne, pp. 1-2).

52. Cf. Lamont, pp. 8 ff.

53. Cf. Jn. 2:25; Mk. 7:27 ff.; Mt. 23:25 ff.; Ja. 4:1 ff.

54. In 1947 Emile Brehiers of the Sorbonne in his *Science et humanisme* spoke of the "Crisis of humanism." He saw Christianity and humanism opposed because Christianity denies to man the ability to save himself, whereas humanism stresses man's ability. Cf. Sciacca, pp. 362 f.

55. Cf. Kingsley Martin, "Is Humanism Utopian?" in *Objections to Humanism*, ed. H. J. Blackham (London: Constable, 1963), pp. 79 ff. The Christian has a surer word of prophecy—a "better hope" founded on "better promises" (Heb. 7:19—8:6). Cf. Brunner, *Eternal Hope*, trans. Harold Knight (London: Lutterworth, 1954); Jürgen Moltmann, *The Theology of Hope*, trans. James W. Leitch (London: SCM, 1967).

56. Blackham, p. 25.

57. Cf. *Religion and Humanism* (London: BBC Pubns., 1965), pp. 64 ff.

58. ". . .a little of the best side of the religious spirit is like salt in cooking—it improves most things" (Julian Huxley, *Religion Without Revelation* [London: Ernest Benn, 1927], p. 306).

59. Huxley, *The Humanist Frame* (London: Geo. Allen & Unwin, 1961), p. 41.

60. The secular interpretation of the gospel got its impetus from Bonhoeffer's "religionless" and "worldly" Christianity. "It is not with the beyond that we are concerned, but with this world as created and preserved, subjected to laws, reconciled, and restored. What is above the world is, in the gospel, intended to exist for this world" (Bethge, p. 777).

61. Cf. Thomas Altizer, *The Gospel of Christian Atheism* (London: Collins, 1966), p. 16.

62. Cf. Paul van Buren, *The Secular Meaning of the Gospel* (London: Pelican Books, 1968), p. 192.

63. Cox, p. 125. Cf. William O. Fennell, "The Theology of True Secularity" in *New Theology No. 2* (New York: Macmillan, 1965), pp. 28-38; Peter L. Berger, *Social Reality of Religion* (London: Faber & Faber, 1969), chaps. 5-7; John J. Vincent,

Secular Christ (London: Lutterworth, 1968).

64. Langdon B. Gilkey, "A New Linguistic Madness" in *New Theology No. 2*, pp. 39-49. Cf. E. L. Mascall, *The Secularization of Christianity* (London: Darton, Longman & Todd, 1965), especially chaps. 2, 4.

65. Cf. R. Bultmann, "The New Testament and Mythology" in *Kerygma and Myth: A Theological Debate*, ed. Hans Werner Bartsch, trans. Reginald H. Fuller (London: SCM, 1953), pp. 1-44.

66. Cf. T. R. Torrance, *Theological Science* (Oxford: U. Press, 1969), pp. 1-54.

67. Eliot, "Four Quartets" in *The Complete Poems and Plays of T. S. Eliot* (London : Faber & Faber, 1969), p. 191.

68. See Quirinus Breen, *Christianity and Humanism* (Grand Rapids: Eerdmans, 1969) for a study of the influence of Renaissance humanism on the Reformers. Note, for example, his remark on Melanchthon: "On the one hand, his work was the means of preserving in Protestantism an appreciation of culture; on the other hand, the special nature of his concern with salvation is ever in the shadow, to neutralize" (p. 92).

69. W. B. Yeats, "The Second Coming," *Selected Poetry* (London: Macmillan, 1967), p. 97.

70. Cf. W. S. Urquhart, *Humanism and Christianity* (Edinburgh: T. & T. Clark, 1945), chaps. 3, 4.

71. Hartshorne, p. 316.

72. Maritain, *True Humanism*, p. 11.

73. M. Buber, *Biblical Humanism: Eighteen Studies*, ed. Nahum N. Glatzer (London: Macdonald, 1968), p. 213.

74. Cf. Boethius' statement: "No man degenerate is unless through sin, he leaves his proper source for meaner things" *(The Consolation of Philosophy* [London: Penguin Classics, 1969], p. 90).

RELIGIOUS CERTAINTY
AND INFALLIBILITY:
A DISCUSSION WITH HANS KÜNG

by Stanley Obitts

In the sixteenth century a leading Roman Catholic theologian in Germany named Martin Luther challenged his church's doctrine of justification. Instead of meeting his challenge head on, the church ultimately repudiated his right to challenge, because John Eck and others maneuvered him into admitting to his belief that the pope and the church councils were not always infallible.

In the mid-twentieth century another leading Roman Catholic theologian in Germany, named Hans Küng, has decided to challenge his church's doctrine of infallibility itself. This time the church has no alternative to meeting the challenge head on, for its very right to repudiate Küng is the point at issue. However, Küng does not limit his attack to the infallibility of the teaching office of the church. In his bold new book entitled *Infallible? An Inquiry* [1] he calls in question the idea of propositional infallibility wherever it is found, which includes the Protestant doctrine of scriptural infallibility.

The basic thrust of Küng's argument is worthy of scrutiny

275

by an evangelical Protestant, for he asserts that the "central problem" of the doctrine of infallibility lies in the church's claim that its infallibility is "dependent on infallible *propositions.*"[2] He is not simply referring to infallible propositions uttered by the Roman pontiffs or ecumenical councils. He is explicitly including infallible biblical propositions which, he argues, Protestants have substituted for the infallible teaching office of the church. It is an unfortunate historical fact, he says, that "on the defensive against the claims of the Church newly reinforced at Trent—Lutheran and Reformed orthodoxy developed systematically the theory of inspiration shared by the Reformers and Trent, without undue strain, in the sense of *verbal inspiration.*"[3]

This Protestant approach to infallibility, as Küng sees it, not only lacks biblical and early historical support, but also entails the identification of revelation "with the production of the word of Scripture as it took place through the Holy Spirit at the time, once and for all, in the biblical author." This, it seems, must mean that the biblical authors would be "unhistorical-phantom beings through whom the Holy Spirit effects everything directly," resulting in the verbal inerrancy of the Scriptures. This view of revelation and of the inspiration of Scripture has in turn, led those who hold it to make the grave mistake of regarding "the infallible word of the Bible," rather than "the Christian message, Christ himself as preached," to be "the real ground of faith." While the Enlightenment has served to keep most Protestant groups from committing this error any longer, Küng feels that American Fundamentalists and certain European pietists have still not seen the light.[4]

Leaving the Roman Curia and Karl Rahner to their own devices to salvage anything of value in the doctrine of papal infallibility, and ignoring the question of the accuracy of Küng's history of Protestant theology, let us focus on the underlying problem he is posing for all forms of infallible religious authority, namely, "the real ground of faith."[5] Could infallible propositions and, specifically for our purposes, biblical propositions, be conceived as "the real ground of faith"? Or is Küng correct in finding it, with Barth, in "the Christian message, Christ himself as preached"?[6]

Küng is not denying that a community of believers, including the apostolic church, must communicate its faith through summary, definitive, and defensive statements of that faith. He recognizes that the New Testament contains brief formulae of faith. But he is concerned to point out that even these formulae, much less later ones sanctioned by the church, are propositions of faith. They are not affirmations of a faith in propositions. As "spontaneous," "free expressions of the faith of the congregation," biblical dogmas of faith were not intended to be interpreted as formulae "a priori free from error and not open to correction, infallible and irreformable."[7]

Why, then, he asks, would "neoscholastic textbook theology, and Lutheran and Reformed orthodoxy affirm the infallibility of biblical expressions of faith? Küng's answer is that Descartes, with his penchant for clarity and distinctness as the ideal of knowledge, is the culprit. His identification of truth with certainty gradually brought about the dominance of theology by rationalism. It was not until Leibnitz and Kant showed the greater richness of concrete knowledge and Hegel called attention to the dynamism of the subject and object of knowledge that some theologians began to realize again the impossibility of particular propositions constituting infallible expressions of religious truth.[8] To think otherwise is to exhibit a lack of faith, which is the "Achilles' heel" of the notion of infallibility, alleges Küng.[9]

Christ's promises of the "Spirit of truth" to lead the believer "to the complete truth" (Jn. 14: 16-17; 16:13) do not make possible inerrant interpretations of God's acts in history, because the human propositions the Spirit must use are caught in "the problematic of human propositions in general." By this Küng means that (1) Propositions can never capture reality fully—there is always a gap between what a language user intends to convey and what he actually communicates. (2) Propositions will always be subject to misunderstanding because of the "ambiguous and fluid meanings" of words. (3) A proposition's translatability is limited. (4) Propositions are not static, for language is dynamic. (5) "Propositions are ideology-prone." [10]

Instead, then, of grasping for "infallible truths" in an attitude of unbelief, the genuine Christian has faith that he "will persist in the truth in spite of all ever possible errors." [11] This faith is certainty, however, for "faith in God's guidance and providence in the history of man and of the world has no room for doubts, even though things of great or of little moment go completely wrong," asserts Küng. [12]

The basis for this certainty yielding faith is "God's promise" that the "Spirit of truth" will never forsake the community of believers "throughout all—even erroneous—propositions." [13] This faith in the indefectibility or perpetuity in truth of the community of believers is not grounded on "evidence" that the believer can "observe," without himself "being personally involved." "It is based on the promise that challenges" him "to venture and commit" himself "confidently." "That from which, in which and for which" the community of believers "lives is hidden." Hence, "the promise of remaining in the truth is a challenge to faith," Küng explains. [14]

Nonetheless, he declares, "Certainty is essential for faith. Faith should give certainty." How can this be possible? The Barthian answer comes again:

> Only the Christian message itself—whoever preaches it—confers certainty of faith. It is Jesus Christ, given us in the Christian proclamation, who bestows faith. He in his person is the invitation, the challenge, the encouragement to faith, so that the individual through his person is placed before God in a way that is un-

parralleled in its critical and promising character, in order to assent before God to his life and death. [15]

But Küng goes further by claiming that the certainty of faith bestowed by Jesus Christ in the Christian proclamation "depends on the *Truth* of the Christian message." Such truth is not to be confused with "evidence or infallibility," for the propositions used in the proclamation of the gospel, as in all propositions of faith, suffer "an ultimate ambivalence." Rather, certainty "emerges only when the person addressed commits himself to the message, whether the individual proposition is more or less true, more or less adequate to this message: when he commits himself to the Person who is proclaimed in this message." Küng goes on to point out that

> believing in this sense does not mean accepting true or still less infallible propositions: believing this or that; nor does it mean accepting a person's trustworthiness: believing this person or that person; but it means, throughout all, perhaps ambiguous or perhaps in particular even false propositions, committing oneself in one's whole existence to the message, to the person proclaimed: believing *in* Jesus Christ. It is this faith alone that can give certainty: the peace that surpasses all reason. . . .I become certain. . .of the love of God only when I myself love. [16]

The believer's certainty can extend to Scripture as well. Says Küng:

> I believe then, not—as it were—*first* in Scripture or still less first in the book's inspired character and *then* in the truth of the gospel, in Jesus Christ. But I believe in the Jesus Christ originally attested in Scripture and, by thus experiencing Scripture as gospel in faith, I become certain of Scripture as Spirit-effected and Spirit-filled. It is in Scripture that my faith in Jesus Christ originates, since this is the testimony of Jesus. But my faith is not based on Scripture: Jesus Christ, not the inspired book, is the ground of faith. [17]

But if the certainty of the faith given by Jesus Christ in the preaching of the Christian message "depends on the *truth* of the Christian message," as seen above, would not the certainty the believer can have concerning "Scripture as Spirit-effected and Spirit-filled" need to depend on the "*truth* of Scripture"? Indeed it does, replies Küng:

> not in the sense of an a priori inerrancy of its propositions, but certainly in the sense of a testimony to Jesus Christ that, through all defects in detail, is sound and faithful as a whole. And even though there are not propositions in the Bible which are a priori free from error, nevertheless there are in fact *true* propositions attesting the gospel. 18

What kind of truth might that be? The "truth of Scripture... means more than simply truth as conformity of intellect with reality." It "means in the last resort truth beyond all true propositions," that is, "the fidelity. . .of the God of the Covenant to his word and to his promise." Through its often erring propositions, Scripture "attests unrestrictedly *the* truth as the perpetual fidelity of God," in other words, "Scripture attests the infallibility of God himself," declares Küng. 19

It would appear, then, that Küng has not rejected the concept of infallibility as an object of faith. But he has changed the entity which is believed to be characterized by infallibility. Propositions, including those regarded by neoscholasticism and Lutheran and Reformed orthodoxy as revealed, have been rejected in favor of the substance of divine encounter. Faith is no longer a propositional attitude; neither is the truth of faith the kind ascribed to propositions which correspond to reality. Propositions counted as false according to the truth criteria applicable to propositions can "attest" *the* truth but cannot convey it. "Truth [is] beyond all propositions." Moreover, because the believer has access to *the* truth by faith, faith yields certainty.

Since the object of certainty yielding faith is God's infallibility, the content of that faith yields an expression of

God's infallibility. This expression is "Jesus Christ, given us in the Christian proclamation." Jesus Christ, being *the* truth by virtue of being the only expression of God's infallibility for man, is thereby the "ground of faith." Faith in God's infallibility, therefore, is faith in Jesus Christ, and the ground of this faith is also Jesus Christ.

With the object, content and ground of faith consisting of the same entity, namely, the person Jesus Christ, the means of acquiring such faith would depend upon an encounter with or other comparable experiences of Him. As we have seen, Küng has drawn out this implication. Moreover, he has postulated that a necessary part of that encounter with Jesus Christ is a response with commitment to the Jesus Christ proclaimed by and within the community of believers.

It is at this point that the logic of Küng's religious faith becomes confused. On the one hand, the proclamation of Jesus Christ, who is *the* truth, the expression of God's infallibility, the object, content and ground of certainty yielding faith, must be done by means of propositions which suffer "an ultimate ambivalence" and are "only more or less true." On the other hand, the certainty of faith in the proclaimed Christ "depends on the truth of the Christian message." However, the "truth of the Christian message" is not propositional, for it is Jesus Christ Himself, *the* truth.

The certainty of faith in Jesus Christ is, then, dependent on the object and content of that faith, who is equally its ground. This places the correctness of the response of commitment to the proclaimed Christ in an absolutely crucial position for the attainment of faith with certainty. Yet this response is faced with a double problem. Not only is the proclamation of Christ itself uncertain, being limited by inherently ambivalent propositions, but also the same limitation precludes any infallible declaration from God as to the nature and marks of an appropriate response, which response is a *sine qua non* of a successful proclamation of Christ.

In trying to solve this problem Küng goes in two directions. One is to appeal to a putative immediate awareness of the reality and identity of the love of God discovered as the believer himself loves. The other is to appeal to the promise of the "Spirit of truth" to lead the community of believers "to the complete truth" (Jn. 14:16-17; 16:13). However, the truth of that promise itself cannot derive from its appearance in Scripture, for all scriptural statements are subject not only to ambivalence, but also to error. Küng is convinced that God gave this promise and will keep it infallibly, but the basis for this conviction is not clear. Surely an immediate awareness of the reality of God's love acquired as the individual believer loves cannot constitute guidance of the community of believers into all truth, unless by "all truth" is meant nothing more than the experience of discovering the reality of God's love by loving someone.

The cognitive relation Küng describes between God and man in certainty yielding faith is now becoming vague. From man's side the relation is initiated through a response of commitment to Christ's presence in the preaching of the Word. But that the form this response should take is one of loving others and that it is really Jesus Christ to whom the response is being made seems somehow to be known prior to the initiation of the relation of response to the Christ proclaimed. Yet no provision for its being known prior to the encounter situation is made. Propositional definition by God of the genuinely effective form the response should take is ruled out. Certainty that it is God in Christ to whom one is responding is apparently conceived to be experientially derived in the response situation. The direct awareness of Christ given in the encounter experience is not claimed to guarantee the veracity of the after reflection on the meaning of the experience. Yet certainty is somehow acquired so that (1) the significance of the experience is to be described in Christological terms and (2) this certainty is the coming to fruition of a promise somehow known to have come from God concerning guidance into truth.

There appears to be, therefore, a confusion in Küng's thinking about the basis for the certainty which faith is supposed to give. If the certainty comes from a self-evidently real, self-explanatory experience of Jesus Christ, then a divine promise of infallible guidance into truth is either irrelevant for the certainty which faith can yield, or else it refers to something other than the Jesus Christ known in and through the encounter experience. But the latter alternative is not an option, since Christ is *the* truth, a truth attested to by scriptural propositions but "beyond all true propositions." Hence, Küng is reduced to arguing both that the encounter experience with Christ is self-evidently real and self-explanatory and is also the object of the infallible God's promise of guidance of the community of believers into all truth. Of course, there is nothing illogical about identifying the self-evidence and self-explanatoriness of an encounter experience in a preaching situation with a promised *special* activity of God. But not only is this an unusual use of concepts and not only is it contrary to what Küng thinks he is saying, but also it has not been given any epistemological foundation. For him, as we have seen, the experience situation is the relevant source of religious knowledge; but, surely he would not argue that the concept of the infallibility of God is an object of experience. The notion of God's infallibility, thus, is actually redundant for Küng. It can be eliminated without loss from his account of the alleged transition from faith to certainty.

So far an attempt has been made to show that instead of substituting, as he claims, the infallibility of God for the infallibility of propositional revelation as the "real ground of faith," Küng has actually introduced the infallibility of the believer's interpretation of an encounter experience. In other words, it has been suggested that Küng's understanding of the logic of a believer's appeal in an infallibly interpreted encounter experience either involves the believer in a *petitio principii*—if he invokes God's promise of guidance into all truth—or assumes the existence of self-verifying, self-explanatory encounter experiences by the believer. The viability of this latter meaning which the concept of infallibility in religious authority has for Küng remains to be ascertained.

Precisely what is meant in the claim by a believer that his faith in Christ has passed into a state of certainty by virtue of his having immediately grasped the epistemological import of an encounter experience with a supernatural being in a preaching situation? Obviously the minimum meaning includes a causal relation between the encounter experience itself and that which is experienced, that is, the object experienced. But it is not so obvious what the nature of this causal relation is taken to be. Even such a metaphysically unpretentious interpretation of cause as the one an empiricist could give is in difficulty here. A standard empiricist view of cause describes it as a condition without which the effect could not occur. The empirical meaning of this definition is limited to this: when C happens (along with other conditions), E also happens; and when C does not happen, E does not happen. Certainly no one can hope to construe the concept of cause and effect in a more metaphysically sterile way than this definition of constant conjunction allows. [20] Yet even the restricted notion of the causal relation derived from this definition is inapplicable to the kind of encounter experience Küng describes. The reason is simply that even the minimal meaning of the causal relation implies the existence of independently defined terms or variables so related. In the case of Küng's encounter experience, the experience itself and that of which it is said to be an experience, namely, Jesus Christ, cannot be known to be independently meaningful. Indeed, they cannot even be believed, much less known, to be more than definitionally related, for the only authentic source of information about the alleged object of the encounter experience, namely, Jesus Christ, is held to be the experience itself.

Assuredly, there is nothing to keep one from arbitrarily asserting that statements about having experiences entail statements about entities putatively causing those experiences. But, of course, not even when measured by the reductive standard of the empiricist's constant conjunction theory of cause, could such entailment be ascribed anything more than formal validity. If no other criterion than the experience itself can be given of the occurrence within the experience of a causal relation between the experience and the object experienced, then the two concepts, not being independently meaningful, are related only by definition.

This much is tacitly admitted by H. H. Price, who otherwise would subscribe to Küng's understanding of an encounter experience as the ground of faith. Price is concerned to point out that as we stand in an encounter experience in the presence of "Someone who seems to be giving us a loving welcome now that we are there," we might better think of our being found by Him rather than our finding Him. But even so, argues Price,

there is still some cognitive factor on our side. If He has found us, still, in some way or other, we are conscious that He has. The word "encounter", which theologians sometimes use, has a similar implication. There is no encounter between A and B unless each of them is in some manner or degree *aware* of the other when they meet. If I encounter the Chief Constable in the lane, or he encounters me, it is not enough that he sees me or hears me say "Good morning." It is also necessary that I should see or hear *him*. Or if I am half-blind and three-quarters deaf (as this analogy would perhaps require) I must have some sort of visual or auditory perception of him, however dim and confused, or feel the touch of his hand if nothing else. And if the Chief Constable was looking for me and contrived the encounter himself, then certainly he has found me. But still in a sense I have found him too, even though he himself arranged that I should. [21]

While rejecting a propositional attitude as the cognitive factor in faith in God, Price at least clearly recognizes the necessity of there being some cognitive factor. Moreover, he is careful not to claim to have found it in a supposedly self-authenticating experience of God.

Küng has not been so careful, thereby leaving himself open to the incisive criticisms of "divine encounters" leveled by Ronald Hepburn several years ago and still uncountered. [22] Granting that someone's claim to have had a personal encounter with God can never be disproven, Hepburn persuasively argues that

> the great problem . . . is to fathom how far this claim is in fact a bare record of the immediate encounter, as it purports to be, and how far that experience has been interpreted (and perhaps *mis*interpreted) by the subject in his very attempt to "make sense" of it. Whom or what was he aware of directly meeting? . . . The judgement, "I encountered the God revealed uniquely in the New Testament" would be an indirect, not a direct judgement. It would depend on inferences that could not themselves claim "self-authentication." [23]

The conclusion to which Hepburn's study comes is that one cannot get around

> the objection that such certainty as the Christian claims for his encounters with God can be had only by "subjective" or "psychological" statements: statements *not* to the effect that such and such exists or is the case, but that I have such and such sensations and feelings, and no more. And from statements as cautious as those one may *not* infer any equally certain statements about the world, about things or persons other than the speaker. [24]

The nearly three decades which have passed since the appearance of John Wisdom's fateful article, "Gods," have seen an almost frenetic discussion of the logical analysis of the nature of religious utterances. [25] The bibliography of one recent book on the topic is all of nine pages long. [26] But now that something of a consensus of opinion is beginning to form, the appropriateness of Hepburn's criticism of theistic "encounter" claims is less and less questioned. In his virtually encyclopedic treatment of the many discussions of the meaning of religious language, R. H. Heimbeck concludes that "classical Christian theism" has now been shown to have all along used "God statements" cognitively in the sense of ordinary, common-sense language. Furthermore, he decides that the "metatheological cognitivist" can continue to rest his case on the following "three good reasons for maintaining that 'G' [God] sentences are cognitively meaningful: the checkability of 'G' [God] statements (sometimes on empirical grounds alone, the fact that they have entailments and incompatibles (sometimes empirical), and the intelligibility of 'G' [God] sentences within cognitive frames."[27]

There can be little doubt that Küng thinks that religious utterances can be cognitively meaningful in the sense ascribed above to classical Christian theism. For example, he has been seen asserting that "even though there are no propositions in the Bible which are a priori free from error, nevertheless there are in fact *true* propositions attesting the gospel."[28] But it is our contention that he is inconsistent when he goes on to define the nature of that "truth" to be "more than simply truth as conformity with reality," to be a "truth beyond all true propositions," and meaning by this definition the person of Jesus Christ of whose identity the believer allegedly has an immediate awareness in the encounter experience. As an "encounter" theologian, Küng simply cannot successfully submit his claims to religious knowledge to the criteria for cognitivity of the kind mentioned above. And his appeal to infallibility has been found ill-suited to serve as a substitute.

Suppose the believer makes no inference about the cause of the encounter experience? John Hick argues that the believer could thereby set up the proper conditions for justifying a *claim* to know the experience really was with

God (Hick wishes to limit the definition of knowledge to cases in which the truth claim *is* true). [29] Religious faith, he says, "is an uncompelled mode of 'experiencing as'— experiencing the world as a place in which we have at all times to do with the transcendent God; and the propositional belief to which it gives rise is correspondingly non-coercive in that it is not only presently unverifiable but also unable to be supported by arguments of probability . . . because the concept of probability is not applicable to total interpretations." [30] On this view of faith one can be said to be experiencing life as a "dialogue with God," and this experiencing would be "the believer's primary reason for being sure that God is real." Thus Hick is quite ready to assert that "the religious man's awareness of being in the unseen presence of God constitutes a sufficient reason *for the religious man himself* to be sure of the reality of God." This is the case, Hick goes on to point out, even if the religious man "does not profess to infer God as the cause of his distinctively religious experience." [31]

It is important to keep in mind that Hick is not arguing that the "vivid religious experience" justifying a believer's *claim* to know God's reality entitles him to knowledge of God. And he admits that a religious experience does not provide an adequate answer to the question of God's existence. He demurs from seeking to establish any more than that a "vivid religious experience" is adequate justification of the claim to know God's reality. [32] As he puts it, he is arguing that

> the primary religious perception, or basic act of religious interpretation, is not to be described as either a reasoned conclusion or an unreasoned hunch that there is a God. It is, putatively, an apprehension of the divine presence within the believer's human experience. It is not an inference to a general truth, but a "divine-human encounter," a mediated meeting with the living God. [33]

Could this understanding of the encounter experience solve the cognitivity dilemma in which Küng has landed himself? Probably not, for his appeal to infallibility rubs against the Kantian regulative overtones of Hick's position. [34] The latter's lack of interest in linking an inference of God as the cause of an encounter experience with the viability of the experience as a proper basis for a knowledge claim is the context of his statements about the experience being dependent upon "an interpretative leap," a "total interpretation, in which we assert that the world as a whole (as experienced by ourselves) is of this or that kind," "an interpretation of the world as a whole as mediating a divine presence and purpose." [35] If Küng were to go Hick's route, therefore, the former's belief in an infallible God's promise to lead the community of believers into the "total truth" will itself have to be part of the "total interpretation" into which the believer must "leap," as Hick describes it. The epistemological role God's infallibility would then play could hardly bear the ontological weight which a meaningful appeal to it must assume. Unless God actually exists as an infallible promise-giver, unless He actually has given the promise in question to the believer, and unless He is actually known by the believer to have done so, any interpretative leap of religious experience to obtain this factual state of affairs, all causal concepts having been eliminated, is nothing more than a vacuous leap. As such, it is nowhere near capable of providing the certainty to which Küng thinks God's infallibility permits the believer's faith to come.

The conclusion must be drawn, therefore, that withdrawal of the concept of cause from Küng's understanding of an encounter experience leaves his use of the notion of infallibility as unsubstantiated as when he is construed as regarding God in Christ as the cause of the experience. In either case he is reduced to appealing, not, as he claims, to God's infallibility, but to the infallibility of the believer's interpretation of the encounter experience. It is the believer's infallibility, then, which actually functions as the "real ground of faith" which allows faith to "give certainty," for Küng.

Küng's treatment of infallibility in the area of religious authority is of special interest to the evangelical Protestant, for the latter thinker, too, is committed to the divine authorization of belief as not only sufficient but also necessary for religious truth. This commitment on Küng's part is obviously indicated by his favorable interest in the concept of infallibility. Hence, he approaches the doctrine of infallibility as a friendly critic. Taking the "central problem" of the doctrine to be its dependency upon infallible propositions, he seeks not to cancel the doctrine but to reformulate it in such a way as to place the infallibility upon God as viewed Christologically in the Barthian fashion. Our faulting of that reformulation neither establishes the position against which he is reacting nor does it preclude the success of other reformulations of the position traditionally accepted by Lutheran and Reformed orthodoxy. But perhaps from our examination of Küng's attempt any future reformulator will learn to take more seriously the difficulty of moving from any alleged encounter experience of Jesus Christ to divinely authorized beliefs about Jesus Christ or about that encounter experience. The distinction between evidenced belief and divinely authorized belief should not be blurred if the concept of infallibility is to have a viable meaning in the logic of religious faith. The believer's experience of God in Christ as he responds in love to the proclamation of the gospel, as Küng describes it, is certainly evidence for something. But only God or those whom He has informed infallibly know for sure. Such information is never experienced, for it is the interpretation of experience. To be infallible, therefore, its veracity would have to be based on divine authority; its evidence cannot be ascertained by the believer. How such information could be available to the believer nonpropositionally is not clear. Certainly Küng has not explained how it could be available.

FOOTNOTES

1. Hans Küng, *Infallible? An Inquiry*, trans. E. Quinn (Garden City, N.Y.: Doubleday, 1971).

2. Ibid., p. 143. Italics his.

3. Ibid., p. 209.

4. Ibid., pp. 209-10.

5. Concerning the struggle over infallibility between the two giants of German Catholic theology, see G. C. Berkouwer, "The Küng-Rahner Debate," *Christianity Today* 15, no. 16 (May 7, 1971): 45-46.

6. Cf. Karl Barth, *Church Dogmatics*, ed. G. W. Bromiley and T. F. Torrance, vol. 1: *The Doctrine of the Word of God*, trans. G. T. Thomson and H. Knight (Edinburgh: T. & T. Clark, 1956), part 2, nos. 13 and 19.

7. Küng, p. 175.

8. Ibid., pp. 162-66.

9. Ibid., p. 176.

10. Ibid., pp. 157-61.

11. Ibid., p. 175.

12. Ibid., p. 177.

13. Ibid., p. 182; cf. p. 186.

14. Ibid., p. 187.

15. Ibid., p. 191.

16. Ibid., pp. 191-92.

17. Ibid., p. 218.

18. Ibid., p. 220.

19. Ibid., p. 221.

20. See Edward H. Madden, *The Structure of Scientific Thought* (Boston: Houghton Mifflin, 1960), pp. 201-8. Cf. Jerome A. Shaffer, *The Philosophy of Mind* (Englewood Cliffs, N. J.: Prentice-Hall, 1968), pp. 97 ff.

21. H. H. Price, "Faith and Belief," *Faith and the Philosophers*, ed. John Hick (London: Macmillan, 1964), pp. 21-22.

22. Ronald Hepburn, *Christianity and Paradox* (London: Watts,

1958), pp. 24-59.

23. Ibid., pp. 30-31.

24. Ibid.

25. See *Proceedings of the Aristotelian Society*, N. S. 45 (1944-45): 185-206. Reprinted in Antony Flew, ed., *Logic and Language*, 1st ser. (Oxford: Blackwell, 1951), chap. 10; and in John Wisdom, *Philosophy and Psycho-Analysis* (Oxford: Blackwell, 1953).

26. See R. S. Heimbeck, *Theology and Meaning* (London: Allen & Unwin, 1969), pp. 261-69.

27. Ibid., p. 251. Cf. the recent work by Stuart C. Brown, *Do Religious Claims Make Sense?* (London: SCM, 1969), pp. 66 ff. and 176 ff., where Barth's view on theistic assertions is examined. We have been implying in the present essay without argument that Küng's and Barth's positions have a strong affinity.

28. See above.

29. John Hick, *Faith and Knowledge*, 2d ed. (London: Macmillan, 1967), p. 208.

30. Ibid., p. 151.

31. Ibid., p. 210.

32. Ibid.

33. Ibid., p. 115.

34. Cf. Immanuel Kant, *Critique of Pure Reason*, trans. N. Kemp Smith (London: Macmillan, 1929), A 670-86—B 698-714, pp. 549-60.

35. Ibid., pp. 114-15.

MISSION AND CULTURAL ENVIRONMENT

by Arthur Glasser

The Christian church is worldwide. Its gospel is being proclaimed in every nation and increasingly to all peoples. Although facing the possibility of total catastrophe in certain Communist-dominated nations, it is growing at an unprecedented rate in the Third World. Indeed, ever since World War II this universal church has been rapidly losing its Western base and becoming steadily more indigenous to African, Asian and Latin American cultures. It is facing today a generation in which hundreds of millions, for a variety of reasons, are changing their religious allegiance.

Religious encounter—this is the crucial problem of our time. What attitude should Christians have toward the non-Christian religions of the world? Some major religions are in resurgence. Others are being assaulted by hostile governments. Still others are struggling to adapt to new conditions. All are in polemic opposition to Christian missions even though they bear marks, in Latourette's phrase, of "mass modification" resulting from protracted contact with their vigor throughout the modern era. [1] Some, more than others, are struggling to disorient themselves from former other-worldly mysticisms and are caught up in the universal concern of war-weary man in his struggle for world brotherhood and social justice. They unitedly sing: "We are alike despite our differences. We all seek to give meaning to our common humanity. We are all striving to affirm the worth of human values."[2]

The closing decades of the twentieth century may well find interreligious cooperation growing throughout the world. Those who participate can be expected to display a mounting hostility toward that segment of the church which will still believe that it must beseech men on behalf of Christ to be reconciled to God. Evangelism will increasingly be denigrated as proselytism, and church-planting slandered as religious imperialism. In the face of this prospect of the triad of unacknowledged indebtedness, hostility toward historic, biblical evangelism, and interreligious cooperation we approach the question: What about Christianity and the non-Christian religions?

Many feel that Evangelicals are incapable of discussing this subject objectively. The argument goes as follows: He who feels he must preach the gospel to all men with the avowed intention of pressing them to embrace Jesus Christ and enter His church cannot but be negative when assessing non-Christian religions. He will be incapable of rising to the demands of "reverence for reverence," scientific accuracy and intellectual honesty. With veiled contempt the question is raised: Where is the Evangelical who is an expert in non-Christian religion? Are you sure he is an Evangelical? Ronald Knox's epigram is quoted to complete the argument: "There is nothing like comparative religion for making a man comparatively religious."[3]

We must take seriously these criticisms. It is true that relatively few evangelical theologians have tackled this complicated subject. All too often they have pursued their theological task within the narrow confines of Western culture with little awareness of the multicultural larger world outside. Few have the breadth of missionary vision to sense its desperate importance. Few have even sensed how hopelessly inadequate from a missionary point of view are the historic creeds for which they have devoted their lives in exposition and defense.

Because of a keen sense of dilemma over the prospect of religious encounter in the days immediately ahead, some Evangelicals are tempted to retreat to one nineteenth-century missionary position which regarded all non-Christian religions as demonic darkness, filled with error and degradation. Can the Evangelical today honestly endorse the Anglican missionary to India who in 1855 described Hinduism as a "fearful system. . .the corrupt heart of man, under Satanic influence, elaborated it out of the depths of its own depravity, and set up as objects of worship the personification of its own vices"?[4]

Contemporary anthropological studies have made a shambles of this position. It is simply neither fair nor true.

What then? The Evangelical can hardly embrace the opposite view which sees these religions as the sublime expressions of man's nobility and creativity. Even secular anthropologists no longer hold this position. In the formative years of their crusade for cultural relativism some argued that the religious system of each culture adequately met the needs of its people. But this is true no longer. Goldschmidt's current call for "comparative functionalism" is closer to reality and Scripture when he states:

> There are enough instances on record of primitive peoples not being happy in their own customs but like many a married couple not knowing how to escape them. . .so that we, too, should begin to understand the phenomenon of destruction and establish relevant criteria for functional efficiency. . . .We must rid ourselves of the Rousseauean "good savage," must cease to use ethnographic data either as an escape or a vehicle for expressing our personal social discontent. . . .[5]

We must also include in this introduction an affirmation of the truth of the Christian faith. It is that God has chosen in His own way and time to disclose Himself as the living and true triune God, perfect in love and righteous in all His ways. He began this revelation through His creation, and has savingly spoken in the words and events of redemptive history, which were fulfilled in Jesus Christ. "There is salvation in no one else, for there is no other name under heaven given among men by which we must be saved" (Ac. 4:12, RSV). The Christian does not stand before the devotees of other gods and merely contend that he possesses something which they do not.[6] Rather, his desire is to confront his generation and point gratefully and humbly to Christ, saying all the while, "It has pleased God to reveal Himself fully and decisively in Christ; repent, believe, and adore."[7]

Missionary work involves the transcultural communication of this Christian message. We should not be surprised that missionaries have long urged the theologians of the church not to study man in isolation, but within his concrete cultural, sociopsychological context. It is unfortunate that this pressure has been largely resisted, for the dimension of culture is one of the crucial elements in the study of Christianity and the religions. For, as soon as one affirms the fact that God is portrayed in Scripture as desirous of communicating Himself to man, it must be recognized that this communication will only take place within culture and on its terms. When Nida speaks of the "necessity of disengaging Christian truth from the cultural forces in which it has been imbedded" he is positing the fact that God, His nature, attributes, will and purpose are supracultural.[8] When a lawyer inquired of Jesus which was the greatest commandment, He cited two commandments in reply: Men are to love God and their neighbor (Mt. 22:34-40). All behavior must be God-motivated, or it is defective. All love must be other-directed, within the context of human culture, or it is mere subjective mysticism. But more, its expression will vary from culture to culture.

This brings us to the place of religion in a culture or society. Every society has some sort of religion, since every society is made up of human beings, created in the image and likeness of God. This means that men are not only capable of self-integration and self-identity. They also possess the desire and capacity for establishing relationships with one another. Ultimately they seek relationship with whatever is regarded as Ultimate, the superhuman power which man believes in and depends on for meaning and security. Burkhardt defines religion as "the expression of the eternal and indestructible metaphysical craving of human nature," and adds that "the grandeur of religions is that they represent the whole supersensual complement of man, all that he cannot himself provide." [9]

In his classic work, *The Idea of the Holy,* Otto explored deeply the existential "creature feeling" in man that has precipitated the universal religious quest. Throughout his history and within every culture, man has been overwhelmed from time to time by what can only be described as the experience of Mystery, quite beyond his conception or understanding. Something extraordinary and unfamiliar impinges upon his life. Not that man deliberately seeks transcendence. Rather, he is overtaken by "the Haunter from Outside," the *"Mysterium Tremendum,"* the *Numinous,* and finds it at once so fascinating and so awefull, that he must respond, or his life will be incomplete and unfulfilled. Otto writes:

> The feeling of it may at times come sweeping like a gentle tide, pervading the mind with a tranquil mood of deepest worship. It may pass over into a more set and lasting attitude of the soul, continuing, as it were, thrilling vibrant and resonant, until at last it dies away and the soul resumes its profane. non-religious mood of everyday experience. [10]

In his *Confessions,* Augustine describes his experience of the Holy: "What is that which gleams through me and smites my heart without wounding it? I am both a-shudder and a-glow. A-shudder insofar as I am unlike it, a-glow insofar as I am like it."[11] In his *Varieties of Religious Experience,* James records a vivid testimony of the reality of the "Wholly Other":

> The perfect stillness of the night was thrilled by a more solemn silence. The darkness held a presence that was all the more felt because it was not seen. I could not any more have doubted that He was there than that I was. Indeed, I felt myself to be, if possible, the less real of the two.[12]

This feeling that the world is haunted by a Presence or Power seeking relationship with men is at the heart of all religious activity. Indeed, it is such a universal, such a "given" in human experience, that the religious quest will always be part of human experience. Despite the current massive invasion of traditional cultures and religions by the climate of secularism, man cannot disorient himself for long from this religious preoccupation.[13]

Many have commented on the disdain with which today's student generation views "the dead symbols of institutional religion." And yet, this same generation is intensely interested in spiritual matters. They seem unable to avoid being caught up in exploring new ways of coming to terms with their inner experience of the *Numinous.* Is their exploration of Eastern religions an expression of the search for new "live" symbols to replace those of Christianity which appear to have lost the Mystery?

At any event, where is God in all this? The old Malinowski dilemma comes before us at this point. This great anthropologist was most insistent that every culture be understood in its own terms. This meant that every institution (e.g., religion) must be seen as a product of the culture within which it developed. This would rule out any cross-cultural comparison of religions as essentially a false enterprise. How can one compare incomparables? How can one generalize about the non-Christian religions and Christianity?

It was Freytag in his compact monograph, *The Gospel and the Religions,* who scuttled forever the simplistic reasoning behind such clichés as "All religions say the same thing"; "All are manifestations of the ascending religious development of mankind"; "In their practical religious experience all religions stand side by side in unity"; "All religions in their imperfection find their perfection in the Gospel"; "The longings expressed in the religions find their fulfilment in the Gospel."[14] Malinowski's dilemma is real; the religions cannot be compared. But where do we go from here?

Fortunately, Goldschmidt again comes to our rescue with his dogmatic assertion that "people are more alike than cultures." Humans require both human interaction (social structures) and symbolization (religious world view). His symbols are particularly pervasive in that they integrate all aspects of his life and give symbolic significance to the world about him and the eternity he faces after death. Goldschmidt concludes:

> Social demands are normative. . .the average behaviour under any culture tends toward the center of the range for humans as a whole. . .there is a good deal of evidence that, for instance, the average Zuni and average Kwatiutl man behave a good deal more like each other than the normative patterns of the two cultures are alike.[15]

In a very real sense, this universal enables us to avoid the criticism that no one is capable of understanding a religion which he himself does not believe. The argument turns on the faith of the believer as of the essence of his religion. The two cannot be separated. How can one expound a religious system if he does not first put himself within its framework, accepting its philosophical orientation and participating in its devotional patterns? How can the Christian evaluate the ultimate understanding which the non-Christian has of himself if he remains outside the other's total experience of reality? These are issues of both mind and heart. And unless the basic realities and meanings which the non-Christian attaches to his existence are traced out and appreciated, how can one have genuine religious encounter with him? For instance, how can the committed Christian enter sympathetically into the vital experience of the committed Hindu? If overly sympathetic, will he not be caught up in an amorphous, confused drift toward syncretism? Conversely, if he becomes increasingly the unbeliever (in Hinduism), will this not fault his capacity for objective understanding?

So then, we are free to turn deliberately from the comparison of religious systems and religious values in order to focus on the universals of the human condition. We shall not think of Hindus or Muslims or animists. We shall only think of men who happen to be members of these separate religious allegiances.

It may appear somewhat of a surprise to refer to Tillich at this point. Actually, in his oft-quoted and oft-criticized *Missions and World History* he states that "in some way and on some level, every human being is longing for a new reality in contrast to the distorted reality in which he is living." He then anticipates Goldschmidt (by five years) and speaks of man's response to the *Numinous* in the context of his culture:

> People are grasped by God on the level in which they can be grasped—in their experience of the Divine, in the realm of holiness in which they are living, in which they are educated, in which they have performed acts of faith and adoration and prayer and cult, even though the symbols in which the Holy is expressed may seem extremely primitive and idolatrous. [16]

In summary, several affirmations are in order. First, every religious system is the result of human activity in response to the *Numinous,* however dimly perceived. The outsider can be most superficial and erroneous in evaluating the religion to which he gives no allegiance. Second, every religious system has its ethical outreach, frequently noble in content, but this nobility can only be discerned within the cultural context. Although these statements are capable of solid defense, they do not tell the whole story. What of the biblical data that bears on the subject? To this we now turn.

THE OLD TESTAMENT AND THE RELIGIONS

It has long been held that when one turns to Holy Scripture in search of positive estimates of non-Christian religions, he turns in vain. Schlette speaks of its witness as "extremely negative." [17] Dewick says its predominate note is "hostility," although he qualifies this somewhat by saying there are some "notable exceptions to this; but they are the exception rather than the rule." [18] We are in essential agreement with this judgment. And yet, this element in the divine revelation can only be appreciated if we keep in mind the redemptive purpose of God touching mankind.

Scripture reveals that there never was a time when fallen man was in a situation of exclusive perdition, totally without divine grace. The early chapters of Genesis contain the record of God's covenant with Noah and the whole of mankind (Gen. 9:8-17), in which He pledged man His grace and providential care. This reminds us of the New Testament affirmation that God wills the salvation of all men (1 Ti. 2:1-6).

From the call of Abra(ha)m onward, however, the focus shifts from the universal to the particular. In order to bless the nations, God chose a particular people as His channel and commenced to prepare them for this task. The sequence was election, redemption, revelation and discipleship. Brunner blasts as wholly untenable the popular opinion that the biblical witness to this divine disclosure has its parallels in the non-Christian religions. He contends:

> The claim of the revelation (by a Revealer) possessing universal validity in the history of religion is rare. The claim of revelation made by the Christian faith is in its radicalization as solitary as its content: the message of atonement. It is this: Only at one place, only in one event has God revealed Himself truly and completely—there, namely, where He became man. . . .No "other religion" can assert revelation in the radical unconditional sense in which the Christian faith does this because no "other religion" knows the God who is Himself the Revealer. [19]

We should not be surprised then that Scripture describes other religious systems as a constant threat to what God was seeking to do with His chosen people throughout the whole Old Testament era. How could it have been otherwise? His people were so few in number, so lacking in moral courage, so wayward in their relation to Him that they were tragically vulnerable to almost every blandishment that came from their pagan neighbors, whether social, political or religious. At times, God had to go to great lengths to guard the growing deposit of truth He was giving them. They treated it so lightly and regarded Him with such contempt. All this, while He was seeking to bring them to the place where they would willingly embrace their God-appointed role as His servant people among the nations. He treated them, not as robots to be manipulated, but as free moral agents to be discipled. Indeed, on occasion He made them reap the fruit of their own folly, even though this meant putting His own saving purpose for the nations in great jeopardy. The Jews had to know the bitterness of decimation in wars, occasional massive disruptions of their civil and religious life through military defeats, and even long years of captivity among pagans far from the land of their destiny.

When the children of Israel came out of the desert and began their conquest of Canaan they were commanded to destroy utterly all aspects of Canaanite religion (Deu. 7:2-5). This intolerance in part grew out of Yahweh's expressed hostility toward the low level of morality practiced by the Canaanites. But more, it grew out of the conviction of the Old Testament writers that all other gods were nonexistent, at the most, "shams and lies" pretending what they were not. The Jews in their particularity never imagined that God revealed Himself to other branches of the human family. They firmly believed that they alone had the true revelation from Him.

All in all, the writers of the Old Testament were uninterested in the nature and meaning of pagan religion, if we are to judge from their silence on the subject. They only recorded a scattering of names of some of the gods the pagans worshiped (e.g., Baal, Ashtoreth, Chemosh, Milcom, Bel, Nebo). Attention is focused not on the gods as active beings but on the idols which represented them. The gods themselves are not deliberately denied existence; they are simply ignored. One also searches in vain for any reference to the popular myths associated with these gods. When the prophets condemned "the worship of the host of heaven" they were explicit in not referring to any astral deities, but to the cultic worship of the actual heavenly bodies. Indeed, when the Old Testament refers to the conflict between Yahweh and the "gods of the nations," in every case the objects of His fury are the idols. When magic and sorcery are mentioned, the idols are regarded as the bearers of occult powers and deserving of Yahweh's wrath. And the sole argument advanced against pagan religion is that it is a fetishistic worship, a senseless deification of wood and stone, what the anthropologist would call "mana-belief."

Idolatry in Scripture, then, is the belief that divine and magical powers inhere in certain natural or man-made objects, and that man can activate these powers through fixed rituals.[20] The prophetic polemic against idolatry is largely taken with taunts against fetishism. It has no place for serious reflection on what might be called "authentic paganism." "The makers of idols are all of them a mockery, their beloved images are good for nothing" (Is. 44:9, Moffatt). Inanimate objects cannot be gods! Yahweh gives His glory to no other. Indeed, Yahweh has no rivals apart from the idols and graven images of the pagans. As a result one cannot find in the Old Testament any polemic against the essence of polytheism, the belief in living gods, or any repudiation of the pagan myths that cluster around these gods.

The central religious encounter of the Old Testament was between Yahweh and Baal. These were not two rival religions, one somewhat superior to the other. Baal worship centered in the nature cycle, particularly in the forces and functions of nature that have to do with fertility, death and rebirth. By ritual involving sacred prostitution, orgiastic and ecstatic practices, man was summoned to sink to the level of his animal nature and remain there. As Bright succinctly summarizes:

> Baalism. . .that religion which posed no moral demands, but provided men with an external ritual designed to appease the deity and to manipulate the divine powers for their own material ends; which was incapable of creating community but rather, by pandering to the selfish desires of the worshipper, was destructive of real community.[21]

The heart of all pagan thought is that prior to the gods and above them is the primordial realm with its preexistent, autonomous forces on which they depend and whose decrees they obey. These gods do not transcend the universe; they are rooted in it, and limited by it. Monotheism, as we meet it in Scripture, is not merely the view that there is a God who is an all-powerful, eternal Creator. Such a belief was variously held throughout the ancient world. Rather, monotheism is the concept of a God who is the source of all being. He is not emergent from a preexistent primordial realm of power, but free of all limitations that magic and mythology forge around the gods. Schmidt and Langdon's "High Gods" (gods of the sun and moon, of nations and empires) discovered in the legends of many primitive peoples should not be regarded as representations of the one prime Cause of all. More often than not they were shrouded in mythology, revealed as dependent on the world, and manipulatable by self-operative forces external to themselves. They are not the intimations of an original monotheism. The central theme of the Old Testament is in sharpest contrast. There is only one God and He is supreme over all. He is subject to no laws or forces transcending Him. He is completely free from mythological traits. He is not surrounded by a heavenly court of angels and demons metamorphosed from gods and goddesses, whom He overcame in earlier cosmic struggles.

Of God's personal life we know nothing. Scripture focuses solely on His relationship to His creation. It says nothing about fate. It knows but one fundamental and supreme law: the will and command of an absolutely good and utterly holy God. Perhaps for this reason Scripture is utterly devastative in its denunciation of the confidence of sinful man in human wisdom. Kaufmann describes the

> biblical religious idea. . .of a supernal God, as above every cosmic law, fate, and compulsion; unborn, unbegetting, knowing no desire, independent of matter and its forces; a God who does not fight other divinities or powers of impurity; who does not sacrifice, divine, prophesy, or practice sorcery; who does not sin and needs no expiation; a God who does not celebrate festivals of His life. An unfettered divine will transcending all being—this is the mark of biblical religion and that which sets it apart from all the religions of the earth. [22]

Although the Old Testament neither approves pagan

religion nor suggests that it possesses any "religious value," it needs to be underscored that it teaches that God is just and impartial in His dealings with men (e.g., Amos 1:3—2:5). Furthermore, it contains many intimations of His outgoing concern for non-Jewish people. In a moving passage from Amos, Yahweh reminds Israel of His unconditional sovereignty in dealing with her, and with neighboring nations:

> "Are you not like the Ethiopians to me, O people of Israel?" says the LORD. "Did I not bring up Israel from the land of Egypt, and the Philistines from Caphtor and the Syrians from Kir?" (Amos 9:7, RSV).

God is concerned with justice and mercy, too. His expressed goodwill toward the Gentile nations culminates in the promise that they shall be converted and incorporated into the family of His people. Isaiah 56:6-7 movingly discloses the heart of this universal concern:

> Foreigners who join themselves to the LORD, who minister to him, to love the name of the LORD, and to be his servants, . . .these I will bring to my holy mountain, and make them joyful in my house of prayer; their burnt offerings and their sacrifices will be accepted on my altar; for my house shall be called a house of prayer for all peoples.

Before we conclude this summarization of the Old Testament regard for religion, we should examine the type of passages which have been used to buttress the view that it is not totally hostile to religious pluralism. Two illustrations will suffice. First, Micah 4:5—"All the peoples walk each in the name of its god, but we will walk in the name of the LORD our God for ever and ever." Dewick argues that the implication is that these other gods had "a legitimate claim" on the loyalty of their own peoples. Hence there must have been a henotheistic period in Israel's religious development.[23] We would counter that Old Testament scholars such as Albright strongly challenge this conjecture.[24] But more, Dewick failed to do justice to the context of this verse. It is a vivid description of the apocalyptic elevation of Jerusalem with all nations streaming into it to worship the true God and learn of His ways (vv. 2-4). Strengthened by this assurance of the final triumph of God in history, the people reasoned, "What if the nations in our day persist in their worship of their national gods, which are not gods at all? We herewith reaffirm our covenantal relation to Yahweh. With His help we will remain true to Him." This is hardly an endorsement of religious pluralism!

The second passage is Malachi 1:11 (RSV)—"From the rising of the sun to its setting my name is great among the nations, and in every place incense is offered to my name, and a pure offering; for my name is great among the nations, says the LORD of hosts." Rowley argues that this text demonstrates "the wider vision"—

> The prophet is here claiming for Yahweh worship that is not offered in His name, worship that is offered to other gods. He is claiming that men who did not call themselves worshippers of Yahweh were really worshipping Him, that worship ignorantly offered to idols could be accepted by Yahweh as offered to His Name.[25]

According to Rowley what matters is not what name a person worships but the quality of his worship. "Sincerity of spirit is the sole factor in true worship. . . .He who lives up to the light he has is accepted by God." Actually, in Malachi's day the name of Yahweh was neither universally known nor widely worshiped. Furthermore, the grammatical form Malachi used allows us to understand the words prophetically as relating to the future missionary extension of the kingdom of God among all nations. This will result in the true God being worshiped "in every place." [26]

THE NEW TESTAMENT AND THE RELIGIONS

We have no evidence in the gospels that Jesus ever expressed a judgment about non-Jewish religions. All we know is that He gave unquestioned allegiance to the Old Testament and largely endorsed the manner in which the Jews understood and expressed their faith. He came not to abolish the law and the prophets but to fulfill them (Mt. 5:17). He saw no possibility of other gods besides the one He knew as His Father in heaven (Mk. 12:32). He believed that His coming into the world to bring redemption to Israel and salvation to the nations was in fulfillment of Old Testament prophecies. It is virtually impossible to contend that His attitude to other religious systems would have been at variance with the Old Testament viewpoint earlier defined.

And yet, Jesus used the Old Testament in a selective and original fashion to attack certain practices of the Judaism of His day. Although He commended in part the expository teaching of the Pharisees, He exposed and rebuked their self-righteousness, religious externalism, and exclusive Jewish nationalism. [27] He was particularly adamant against the legalistic use Jews made of the law in hope of bartering with God to secure His favor. As Baago rightly affirms:

> He accepted and rejected at the same time the religion of His forefathers realizing that man can never relate himself to God without religious forms (symbols and rites, worship and institutions) but also realizing that it is man's temptation to absolutize these forms in order to win security for himself. [28]

308

Jesus' constant effort to make a sharp distinction between the infallible truth of Scripture and the fallible practice of that truth by people must be taken very seriously. It is basic to this study. It keeps us from the temptation of equating Christianity with the Christian gospel. The former is but the human formation, the earthly community, the answer of sinners to the revelation of Jesus Christ. The latter is the faith which was once for all delivered to the saints (Jude 3).

Christianity as a religious movement has much in common with other religious movements. Its history contains the familiar sequence of the Founder, His privileged circle of disciples, the growing tradition, the organized community, confessional statements and structured rituals. The great themes of Christianity likewise have their parallels in other religions: law and grace, sin and righteousness, judgment and salvation, death and life. Between Christianity and other religious communities there are also correspondences in forms and functions.

Even though its human dimensions give Christianity its solidarity with other human institutions, this is only one aspect of its total reality. Because it represents God's redemptive activity and is under the judgment of His Word, Christianity also has a divine dimension seen in the body of Christ, the regenerates whom the Lord knows as His own but which no man can distinguish with certainty. [29]

We are not surprised, then, that Jesus balanced His criticism of Jewish externalism with commendations of those who within Judaism served God faithfully. Although He regarded the Samaritan offshoot of Judaism to be inferior (Jn. 4:22), He commended certain individual Samaritans for their personal morality and social concern (Lk. 10:25-37; 17:16). He also rejoiced over the genuine faith of a Roman centurion (Mt. 8:10). Because of His willingness to speak positively of all who were outgoing in their love and who were devoid of the spirit of retaliation toward others, the early church Fathers came to recognize that "all that is good, true and beautiful, wherever it is found, comes from the Holy Spirit."[30]

This brings us to the final aspect of the ministry of Jesus that is related to our subject. He unmasked the spirit world that opposes the ongoing of God's purpose among men. The gospels contain frequent references to evil spirits. We are hard put to know how to interpret the existence and significance of these malevolent beings. How can any of God's creatures be the embodiment of evil? At any event, Jesus challenged and overcame their destructive activities among men to a degree unknown in the Old Testament

We do not sense the part played by these nonhuman intelligences in the religious activity of men until we turn to the writings of the apostle Paul. There we learn that originally the unseen world of "principalities, powers, thrones and dominions" was created by Christ to serve as the instrument of His dominion, as the "invisible, weight-bearing substratum of the world," the "underpinnings of creation," as Berkhof explains. Prior to the revolt they were not evil in essence (Col. 1:15-17). Apparently God's design was that they would provide the linkage between His loving providence and man's creaturely existence. They were to serve as hedges by which He would encircle His good creation, keep it in His fellowship, and protect it from anarchy. They would bring stability to its cultural forms by incarnating themselves within its customs, institutions, ethical rules, ordering of the state, and religious patterns. By these powers, God would rule His creation.

When the revolt took place, with many of these invisible intelligences participating in Satan's challenge of God's sovereignty, their stabilizing function continued, but in a negative fashion. They now seek to keep men from the love of God. Berkhof argues that this understanding is especially illuminating when we think of the religio-social structures by which the world outside Christ has been and is carried along. . . .However pointed the Bible teaches us to see this as slavery, we should not forget that it is still a part of God's preserving mercy, holding life in line where men do not know Christ's liberation. The manifold traditions and codes of which moral life is full are examples. . . .To see the pre-Christian faiths as being in subjection to the Powers (Gal. 4:1-11) will preserve us from illegitimate rapprochements with Christian faith (for example, as if it were the "highest form" of religiosity), as well as from an equally illegitimate condemnation of "blind heathendom."[31]

The theology of the apostle Paul does not make much sense if one fails to allow for the existence, power and organized intent of these spirit beings. His writings are replete with references to "the elemental spirits of the universe" (Col. 2:8, RSV), "the world rulers of this present darkness. . .the spiritual hosts of wickedness in the heavenly places" (Eph. 6:12, RSV). When he rebukes the Christians in Colosse for having turned away from Christ and exposed themselves once again to the former pattern of life in which these powers held sway, we cannot but conclude that the religious activity of men is to a greater or lesser degree under this spirit influence.

In this day of careless tolerance and religious relativism we can all too easily dismiss this scriptural witness. Doubtless the Christians in Ephesus did not like to have Paul tell them that they once had been "following the course of this world,. . .the prince of the power of the air, the spirit . . .now at work in the sons of disobedience" (Eph. 2:2, RSV). Who likes to be told that all his religious activity prior to conversion was locked in a system dominated by intelligences hostile to God?

Strange as it may seem, however, when Paul gave his most comprehensive exposition of the spiritual plight of man in his epistle to the Romans he mentioned neither Satan nor the powers. Rather, he attributed all sinful conduct and false religion to the human heart. Because his exposition is crucial to our understanding of the relation between God and man, we must mention its major emphases. They are as follows:

1. The gospel of Christ is of universal applicability and is able to transform all who believe (1:16-17).

2. The wrath of God, His "holy love in action against sin" (Miller), has brought all men under judgment (1:18).

3. The evidence of creation points to a supreme Being to whom worship and obedience are due (1:19).

4. The sinfulness of man is vividly apparent in his unconscious and unintentional suppression of the truth regarding God (1:18).

5. The judgment of God is to give man up to the destructive dynamics of his reprobate mind (1:24 ff.).

6. The religions of man reflect his feverish preoccupation with created things in his desire to banish God from his consciousness (1:25).

We must ponder the implications of these statements. Bavinck contends that the truth of God's everlasting power and divinity has been exiled to man's unconscious. But this does not mean, he adds, that it has vanished forever:

> Still active, it reveals itself again and again. But it cannot become openly conscious; it appears in disguise, and it is exchanged for something different. Thus all kinds of ideas of God are formed; the human mind as the *fabrica idolorum* is not intentional deceit—it happens without man's knowing it. He cannot get rid of them. So he has religion; he is busy with a god; he serves his god—but he does not see that the god he serves is not God Himself. An exchange has taken place—a perilous exchange. As essential quality of God has been blurred because it did not fit in with the human pattern of life, and the image man then has of God is no longer true. Divine revelation indeed lies at the root of it, but man's thoughts and aspiration cannot receive it and adapt themselves to it. In the image man has of God we can recognize the image of man himself. [32]

Before concluding this brief review of the New Testament's regard for religion, we should examine two texts that have been used to command religious pluralism. First, Acts 10:34-35 (RSV)—"God shows no partiality, but in every nation any one who fears him and does what is right is acceptable to him." The temptation has been to extract this statement from its context and force it to carry the heterodoxy of salvation by works. Actually, the text is part of the opening section of Peter's message in the house of Cornelius, a message that clearly affirmed the great theme of Scripture, justification by faith (v. 43).

The second text is found in Paul's comments on the altar inscription, "To the Unknown God," in his address on Mars Hill (Ac. 17:23): "Whom therefore ye ignorantly worship, him declare I unto you." The King James Version is cited because it has given encouragement to those who want to see in this statement endorsement for the view that all religious worship ultimately has to do with the one, true and living God. The claim is that all men are already in Christ; the mission of the church being merely to announce this fact. As Panikkar says,

> The good and bona fide Hindu is saved by Christ and not by Hinduism, but it is through the sacraments of Hinduism, through the message of morality and the good life, through the *mysterion* that comes down to him through Hinduism, that Christ saves the Hindu normally. . . .Hinduism is the starting point of a religion that culminates in Christianity.[33]

Actually, when Paul's statement is critically examined, it becomes apparent that he did not unreservedly identify this "unknown god" of the altar inscription with the God whom he proclaimed. Rather, he announced that "since they acknowledged their ignorance of the divine nature, he would tell them the truth about it. . . . The ignorance rather than the worship is thus underscored."[34]

313

CONCLUSION

This is a day in which churchmen are attacking the biblical mandate to disciple the nations through preaching the redemptive gospel and calling for repentance and faith. They contend "mission" should be reinterpreted to mean service and not evangelism. The general argument, in Macquarrie's words, is that the church should "abandon arrogant claims to be in exclusive possession of the truth" and should "put an end to proselyting." Conversion to Christ is too disruptive to one's sense of identity; it exposes him to the possibility of cultural disorientation. What does the Asian or African gain by being baptized into a Christianity that is alien to his own tradition? Hasn't Christianity compromised itself too much in the past? Isn't it too fragmented today? What superior spiritual benefits can it offer those who are faithful adherents to their ethnic religions?

In the debate, participants candidly admit that "much reluctance among Christians to engage in evangelism stems from the lack of any strong desire to share the love of God in Christ."[35] But the end point is that conversion is "out," and the sort of interreligious dialogue that stops short of conversion is "in."[36] Whenever the Evangelical considers the liberal option, he tends to grow weary with the churchman like Canon M. A. C. Warren who says that God "revealed Himself uniquely in Jesus Christ our Lord," then presses us to

> be bold enough to insist that God was speaking in that cave in the hills outside Mecca; that God brought illumination to the man who once sat under the Bo tree (Buddha); that the insight into the reality of the moral struggle and of man's freedom to choose the right, which was given to Zoroaster, came from God; that it was God who spoke to a simple Japanese peasant woman, a hundred years ago, of sin, of righteousness, and of judgment, and that God is at work among the four million Japanese who follow her teaching; that indeed, the God of a hundred names is still God. [37]

314

Suppose the above were true. What then? Canon Warren was roundly criticized when he uttered these words. The criticism was not provoked because he was too sympathetic in his approach to other religions; rather, it came because he made too small an effort in this address to generate interest in proclaiming the gospel of Jesus Christ to the devotees of these religions, with a view to persuading them to become Christ's disciples and members of His church.

The traditional option is more attractive and realistic for Evangelicals. Is it hopelessly unrealistic or mentally suicidal to cling to the conviction that all men everywhere must be born again? Was Bishop J. C. Ryle wrong in his conviction that "a day will come when those who are not born again will wish that they had never been born at all"? Not if one takes seriously the words of Jesus Christ.

All of which brings us back to our task. What do we actually do when confronting men of a religious allegiance different from our own? Earlier we noted that leading anthropologists like Goldschmidt hold the human dimension to transcend the cultural. Men as individuals are more important than men as members of cultures.

All which brings us back to the apostles and their performance of Christian mission. At Athens Paul did not descend to the level of his philosophically oriented hearers. He did not argue from first principles as they might have done. Christianity is not just another philosophy, a mere system of ideas. As the witness to Jesus Christ he refused to demean his proclamation of the gospel to the low level of mere intellectual dialogue.

Furthermore, Paul saw no point in blasting the worship of idols, exposing to ridicule its foolishness, and scolding the Athenians for their stupidity. Why give needless offense through assaulting head on the radical errors of idolatry? Paul wanted to win men, not fight them. So he reached out after the hungry-hearted, the groping—those who like blind men confessed their blindness as they fumbled to find the latch of the door. The altar and its inscription "To the Unknown God" revealed to Paul the ultimate agony of idolatry. But it was the one hopeful sign he could find in all Athens. In seizing on it, he accepted the validity of the universal religious consciousness of man. Were he among us today he would say, "Don't preach to Buddhists, to Muslims, to Hindus. Just preach to men. Reach out to men in the tragedy of their need. And you will win them to Christ."

Of course, there are those who will challenge this approach as wholly unsuited to today. But is their challenge valid? In his excellent book *Christianity and History,* Butterfield encourages us to believe that the present day is the "most important and the most exhilarating" period in the history of Christianity for fifteen hundred years. He adds that "we are back for the first time in something like the earliest centuries of Christianity, and those early centuries afford some relevant clues to the kind of attitude to adopt."[38]

We conclude, then, by calling for a serious search for those "relevant clues." What shall be found? We feel Blaicklock is right in his summarization:

> An easy-going Christianity could never have survived; it could not have conquered and trained the world; only the most convinced, resolute, almost bigoted adherence to the most uncompromising interpretation of its own principles could have given the Christians the courage and self reliance that were needed. For them to hesitate or to doubt was to be lost.[39]

As then, so now.

FOOTNOTES

1. "The great non-Christian religions have utilized the permeation of Christian ideas and ideals for their own internal and external strengthening" (Hendrik Kraemer, *The Christian Message in a Non-Christian World* [Grand Rapids: Kregel, 1969], p. 291).

2. Paul David Devanandan, *The Shock of the Discovery of World Religions: History's Lessons for Tomorrow's Mission* (Geneva: World Student Christian Federation, 1960), p. 221.

3. Eric F. Sharpe, *The Spirit and the Religions: The Church Crossing Frontiers* (Uppsala: Swedish Institute of Missionary Research, 1959), p. 113.

4. *Church Missionary Intelligencer* 6 (1855): p. 76, as quoted by Eric F. Sharpe, *Not to Destroy but to Fulfill* (Uppsala; Swedish Institute of Missionary Research, 1965), p. 27.

5. Walter Rochs Goldschmidt, *Comparative Functionalism* (Berkeley: U. California, 1966), p. 138.

6. This is not to deny Deu. 29:29 (RSV): "The secret things belong to the LORD our God; but the things that are revealed belong to us and to our children for ever, that we may do all the words of this law."

7. Kraemer, p. 119.

8. Eugene A. Nida, *Message and Mission* (New York: Harper, 1960), p. 208.

9. Quoted by Hans-Joachim Schoepps, *The Religions of Mankind* (Garden City, N. Y.: Doubleday Anchor Book, 1966), p. 2.

10. Rudolf Otto, *The Idea of the Holy* (London: Oxford U., 1923), p. 12.

11. Augustine, *Confessions*, 2, 9, 1.

12. William James, *The Varieties of Religious Experience* (New York: Longmans Green, 1928), p. 66.

13. "Indifference towards the question of the meaning of one's existence is a transitory state. . .it cannot last, and it never lasted longer than one moment in which a sacred tradition lost its meaning and new answer had yet to appear" (Paul Tillich, *Christianity and the Encounter of the World Religions* [New York: Columbia U., 1964], p. 13.

317

14. Walter Freytag, *The Gospel and the Religions* (London: SCM, 1957), pp. 14-28.

15. Goldschmidt, p. 134.

16. Tillich, *Missions and World History* (The Theology of the Christian Mission) New York: McGraw-Hill, 1961), p. 287.

17. Heinz Robert Schlette, *Towards a Theology of Religions* (New York: Herder & Herder, 1966), p. 25. He quotes such texts as 1 Ki. 11:1-13; Jer. 2:26-29; 10:1-16; Is. 40:18-20; 44:9-20; 46:6 f.

18. C. Dewick, *The Christian Attitude to Other Religions* (Cambridge: U. Press, 1953), p. 63.

19. Emil Brunner, *Revelation and Reason* (Philadelphia: Westminster, 1946), pp. 235-36. Chap. 15 is devoted to the development of this thesis.

20. Yahezkel Kaufmann, *The Religion of Israel* (Chicago: U. Chicago, 1960), p. 64. Chap. 2, "Pagan Religion," is a gold mine of helpful insights on this subject.

21. John Bright, *The Kingdom of God* (Nashville: Abingdon, 1963), pp. 52-53.

22. Kaufmann, p. 121.

23. Dewick, p. 64.

24. W. S. Albright, *From the Stone Age to Christianity* (Baltimore: Johns Hopkins U., 1946), p. 219.

25. H. H. Rowley, *Israel's Mission to the World* (London: SCM, 1939), p. 31.

26. Carl Friedrich Keil, *The Twelve Minor Prophets* (Grand Rapids: Eerdmans, 1951), 2:438. See also Johannes Blauw, *The Missionary Nature of the Church* (New York: McGraw-Hill, 1962). "No theory of general revelation or of general grace can be built on this passage" (p. 143).

27. Contrast Mt. 16:12 with Mt. 23:2-3.

28. Kaj Baago, "The Post-Colonial Crisis of Missions," *International Review of Missions* 55, no. 219 (July, 1966): 327.

29. Mt. 7:21-23; Ro. 11:1-6; 2 Co. 13:5; 2 Ti. 2:19, etc.

30. Schlette, p. 36.

31. H. Berkhof. *Christ and the Powers* (Scottdale: Herald, 1962), pp. 27, 56.

32. Johannes H. Bavinck, *The Church Between Temple and Mosque* (Grand Rapids: Eerdmans, 1966), p. 122.

33. Quoted by Lesslie Newbigin, *The Finality of Christ* (Richmond: John Knox, 1969), p. 42.

34. F. F. Bruce, *Commentary on the Book of Acts* (Grand Rapids: Eerdmans, 1966), p. 355. For an extensive study of Ac. 17 and Ro. 1, consult Bertil Gartner, *The Areopagus Speech and Natural Revelation* (Uppsala: Gleerup, 1955), p. 289.

35. Ian H. Douglas and John B. Carman, "Comments on the Post-Colonial Crisis of Mission," *International Review of Missions* 55, no. 220 (Oct., 1966): 489.

36. The literature on the debate is vast. For a good summarization of the secular-theological understanding of mission see Carl F. Hallencrentz, *New Approaches of Men of Other Faith. 1938-1968* (Geneva: World Council of Churches, 1970), p. 95, and Donald A. McGavran, ed., *Eye of the Storm: The Great Debate in Mission* (Waco: Word, 1971).

37. From an address delivered at the 1963 Anglican Congress reported by Peter Whitely, *Frontier Mission, An Account of the Toronto Congress* (London: SPCK, 1963), p. 18.

38. Herbert Butterfield, *Unity and History* (London: Bell, 1954), p. 135.

39. E. M. Blaiklock, *The Christian in Pagan Society* (London: Tyndale, 1951), p. 29.

CONTRIBUTING AUTHORS

Roland K. Harrison is Professor of Old Testament at Wycliffe College, the University of Toronto. He holds the B.D., Th.M. and Ph.D. from the University of London and the D.D. from Huron College. He is the author of many scholarly articles and books, including *Introduction to the Old Testament, Old Testament Times, Archaeology of the Old Testament* and *The Psalms for Today.*

Everett F. Harrison is currently Senior Professor of New Testament at Fuller Theological Seminary. He gained the B.A. degree from the University of Washington, the M.A. from Princeton University, the Th.B. from Princeton Seminary, the Th.D. from Dallas Seminary and the Ph.D. from the University of Pennsylvania. He has written extensively; included among his books are *Introduction to the New Testament, A Short Life of Christ* and *Jesus and His Contemporaries.*

Palmer Robertson is serving as Associate Professor of Old Testament Theology at Westminster Theological Seminary. His B.A. was gained from Belhaven College, the B.D. from Westminster Theological Seminary, and his Th.M. and Th.D. from Union Theological Seminary in Virginia.

Clark H. Pinnock, formerly Assistant Lecturer in New Testament Studies at the University of Manchester, is now Professor of Systematic Theology at Trinity Evangelical Divinity School. He holds the B.A., University of Toronto, and Ph.D., University of Manchester. He is the author of *Set Forth Your Case* and *Biblical Revelation: The Foundation of Christian Doctrine.*

Geoffrey W. Bromiley is Professor of Church History and Historical Theology at Fuller Theological Seminary. He holds the M.A. from Cambridge University and the Ph.D. from Edinburgh University. Edinburgh University, where he formerly taught, also honored him with the D.Litt. He is the editor and part translator of Barth's *Church Dogmatics,* and he is also translating Kittel's *Theological Dictionary of the New Testan ent,* and some of Zwingli's and Bullinger's writings foɪ the *Library of Christian Classics.* In addition, he is the author of several books, including *Thomas Cranmer, Theologian* and *Sacramental Teaching and Practice in the Reformation Churches.*

David F. Wells is Associate Professor of Church History and the History of Christian Thought at Trinity Evangelical Divinity School He first studied at the University of Cape Town, South Africa, and then turned to theology, gaining the B.D., University of London; Th.M., Trinity Evangelical Divinity School; and Ph. D., University of Manchester.

Bernard L. Ramm is serving as Professor of Systematic Theology and Christian Apologetics at the American Baptist Seminary of the West at Covina. He holds the B.D. from Eastern Baptist Theological Seminary and his M.A. and Ph.D. are both from the University of Southern California in Los Angeles. He also pursued graduate studies abroad under Karl Barth at the University of Basel, Switzerland. He is the author of over a dozen books, which include *The Christian View of Science and Scripture, Protestant Christian Evidences, Special Revelation and the Word of God* and *A Handbook of Contemporary Theology.*

321

Harold J. Ockenga,who was formerly President of Fuller Theological Seminary, is now President of Gordon College and Gordon-Conwell Theological Seminary. He holds the A.B., Taylor University; B.D., Westminster Theological Seminary; and both the M.A. and Ph.D. from the University of Pittsburgh. He is the recipient of many honorary doctorates and the author of over a dozen books, including *Protestant Preaching in Lent, Power Through Pentecost, Preaching in Thessalonians,* and *No Other Lord.*

H. Dermot McDonald is chairman of the Philosophy department at London Bible College in England. His B.A., B.D., and Ph.D. were all gained from the University of London, which subsequently honored him with the D.D. He is the author of *Ideas of Revelation, Theories of Revelation* and *I and He* as well as some important scholarly articles.

Stanley R. Obittsis Associate Professor of Philosophy at Westmont College. His B.A. was granted by Wheaton College, his B.D. by Wheaton Graduate School of Theology, and the Ph.D. by the University of Edinburgh.

Arthur F. Glasser has recently been appointed Associate Dean and Associate Professor of Missions, Graduate School of World Mission, Fuller Theological Seminary. His first degree, the C.E. in engineering, was granted by Cornell University. Subsequently he was granted the B.D., Faith Theological Seminary; S.T.M., Union Theological Seminary in New York. He was awarded the D.D. by Covenant College and Theological Seminary. He is joint author of *Missions in Crisis* and has written many articles for journals and periodicals.

322

INDEX OF NAMES

Abbot, 183n, 24.
Albright, 37n, 4, 38n, 21, 39n, 41, 307, 318n, 24.
Allis, 87n, 16.
Altizer, 162, 182n, 17-18, 263, 264, 273n, 61.
Alves, 190, 194, 197, 198, 199, 213n, 20, 214n, 38-40.
Andrewes, 132, 144.
Anselm, 254, 271n, 39.
Apelles, 146.
Aristophanes, 102.
Aristotle, 175, 266.
Astruc, 12.
Athanasius, 137, 138, 153n, 34, 154n, 46.
Augustine, 10, 126, 139, 141, 153n, 37, 154n, 51, 155n, 72, 159, 175, 252, 259, 271n, 35, 298, 317n, 11.
Aulén, 149.

Baago, 308, 318n, 28.
Bainton, 186n, 49, 236n, 12.
Baird, 49, 63n, 15.
Baker, 271n, 37.
Balthasar, Hans Urs von, 165, 169, 185n, 33.

Bambrough, 263.
Barnabas, 133, 155n, 90.
Barth, 87n, 18, 105, 112, 119n, 1, 122n, 35, 140, 142, 154n, 54, 154n, 66, 159, 160, 164, 182n, 10-11, 189, 195, 202, 211n.i, 277, 291n, 6, 292n, 27.
Basilides, 146.
gbaum, 168.
Bavinck, 312, 319n, 32.
Baxter, Batsell, 226, 237n, 38, 238n, 43.
Beal, 269n, 8, 269n, 10.
Beecher, Henry, 236n, 1.
Beecher, Lyman, 226.
Beker, 87n, 19.
Bellamy, 184n, 29.
Bennet, J.C., 251.
Berdyaev, 183n, 23.
Berg, 37n, 5.
Berger, Peter, 119n, 2, 120n, 17, 181n, 2, 182n, 15, 273n, 63.
Berkhof, 310, 319n, 31.
Berkouwer, 291n, 5.
Bernard of Clairvaux, 186n, 49.
Bethge, 270n, 27, 273n, 60.
Bettenson, 153n, 18, 153n, 32-33,

323

153n, 35, 154n, 52-53, 155n, 72, 155n, 74.
Betz, 190, 195, 197, 207, 209, 214n, 32, 214n, 35.
Blackham, 262, 273n, 55-56.
Blaicklock, 316, 319n, 39.
Blauw, 318n, 26.
Bloch, 189, 190-93, 194, 195, 197, 200, 201, 202, 204, 205, 208, 211n, 5, 212n, 10, 212n, 13-15, 213n, 16, 213n, 18, 215n, 51.
Bochert, 122n, 34.
Boethius, 274n, 74.
Boettner, 119n, 1.
Bonhoeffer, 183n, 24, 250, 270n, 27, 273n, 60.
Boniface VIII, 270n, 24.
Bonnett, 187n, 56.
Bornkamm, 250, 270n, 29.
Bouillard, 165.
Bounds, 238n, 46.
Braaten, 190, 198, 200, 203, 206, 207, 214n, 37, 215n, 44-5, 215n, 56.
Breen, 274n, 68.
Bréhiers, 272n, 54.
Bright, 30, 39n, 31, 304, 318n, 21.
Brinkmann, 240.
Bronislaw, 240.
Brooks, 226, 236n, 1, 237n, 39.
Brown, Peter, 271n, 35.
Brown, Stuart, 292n, 27.
Bruce, 52, 84n, 8, 90n, 30, 319n, 34.
Brunner, 106, 189, 244, 251, 269n, 13, 270n, 21, 271n, 32, 273n, 55, 302, 318n, 19.
Buber, 266, 274n, 73.
Buckle, 254, 271n, 40.
Bulgakoff, 272n, 45.
Bultmann, 43, 47, 62n, 6, 79, 81, 89n, 23-24, 98, 99, 100, 103, 105, 107, 112, 119n, 7, 123n, 39, 195, 205, 210, 211n, 1, 264, 274n, 65.
Burckhardt, 240.
Buri, 108, 121n, 27.
Burrows, 32, 39n, 34.
Butterfield, 316, 319n, 38.
Buttrick, 217, 236n, 7.

Cadman, 217.
Calvin, 126, 152n, 3, 176, 177, 178,

179, 186n, 52-55, 253.
Capps, 190, 211n, 5, 212n, 7.
Carman, 319n, 35.
Cauthen, 190 212n, 7
Celsus, 146.
Childs, 38n, 22, 90n, 30, 90n, 33, 122n, 36.
Chrysostom, 221.
Clark, Henry, 240, 268n, 2.
Claudel, 185n, 35.
Clement of Alexandria, 138, 154n 45, 154n, 50, 248.
Clement of Rome, 152n, 12, 154n, 48, 154n, 63.
Cobb, 211n, 3.
Cochrane, 252, 271n, 34.
Cole, 187n, 56.
Comte, 11, 166, 259.
Conzelmann, 79, 89n, 26.
Cox, 121n, 28, 162, 182n, 16, 190, 194, 208, 211n, 5, 212n, 16, 213n, 21, 215n, 59, 218, 263, 264, 273n, 63.
Cragg, 37n, 9.
Craig, 271n, 37.
Cranmer, 126, 127, 140, 143, 144, 152n, 5, 152n, 15-16, 153n, 17, 154n, 55-59, 155n, 73, 155n, 75.
Cross, 39n, 35.
Cullmann, 56, 63n, 22, 79, 80, 89n, 27, 89n, 29, 113, 123n, 39.
Cyprian, 134, 141, 153n, 23, 153n, 26, 154n, 69.
Cyril, 138, 154n, 42-43.

Darius the Mede, 28, 29, 38n, 30.
Darwin, 13, 37n, 5.
Davies, Merlin, 269n, 15.
Davies, W. D., 43, 62n, 5.
Day, 230.
Descartes, 277.
Devanandan, 317n, 2.
Dewart, 185n, 34.
Dewick, 301, 307, 318n, 18, 318n, 23.
Dinkler, 90n, 33.
Dix, 130.
Dodd, 63n, 23, 90n, 30, 194, 210.
Donne, 9, 10n, 2.
Dorner, 243.
Douglas, Ian, 319n, 35.
Driver, S. R., 34, 39n, 39.

324

Dubos, 203, 215n, 54.
Dubcek, 215n, 51.
Durkheim, 171.

Eadie, 88n, 21.
Eck, 129, 275.
Edwards, David, 258, 272n, 45.
Eichhorn, 12.
Eichrodt, 84n, 1, 87n, 20.
Eliot, 240, 241, 268n, 3, 274n, 67.
Ellis, E. E., 90n, 30.
Eudoxia, 221.
Eusebius, 154n, 62.
Eutyches, 144.

Fackre, 182n, 15.
Fairweather, 269n, 12.
Farrer, 62n, 9.
Fenelon, 218, 219.
Fennell, 273n, 63.
Feuerbach, 99.
Finney, 231.
Fisher, 217.
Flew, 291n. 25.
Foley, 203, 215n, 53.
Forsyth, 270n, 25.
Frederick the Wise, 223.
Freedman, 26, 38n, 24.
Freeman, E., 183n, 21.
Freud, 171.
Freytag, 299, 318n, 14.
Fromm, 263.
Froude, 37n, 9.

Gabler, 65, 84n, 6.
Gardiner, Samuel, 215n, 49.
Gardner, p., 53, 63n, 18.
Garrigou-Lagrange, 184n, 28.
Gartner, 319n, 34.
Geddes, 12.
Geiselmann, 124n, 44.
Gerhardsson, 42, 55, 62n, 2, 63n, 20,
   63n, 28.
Gilkey, 108, 119n, 4, 119n, 6, 121n,
   20, 121n, 29-30, 159, 264, 274n,
   64.
Glasson, 90n, 30.
Glicksburg, 100, 120n, 13.
Glock, 158, 170, 171, 181n, 1, 181n,
   6-7.
Gobryas, 28.

Goguel, 47, 48, 62n, 12.
Goldschmidt, 295, 299, 300, 315,
   317n, 5, 318n, 15.
Golffing 211n, 5.
Goppelt, 48, 62n, 13, 87n, 5, 90n, 30.
Gordon, C. H., 38n, 16.
Gordon, George, 236n, 1.
Gore, 130, 155n, 72.
Gorresio, 270n, 24.
Graf, 19.
Graham, Billy, 224, 231.
Graham, R. P., 37n, 9.
Grandmaison, Léonce de, 184n, 28.
Grounds, Vernon, 200, 213n, 22,
   215n, 46.
Greeley, 119n, 5.
Gubarv, 28, 29.
Gundry, 63n, 27.
Gunkel, 20, 21, 25, 27.
Gwatkin, 129, 152n, 8.

Hadden, 119n, 3.
Haldane, J.B.S., 37n, 5.
Hallencrentz, 319n, 36.
Hamilton, 119n, 2, 121n, 23.
Handy, 269n, 14.
Hanson, R.P.C., 90n, 30.
Hardy, 236n, 13.
Harnack, 105, 108.
Harrison, R.K., 37n, 1, 37n, 11, 38n,
   19, 38n, 23, 39n, 32, 122n, 36.
Hartshorne, 183n, 21, 266, 272n, 49,
   273n, 51, 274n, 71.
Haseldon, 236n, 2.
Harvey, Van A., 100, 119n. 4, 120n,
   10, 159, 179, 187n, 58.
Hayes, 63n, 26.
Hefner, 184n, 24.
Hegel, 190, 195, 202, 205, 277.
Hegesippus, 154n, 62.
Heidegger, 194, 208.
Heimbeck, 287, 292n, 26.
Henry, 122n, 33, 123n, 42.
Hepburn, 286, 291n, 22.
Herder, 240.
Herodotus, 28, 38n, 28.
Hick, 287, 288, 289, 292n, 29-33.
Higham, 269n, 15.
Hilary, 143.
Hippolytus, 155n, 83.
Hocedez, 184n, 25.

325

Hoffman, 214n, 41.
Hoggart, 268n, 1.
Hoijer, 269n, 8.
Holtby, 218.
Holyoake, 258.
Hordern, 202, 215n, 52.
Horosz, 254, 271n, 38.
Howley, 63n, 17.
Hügel, Friedrich von, 184n, 26.
Hume, 99, 101.
Huxley, Julian, 263, 273n, 58-9.
Huxley, T. H., 16.
Hyatt, P. 39n, 35.

Ignatius, 133, 153n, 20, 153n, 30, 154n, 47, 154n, 60.
Iremonger, 271n, 37.
Irenaeus, 131, 132, 138, 140, 142, 143, 146, 152n, 9, 152n, 13, 153n, 19, 153n, 31, 153n, 36, 153n, 38-9, 154n, 40, 154n, 61, 155n, 68, 155n, 90, 183n, 24.
Irwin, 24.
James, William, 298, 317n, 12.
Jaspers, 108.
Jenson, 198, 214n, 36.
Jeremias, 43, 62n, 7, 62n, 8.
Jewel, 126, 129, 141, 142, 143, 144, 152n, 4, 154n, 64.
Joad, 269n, 19.
Johann, 271n, 44, 272n, 48.
John of Damascus, 154n, 44, 155n, 76.
Jones, Edgar, 217, 236n, 1, 236n, 3, 236n, 8.
Josephus, 30.
Justin, 131, 152n, 11, 154n, 50, 155n, 82.

Kaehler, 112.
Käsemann, 91n, 34.
Kallas, 122n, 31.
Kant, 102, 240, 245, 277, 292n, 34-5.
Kantzer, 186n, 51.
Kaufman, Gordon, 102, 120n, 15-6, 173, 174, 182n, 13.
Kaufmann, Yahezkel, 305, 318n, 20, 318n, 22.
Keil, 318n, 26.
Keller, Ernst, 120n, 8.
Keller, Marie-Louise, 120n, 8.

Kelly, 153n, 27.
Kidd, 130.
Kierkegaard, 251.
Kirk, 130.
Kirstein, 215n, 51.
Kitchen, 27, 38n, 15-16.
Knox, Ronald, 294.
Koopmans, 39n, 38.
Kraeling, 39n, 38.
Kraemer, 317n, 1, 317n, 7.
Kümmel, 45, 62n, 11.
Küng, 155n, 88, 275-290, 291n, 1-4, 291n, 7-19, 292n, 27.
Kuitert, 213n, 24.

Laberthonnière, 165.
Ladd, 58, 63n, 25.
Lamont, 260, 272n, 50, 273n, 52.
Lampe, 90n, 30.
Langdon, 305.
Latourette, 293.
Leenhardt, 63n, 24.
Lessing, 112, 153n, 28.
Lewis, C. S., 111, 122n, 33.
Lewis, H. D., 270n, 28.
Leo XIII, 165.
Lindars, 90n, 30.
Lindbeck, 124n, 45.
Loisy, 165, 184n, 26.
Lombard, 129.
Lombardi, 193, 211n, 5, 213n, 18.
Long, Edward, 212n, 8.
Lubac, Henri de, 165, 185n, 35, 186n, 48, 259.
Lunn, 237n, 13.
Luther, 126, 129, 175, 176, 222, 250, 251, 275.

Macartney, Charles, 232, 238n, 45.
Macartney, Clarence, 217, 229.
MacIver, 240.
Macquarrie, 182n, 16, 197, 208, 214n, 29, 215n, 58, 314.
McDonald, H. D., 270n, 25.
McGavran, 319n, 36.
Madden, 291n, 20.
Madiran, 184n, 27.
Malevez, 122n, 31.
Malinowski, 240, 298, 299.
Manson, T. W., 62n, 3.
Marcuse, 195.

326

Maritain, 266, 270n, 26, 272n, 47, 274n, 72.
Marlé, 184n, 26.
Marsch, 190, 211n, 4.
Martin, E. D., 268n, 6.
Martin, Kingsley, 261, 262, 273n, 35.
Martin, W. J., 34, 39n, 40.
Marty, 158, 171, 181n, 4, 185n, 38, 213n, 22, 272n, 45.
Martyr, Peter, 126, 143, 144.
Marx, 164, 190, 195, 202, 205, 259, 272n, 47.
Mascall, 159, 182n, 9, 274n, 64.
Matthews, Mark, 217.
Maurice, F. D., 245, 269n, 15.
Melanchthon, 274n, 68.
Mendeléeff, 18, 19.
Michel, 113, 123n, 38.
Milton, 259.
Möhler
Moltmann, 161, 162, 163, 164, 182n, 14, 183n, 22, 189, 190, 193, 195-203, 205, 206, 207, 209, 211n, 2, 212n, 6, 213n, 22-27, 214n, 28, 214n, 30-34, 215n, 42-3, 215n, 47-8, 215n, 51, 215n, 55, 215n, 57, 216n, 61, 273n, 55.
Montogomery, 117, 120n, 18, 121n, 24, 122n, 33, 124n, 46.
Moody, 231.
Morgan, Campbell, 217, 227.
Morison, S. E., 259, 272n, 49.
Morrison, Charles, 217.
Mosbacher, 270n, 27.
Moule, C. F. D., 56, 63n, 21.
Munck, 49, 63n, 14.
Murdock, 271n, 43.
Murray, John, 85n, 11.

Nelson, 186n, 50.
Newbigin, 319n, 33.
Newman, 129, 130, 145.
Newton, Joseph, 217.
Nida, 296, 317n, 8.
Niebuhr, Carsten, 19.
Niebuhr, H. Richard, 122n, 32, 181n, 2, 240, 241, 242, 244, 248, 268n, 5, 270n, 22-23.
Niebuhr, Reinhold, 218, 251, 252, 269n, 11.
Nielsen, 38n, 25.

Nietzsche, 259.
Novak, 108, 121n, 26.
Nygren, 134.

O'Collins, 211n, 5.
Oecolampadius, 126, 143.
Ogden, 120n, 11-2, 123n, 42, 158, 163, 172, 173, 174, 176, 179, 181n, 5, 182n, 19, 183n, 21, 185n, 37, 185n, 39-40, 185n, 42, 185n, 44-6.
Ollé-Laprune, 165.
Opler, 242.
Origen, 134, 146, 153n, 24-5, 153n, 37, 154n, 49-50, 155n, 78-81, 155n, 84-5, 156n, 91.
Orlinsky, 36, 39n, 44.
Orr, James, 123n, 43.
Otto, Rudolph, 297, 317n. 10.
Ourslev, 236n, 4.
Outka, 212n, 8.

Panikkar, 313.
Pannenberg, 113, 121n, 22, 123n, 40-1, 190, 213n, 19.
Parker, T. H., 186n, 51, 236n, 1.
Pascal, 158, 181n, 3.
Pattison, T. H., 236n, 10-1.
Payne, J. Barton, 84n, 4.
Pedersen, J., 20, 37n, 2, 37n, 12.
Peerman, 158, 181n, 4, 213n, 22, 272n, 45.
Pelagius, 139.
Perrin, 61, 63n, 29.
Perry, 258.
Petre, 184n, 31.
Pittenger, 173, 174, 176, 183n, 21, 185n, 47, 211n, 3.
Pius IX, 270n, 24.
Plato, 248.
Plessix Gray, Francine du, 173.
Pollock, 237n, 14.
Porphyry, 29.
Porteous, N. W., 31, 33, 39n, 33, 39n, 36, 84n, 2.
Price, 285, 291n, 21-2, 292n, 23-4.
Procter, 128, 152n, 7.
Pusey, 130.

Rad, Gerhard von, 38n, 22, 38n, 28, 84n, 1, 84n, 3, 86n, 12, 87n, 8.

Radbert, 143.
Rahner, 119n, 1, 123n, 37, 124n, 44, 166, 169, 184n, 29, 185n, 35, 190, 276.
Ramsey, Ian, 212n, 8.
Ramsey, Paul, 212n, 8.
Rashdall, 128.
Ratramn, 143.
Ratzinger, 124n, 44.
Rauschenbusch, 245.
Reardon, 184n, 28.
Reese, W. L., 183n, 21.
Reicke, 51, 63n, 16.
Reimarus, 99.
Rhegius, 152n, 2.
Richardson, Alan, 86n, 13, 122n, 32.
Richardson, Leigh, 152n, 2.
Ridderbos, 89n, 28.
Ridley, 143, 155n, 71.
Riesenfeld, 42, 62n, 2.
Ritschl, 105.
Rizzo, 268n, 4.
Robinson, James, 90n, 32.
Rookmaaker, 269n, 12.
Rooks, 236n, 9.
Rordorf, 122n, 34.
Rowley, 28, 29, 35, 38n, 14, 38n, 27, 307, 318n, 25.
Rubin, 214n, 41.
Rubinstein, Richard, 121n, 25, 181n, 1.
Rühle, 190, 211n, 5, 212n, 6, 212n, 12.
Ryle, 315.
Ryrie, 85n, 10.

Sangster, 217.
Savonarola, 221.
Schaff, 128.
Schillebceckx, 168, 170, 185n, 36, 135n, 43.
Schiller, 16, 37n, 7.
Schilling, 190, 211n, 5, 212n, 11, 215n, 51.
Schippers, 54, 63n, 19.
Schleiermacher, 105, 106, 164, 245.
Schlette, 301, 318n, 17, 318n, 30.
Schmidt, 305.
Schneider, Herbert, 272n, 49.
Schultz, 37n, 6.
Sciacca, 259, 272n, 46, 273n, 54.

Searles, 37n, 8.
Senacleus, Jacques de, 152n, 1.
Shaffer, 191n, 20.
Sharpe, Eric, 317n, 3-4.
Shedd, 128.
Scherer, 237n, 40.
Shinn, 182n, 12.
Shoepps, 317n, 9.
Simpson, C. A., 38n, 14.
Simpson, Matthew, 236n, 1.
Smart, 121n, 21, 211n, 1.
Smith, Adam, 205.
Smith, Morton, 62n, 3.
Socinus, Lelio, 187n, 56.
Solzhenitsyn, 213n, 17.
Spinoza, 99.
Stählin, 122n. 35.
Stark, 158, 170, 171, 181n, 1, 181n, 6-7, 185n, 37, 185n, 39-40.
Stauffer, Ethelbert, 79, 89n, 25.
Stendahl, 90n, 30.
Strauss, 99.
Swanson, Guy, 97, 119n, 5.
Symonds, 186n, 49.
Synge, 90n, 30.

Tanquerey, 184n, 29.
Tavard, 124n, 44.
Teeple, 42, 62n, 1.
Temple, 245, 253, 269n, 17-8, 270n, 20, 271n, 37.
Terrien, 181n, 8.
Tertullian, 131, 138, 140, 142, 146, 147, 152n, 14, 154n, 41, 154n, 50, 154n, 65, 155n, 86-7, 242.
Theodoret, 143.
Thiele, 23, 24, 25, 38n, 18, 38n, 20.
Thomas Aquinas, 129, 248, 249.
Tillich, 112, 163, 182n, 20, 190, 213n, 18, 254, 271n, 41-2, 272n, 48, 300, 317n, 13, 318n, 16.
Tolstoy, 242.
Torrance, T. R., 265, 274n, 66.
Troeltsch, 99, 100, 101, 106, 120n, 9, 164, 253, 271n, 36.
Trueblood, 236n, 5, 237n, 41, 238n, 42.
Truett, 217.
Trypho, 146.
Turner, William, 152n, 2.
Tyrell, 165, 167, 169, 184n, 26, 184n, 30.

Ugbaru, 28, 29.
Unseld, 190.
Urquhart, 266, 274n, 70.

Van Buren, Paul, 108, 121n, 28, 172,
    181n, 1, 185n, 41.
Vance, 217.
Venable, 209, 216n, 60.
Vidler, 269n, 15.
Vincent, John, 273n, 63.
Vincent of Lerins, 155n, 77.
Vos, 71, 84n, 7, 85n, 9.

Waddy, 268n, 1.
Wallace, 13.
Ward, 240.
Warfield, 85n, 11, 88n, 22, 123n, 43,
    128, 152n, 6.
Warren, 314.
Webb, Beatrice, 259.
Webber, 218.
Welch, 10n, 1.
Wellhausen, 12, 13, 14, 19, 21, 31, 33,
    34.
Wesley, John, 223, 231.
Wesley, Samuel, 179.
Westermann, 87n, 17.
Wette, de, 12, 19.
Whitcomb, 29, 39n, 30.
White, Alexander, 229.
White, Leslie, 268n, 7, 268n, 10.
Whitefield, 223.
Whitehead, 183n, 21.
Whitely, 319n, 37.
Wilder, 62n, 4.
Williams, C. S. C., 45, 62n, 10.
Williams, J. R., 104, 120n, 19.
Wilson, R. D., 37n, 3.
Winckler, 15.
Wisdom, 286, 292n, 25.
Wiseman, D. J., 39n, 37.
Wittgenstein, 120n, 18.
Wolfe, 84n, 8.
Woolcombe, 90n, 30.
Wood, A. Skevington, 236n, 6.

Xenophon, 28, 38n, 28.

Yeats, 265, 274n, 69.
Yinger, 181n, 2.

Zwingli, 126, 143, 22 .